CAPTAIN JACK AND
THE DALTON GANG

CAPTAIN JACK & THE DALTON GANG

The Life and Times of a Railroad Detective

JOHN J. KINNEY

UNIVERSITY PRESS OF KANSAS

© 2005 by the University Press of Kansas

Photographs in this book not otherwise credited are from the author's collection.

Published by the University Press of Kansas (Lawrence, Kansas 66045), which was organized by the Kansas Board of Regents and is operated and funded by Emporia State University, Fort Hays State University, Kansas State University, Pittsburg State University, the University of Kansas, and Wichita State University

Library of Congress Cataloging-in-Publication Data

Kinney, John J., 1950–
Captain Jack and the Dalton Gang : the life and times of a railroad detective / John J. Kinney.
p. cm.
Includes bibliographical references and index.
ISBN 0-7006-1414-1 (cloth : alk. paper) —
ISBN 0-7006-1415-X (pbk. : alk. paper)
1. Kinney, John Joseph, 1852-1918. 2. Railroad police—West (U.S.)—Biography. 3. Detectives—West (U.S.)—Biography. 4. Dalton family. 5. Outlaws—West (U.S.) 6. Frontier and pioneer life—West (U.S.) I. Title.
HE1771.K56 2005
363.28′74′092—dc22   2005013308

British Library Cataloguing-in-Publication Data is available.

Printed in the United States of America

10 9 8 7 6 5 4 3 2 1

The paper used in this publication meets the minimum requirements of the American National Standard for Permanence of Paper for Printed Library Materials z39.48-1984.

For Judy

CONTENTS

ACKNOWLEDGMENTS

The staff at both the Oklahoma Historical Society and the University of Oklahoma Western History Collection were professional and helpful. The University Press of Kansas deserves my thanks, particularly Nancy Scott Jackson. This book began in the lifelong correspondence I still enjoy with my friend James Hans. The Oklahombres historical group certainly deserves mention, as there the real experts in Oklahoma history exchange ideas and research. Diron Ahlquist especially went out of his way to help me, for which I remain most grateful. Above all, thanks to my mother and father, who took the time to pass along the family story.

INTRODUCTION

*What song the Syrens sang, or what name Achilles assumed when he
hid himself among the women, though puzzling questions,
are not beyond all conjecture.*
—*Sir Thomas Browne*

Families share far more than blood. They share experiences, usually
in the form of stories. Often these stories will transcend generations,
achieving the status of oral heirlooms, narratively memorializing the
past for the edification of the present. I suspect most families have
such a story, told repeatedly to children, about the exploits of their
ancestors, famous or otherwise. In almost every family, there is probably at least one person whose past deeds or life is kept alive as a caution or an inspiration to a younger generation. For example, I am very
distantly related through my mother to former British Prime Minister David Lloyd George, which would be more of a thrill if anybody
now remembered who Lloyd George was. Even such a distinguished
genealogy, however, does not necessarily make a good story, because
few children can appreciate the negotiations, important as they were,
leading to the creation of the Irish Free State or the arduous experiences of a minister of munitions during World War I.

Far more inspiring to me were the storied deeds of my father's ancestors, particularly those of my great-grandfather, John Joseph Kinney, whose name I share—how he heroically foiled a train robbery in
his capacity as a Pinkerton agent or a railroad detective (nobody was
quite sure which); how he was grievously wounded by the James Gang
or the Dalton Brothers and had to be carried home on a bloody door;
how he would have captured the outlaws except for the unfortunate
fact that the members of the posse he commanded were all Indians
and, conforming to their stereotypes, were dead drunk when the
posse was supposed to leap as a body from its place of concealment on
the train and confront the criminals; how only great-grandfather

leapt, and got the hell shot out of him; and how his courageous actions nevertheless scared the villains away before they could rob the express car, thus affirming my proud lineage with a true Hero of Capitalism, making the world safe for Wells Fargo. All this was tasty food indeed for a hungry young imagination.

Because we are told such stories so often, we probably never forget them entirely, although as we age, they recede in importance, unless we have children of our own we wish similarly to awe or impress—and I don't. This all came to mind several years ago when, driving from Denver to Chicago on Interstate 80 for a visit to my family, I happened to pass by the small town of Adair, Iowa. Wasn't Adair where the family story was supposed to have happened? Yes, Dad later confirmed, it was Adair, but he didn't think it was Iowa. Kansas, perhaps? I asked for and got the whole story again, but this time, I pressed for as much detail as Dad could recall. Drunken, cowardly Indians. Carried home on the bloody door. Dad clearly remembered his own father's view that Captain Jack—so my great-grandfather was familiarly known—was the "bravest man he ever knew." Still, a child's admiring testimony about his own father cannot command much authority. I asked whether anyone had actually researched the details of the family story, and I received a look of surprise. Who could doubt the veracity of a story that had passed through three generations? Don't question the past, for it cannot answer.

But now I was curious. Did anything like the story ever really happen? Would there be any historical record of so minor an incident? Surely this was worth what I then thought would be a brief investigation, which almost immediately turned up an amazing coincidence: there actually *was* a famous train robbery—one of the first west of the Mississippi River—at Adair, Iowa. On July 21, 1873, the James-Younger Gang (including Jesse and Frank James, and Bob, Jim, John, and Cole Younger) derailed a Chicago, Rock Island, and Pacific train rumored to be carrying $75,000 just to the southwest of Adair. Much of the train, which was wrecked beyond salvage, is today buried under a mound near that location, with the robbery commemorated by a historical marker. Engineer John Rafferty was crushed and killed by the derailment, and fireman Denis Foley was badly scalded by escaping steam. The gang forced express guard John Burgess to open the safe but only found $2,000 or so inside. Perhaps another $1,000 was stolen from the passengers for a grand total of $3,000 (which in today's dollars would roughly equal about $60,000).[1]

Still, even the most rudimentary investigation into the family story soon revealed that it must have happened on the night of July 14, 1892, in what was then Adair, Indian Territory (later Oklahoma), and even a cursory search discovered that the robbers were members of the infamous Dalton Gang. Given the notoriety of the Daltons, it is not surprising that the incident attracted a fair amount of attention from historians of the West, because Adair was the first train robbery in which the gang encountered any real organized resistance. It was the last major robbery before, deciding it would be interesting and profitable to rob two banks simultaneously, the Daltons tried to do just that at Coffeyville, Kansas, where most of them were gunned down in the streets by outraged citizens. (Another interesting coincidence is that much the same fate befell the James Gang, some of whom were related to the Daltons, in the town of Northfield, Minnesota, on September 7, 1876.)

Contrary to Dad's good advice, we can question the past—indeed, we must question the past, although it seldom answers in a single or clear voice. Herodotus sensibly taught that the point of writing history is "to preserve from decay the remembrance of what men have done." But this is a task far more difficult than might initially appear. Throughout my own research, I have been, perhaps naively, astounded by the extent to which seemingly reputable sources, although able (usually) to agree on the broad scope of things, nevertheless differ substantially about the requisite details. They agree the Syrens sang, but they cannot name the song. Is this accounted for by the seemingly obvious observation that some sources are right, and some are wrong? No doubt that is so. But time enshrouds facts, and although one might not agree with Nietzsche (who famously argued that there are no "facts," only interpretations), it does appear likely that historical facticity is less an immutable objectivity and more the result (as E. H. Carr observed) of an ever-shifting consensus. A further complication is that usually the only criterion we have for judging the veracity of historical information is other bits of historical information.

This can easily lead to a spurious numbers game. If one source says (as it does) that Captain Jack's posse aboard the train that night numbered thirteen men, but two other sources put the number at eight, are the latter necessarily correct by virtue of repetitive weight? Should a prudent historian average the difference? Is historical research therefore necessarily a partisan activity, however disguised, in which we promote those details that advance our preconceived theory but must reject from the ranks any divergent "facts" (often of a standing entirely equal to those we approve) that do not pledge allegiance to our cause?

Puzzling questions, perhaps beyond all conjecture. My original focus in writing this was the incident itself. What exactly, or even approximately, happened that night of July 14, 1892, in Adair? To what extent is it possible now, more than 110 years later, to recreate those events? What confidence can one have that any recreation would reasonably resemble what actually occurred? Is it possible now, or was it ever possible, to "preserve from decay" with any accuracy the "remembrance" of what happened?

From the incident, my focus necessarily broadened to the man involved, Captain Jack. Character grows out of action, but just as inexorably, action can grow from character, and either can arguably serve as evidence of the other. This becomes important because historians examining the same event have variously concluded that Captain Jack was either a brave man performing heroic deeds or a coward and very probably a killer. But evidence of the man can be legitimately offered as evidence interpreting his action. Whatever happened that July night did not occur in a vacuum devoid of character. And although even the bravest can act in a cowardly fashion—Achilles did hide among the women—it seems prudent to judge events in the wider context of those engaged in them. Events shape men, but men can shape events.

Still, to know the man, one must have some sense of his times, and exciting times they certainly were. Much of what we now take for granted in our own world first appeared during Captain Jack's life. He was born in Glasgow, Scotland, in 1852. He died in Kansas City, Missouri, in 1918. During that period, in addition to experiencing two major wars, one would (as Thomas J. Schlereth writes)

have lived through an era marked by the assassination of three American presidents, the impeachment of a fourth, and a stolen election by a fifth. In the years between the Civil War and World War I, the nation admitted twelve new states, which doubled its geography, making it by 1912 the largest continental republic in the world. Americans voted on ten different constitutional amendments, seven of which were law by 1920. The country's population, number of foreign born, suicides, industrial laborers, divorces, gross national product, and white-collar workers all doubled.[2]

Another social historian, focusing more narrowly on the 1890s, observed that "in 1889 the United States produced 1,705,000 tons of rails; in 1900, 2,672,000 tons. In 1889 factories, mines, and railroads used 23,679,000 horsepower; in 1900, 37,729,000, not counting the use of the popular new electric motors."[3] Changes of such enormous scope must have profoundly affected those who lived through them, with the result that any single incident, such as what happened the night of July 14, 1892, cannot be understood isolated from the surrounding social and cultural dynamics, the energy from which arguably drives all events.

Sir Thomas Browne is surely right that "our fathers find their graves in our short memories."[4] What follows is an attempt to recover what oblivion will now share with remembrance. The little that now remains of Captain Jack's life is at best fragmentary, odd historical bits and pieces, fleeting references by turns suggestive and obscure, faint traces of a life whose coherency and continuity have long since decayed. One attempts the reassembly of such into a mosaic, knowing from the outset the result will be at best incomplete. But although most of that I now want to know can probably never be known, it does not follow that everything is beyond all answer. I can hope to resurrect, if not the full flesh, then at least a partial skeleton of a man's life, and in the process I can receive a glimpse, dim though it is, of how the events of his life may have looked to him. Thomas Carlyle's pronouncement that "History is the biography of great men" has often, and justifiably, been attacked (what about women?). I'm not at all sure that "History" is subject to any single, let alone useful, definition. But whatever history is, it must somewhere include the lives of people, some famous but most not, and my goal here is to present a portion of one such life, a mostly ordinary man, who on the night of July 14, 1892, found himself in extraordinary circumstances.

A DAIRING ADVENTURE

The night of time far surpasseth the day.
—*Sir Thomas Browne*

July 14, 1892. Early evening, perhaps about 8:00 P.M. A man nervously paces outside the railroad depot in Wagoner, Indian Territory (later Oklahoma), which was then, and remains, a tiny flyspeck of a town. As he glances to the south, which he does repeatedly, he impatiently pulls a pocket watch from his vest; it is still light enough to see the time. Periodically, he checks the depot to see whether the telegraph operator has received any new messages, and to confirm that the messages he has sent have been acknowledged. He is a man of above-average height, with a prominent mustache to offset his balding head. He is forty years old, experienced in his job, and carries a Winchester Model 1873 rifle—but not, inexplicably, a sidearm.[1] Many of his friends, and he has many friends, call him "Captain Jack"; his full name, as is mine, is John J. Kinney Jr., and he is my great-grandfather. He is the chief of the Missouri, Kansas, and Texas ("Katy") Railroad detectives,[2] and that night he is expecting, even hoping, to be robbed. That night, he would become, in a very small way, a part of history—a parenthetical person, a human footnote.

Earlier that evening, the Missouri, Kansas, and Texas northbound train No. 2, pulled by Engine No. 115, left Muskogee, thirty miles to the south of Wagoner, on its regular run to Parsons, Kansas. Driving the train is Mr. Glen Ewing, engineer. Behind him in the cab, shoveling coal, is fireman L. Brandenburg. Mr. George Scales is the train's conductor. We no longer know the exact composition of the train, nor has it much importance, but it must have included a number of passenger cars, a few sleeping cars, a "smoker" (that is, a lounge), and

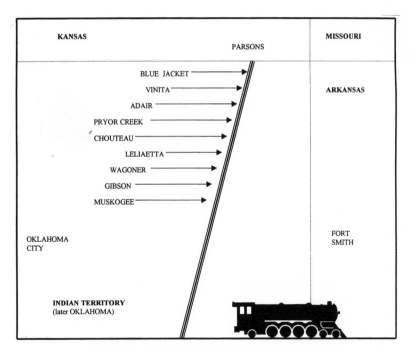

MISSOURI, KANSAS & TEXAS ("KATY") RAILROAD
CHEROKEE (east) LINE
CIRCA 1892

an express car, locked in which were probably both a "local" and a "through" safe and the express messenger, Mr. George P. Williams, who was responsible for them.[3]

The train may also, although this point is in dispute, have included a number of freight cars, or boxcars, one of which would have been modified to unobtrusively carry a contingent of special guards who boarded at Muskogee. These eight or nine (accounts vary) heavily armed men, many of American Indian ancestry, were led by Captain Charles La Flore (also spelled "LeFlore"[4]), himself half Choctaw, who was then both a special agent for the Katy Railroad and the chief of the Union Agency Indian Police for the Indian Territory. He and Captain Jack were friends and colleagues, and they had collaborated on a number of notable criminal cases, one of which made legal history in the form of a Supreme Court decision overturning a case Captain Jack, with La Flore's assistance, brought before the notorious "Hanging Judge" Isaac Parker (*Lewis v. United States*, 146 U.S. 370 [1892]).

Very probably, one of the telegrams Captain Jack was awaiting in Wagoner was from La Flore, assuring him that the special force of Indian police and railroad guards was en route. Aside from La Flore, this posse included Sid Johnson, deputy U.S. marshal for the Wichita district, and Mr. Alf McCay and Bud Kell of the Union Indian Police. A railroad guard known only as Mr. Ward had also joined the group. The other members of the detachment are unknown, at least to me.

Yet another telegram, sent days earlier, was responsible for all this activity. One of the legends of Oklahoma law enforcement, a member along with Bill Tilghman and Heck Thomas of the "Three Guardsmen," was a former Danish soldier named Chris Madsen, who had fought in the Franco-Prussian war and who also served in the French Foreign Legion—or so he said. An attractive feature of the West was that, within reason, people were allowed to reinvent themselves. Other evidence suggests that Madsen never enlisted in either the Danish army or the Foreign Legion, and that he was deported from Denmark as a habitual criminal after serving prison sentences for fraud, forgery, begging, and vagrancy.[5] Whatever his past, by 1892 Madsen was a highly respected and effective lawman, accolades not easily achieved in that time and place.

In any event, Madsen had a network of informants in the area, one of whom had reported to him that the infamous Dalton Gang was planning to rob the Katy train (the train Kinney was then awaiting) at the Pryor Creek[6] station, thirty miles north of the Wagoner depot where Captain Jack paced. But Madsen was suspicious of his informant, believing that he might be concocting the story about the Daltons to court favor for himself. "We were so used to those tips that I paid little attention to his story," Madsen is reported to have said, but he did "send a telegram to the head of the railroad police, Mr. J. J. Kinney, and he organized a posse of thirteen men, who were placed in a special car."[7] In addition to the guards aboard the train, a separate posse had been assembled and then hidden about the Pryor Creek depot, anxiously awaiting the rumored appearance of the Daltons. Surely this seemed enough manpower and firepower to prevail over a gang of train robbers who probably didn't number more than eight.

This was not the first time Kinney and La Flore had encountered the Dalton Gang, although it would be the last. On Monday, September 14, 1891, Captain Jack left his home at 4214 South Prospect Street in Sedalia, Missouri, and took the Katy Flyer to Denison, Texas, where, after breakfast the next morning, he met Captain La Flore on the train and told him "he might look out for a train robbery any night." What evidence he had for such a prediction is not known, but that evening, while still in Denison, he "got a message at 10 P.M. stating that No. 3 was held up by train robbers at Leliaetta at 9 P.M." He immediately left on Katy No. 4 for the scene of the crime, and the next day, he attempted to organize a posse of ten men to trail the robbers (whom he did not then know, although he may have suspected that they were the Daltons). After borrowing a pack of bloodhounds owned by Deputy Marshal Andy Fryers, he prepared to set off in pursuit, but because the hounds would not take the scent and he did not have enough horses to mount all his posse, he was forced to abandon the chase. Leliaetta was very near Wagoner where, some ten months later, Kinney now awaited La Flore and his guards.

Exactly how much the Daltons got at Leliaetta from the express car is subject to argument. As we shall see, accounts by the outlaws themselves greatly exaggerated their proceeds, in order to magnify their success and daring, while the official accounts from the railroads and express companies tended to minimize amounts, in order to discourage future bandits. Thus, the take from Leliaetta is estimated to have been anywhere from $2,500 to $10,000, which in 2005 dollars would be valued at between $50,000 and $200,000. But this would have to be split six ways among the gang's members: Bob Dalton, Emmett Dalton, "Bitter Creek" Newcomb, Dick Broadwell, Charlie Pierce, and Bill Doolin.[8]

Nor was Leliaetta an isolated incident. On June 1, 1892, the same gang, now joined by Grat Dalton, who had just escaped from jail, received intelligence (just as the railroad had spies among them, they may have had spies in the railroad) that a large shipment of cash ($70,000, or $1,400,000 in 2005 dollars) was due to ship through Red Rock. In fact, two trains were scheduled to pass through Red Rock that night, a regular preceded by a special carrying both the cash, an annuity for the Sac and Fox tribes, and a large company of guards. But because of the suspiciously dark windows in the passenger cars, the gang sensed trouble and, correctly suspecting a trap, let it pass unmolested.

The second train was not so lucky. Shortly after it pulled out of the station at 10:00 P.M. (according to this report in the *Atlanta Constitu-*

tion, June 3, 1892, 2), two masked men crawled over the tender and, at gunpoint, compelled engineer Carl Mack to divert onto a siding, where another five robbers appeared. Fireman Frank Rogers was then ordered to break down the express car door with his coal pick, but before he could comply, the express messenger (F. C. Whittlessy[9]) and guard (J. A. Riehl), by then aware that a robbery was in progress, began firing through the door, provoking a fierce return volley, with some of the robbers even crawling under the car and firing up through the floor. Although some 200 shots were exchanged, miraculously, nobody was hurt. The robbers finally succeeded in chopping a large hole through the door, and stood in front of it the hapless fireman, who quickly persuaded his barricaded colleagues of the futility of further resistance. During all this, bizarrely, the bandit leader made polite conversation with the captive engineer, even profusely apologizing to him for "rough remarks" his associates had uttered. The outlaws then broke open and robbed both safes, and after securing a few hundred dollars and an occasional watch from the passengers, they rode off.[10]

Needless to say, such robberies presented a problem to the authorities far larger than the specific sums involved.[11] It's hard for us to understand, at a time when our wallets are stuffed with credit cards and ATMs seemingly dot every street corner, the importance then of cash and liquidity. Most businesses of any size in the 1890s kept safes on their premises, as workers expected to be paid in cash. Small banks—and most banks were small—had to perfect the art of estimating just how much cash to keep on hand. If they kept too much, they risked robbery, at a time when private insurance was often unreliable and federal deposit insurance did not exist. If they kept too little, they risked bank runs. Consequently, cash had to be constantly on the move, precisely the function of the railroads and express companies, and precisely the target of gangs such as the Daltons. In addition, during these times, various treaties with the Indians stipulated the regular dispersal of large sums of cash to the various tribes. These funds were usually transported by the railroads, presenting attractive opportunities for the many bands of thieves and robbers then infesting the territories. Of all men, Kinney and La Flore knew this, and they also knew that if they did not succeed in protecting the railroads, their superiors would quickly find men who would.

So when the No. 2 arrived on time at the Wagoner depot, Captain Jack must have felt both relieved that, at least so far, the plan was on schedule but also some apprehension as to what might lie ahead. To this point, insofar as Kinney knew, the Daltons had not actually physically hurt anyone during their previous train robberies. I am here assuming that the Daltons were not responsible (and the evidence I've seen convinces me that they were not) for an earlier train robbery in Alila, California, during which fireman George W. Radcliff (also spelled "Radliff") was killed.

One reason for believing this is that shortly after the Coffeyville raid (in which four members of the Dalton Gang were killed in addition to four Coffeyville citizens), Ben Dalton, eldest of the Dalton brothers and one of the "honest" members of the family, gave an interview to the *Saint Louis Globe-Democrat* (October 16, 1892). By this time Emmett Dalton, who survived the raid but was thought by everybody, probably including himself, to be on his deathbed, had confessed to the train robberies at Wagoner, Leliaetta, Red Rock, and Adair. But he denied any involvement in Alila. Ben supports this story:

> There was no claim that Grat Dalton was at Alila. Fifty men were ready to swear to an alibi for him. When the robbery took place he was playing cards in a crowd many miles away.
>
> "Now, this is the true story of that Alila business," continued Ben Dalton. "My brothers had nothing to do with it, but the crime was sworn on them by bribery and perjury, and then they entered on a life which ended here at Coffeyville. I haven't a word to say against the people of Coffeyville—not a word, but those two men who hired a perjurer in California to swear that train robbery on the boys I believe are responsible for what has happened since."

I'm inclined to believe this, because I can think of no good reason why one would confess to four train robberies but not five.[12]

However, Kinney may have known that the Daltons, whatever their past crimes, had never been challenged in quite the fashion he and La Flore had planned. And gunplay during such robberies was common. Captain Jack had spent much of 1891 traveling between Sedalia and Ft. Smith, Arkansas, for the trial of Alexander Lewis, whom he suspected of robbing a Katy train on June 15, 1888, at the Verdigris water tank, during which the express messenger, Mr. A. B. Codding, and Harry

Ryan, a "train boy," were both wounded, and Mr. Benjamin C. Tarver, a stockman from Rosebud, Texas, was fatally shot through the head.

Nor is it clear what experience Kinney may have had in gunfights. Although he had successfully confronted and arrested many dangerous men during the course of his career, there is no evidence that he had ever done so at the point of a gun, nor that he even routinely carried a sidearm. His colleague arriving aboard No. 2, Captain Charles La Flore of the Indian Police, had far more experience in such matters. La Flore, born in 1841, had served in the Civil War, rising to the rank of captain. He then built and operated both a lucrative toll bridge and a water-powered grain mill in Atoka County. Some evidence suggests that, formally or informally, La Flore was acting in a legal or law enforcement capacity as early as 1878. The *Sedalia Daily Democrat* published an article (March 7, 1878, 4) about the "hundreds" of people killed in the territories "in the past few years," presenting both judicial and sanitary challenges, as their skeletons were often left "to bleach where they fell." Because this was at a time before morgues were common outside of large cities, authorities had to decide what to do with the bones. One skeleton was discovered three miles south of Limestone Gap; such of it as remained, along with its hat and shoes, was transported to the house of Charles La Flore. The skeleton was judged to be about five or six months old, so "if any one knows any person being missing about that length of time," the paper advised, "they can call and examine the remains."[13]

La Flore later joined the Choctaw Lighthorse Police in 1882, and in 1883 he became a U.S. deputy marshal. Soon thereafter, he led a posse that surprised the Christie Gang as they attempted to rob a train at Reynolds near his home in Limestone Gap, resulting in a furious battle in which five outlaws were killed and a number of deputies wounded.[14] In 1885 he and Captain Sam Sixkiller pursued and confronted the notorious bandit Dick Glass, who was killed during the encounter. In 1886 he shot and killed Jess Nicholson, wanted in connection with the murder of Sixkiller, in Muskogee. The next year he successfully pursued and captured Gus Bogles, one of the most dangerous men in the territory, who was subsequently executed by Judge Parker's court. In 1898 he captured outlaw Henry Whitefield, who was later hanged. A reporter for the Ada, Oklahoma, *Evening News* (August 9, 1910, 1), describing witnesses testifying before a hearing, observed that "a singular appearance was presented by Charles La Flore, a

Choctaw, who as captain of police, had figured in many a battle of the plain. He had only one eye, three of his fingers were shot off, and his body was covered with bullet wounds."

Captain La Flore was fifty-one years old that night in 1892, and he would live until September 10, 1920, when he died in his home in Limestone Gap at age seventy-nine. La Flore was the son of Forbes (also spelled "Forbis") La Flore, described as a "leading citizen" of the Indian Territory.[15] Kinney's diary indicates that he and his wife Elizabeth occasionally entertained the La Flores socially. Like Captain Jack, La Flore had married into a prominent family, his wife Mary Angelina being "a sister of ex-Governor Guy, and a niece of the late ex-Governor Harris."[16] A further bond between the two men is that both had fathered twins: Captain Jack had twin sons (Rolland and Raymond), and La Flore had twin daughters (Chick and Chock). Both had worked, along with Captain Sam Sixkiller, under Tom Furlong at the Missouri Pacific. La Flore's position as the head of the Indian Police was dangerous: one contemporary writer cautioned that "both his predecessors in this office were killed within one year and a half."[17]

Captain Sam Sixkiller, one of the bravest and most effective law officers in the territories, certainly deserves more than a brief mention. Born in the Going-Snake District of the Cherokee Nation in 1842, Sixkiller served on both sides during the Civil War, with Stand Watie's Mounted Confederate Cherokee Rifles and later with a Union artillery company commanded by his father, Redbird Sixkiller. In 1879 he was appointed the chief of the Union Agency Indian Police, a position later occupied by La Flore, having jurisdiction over the five "civilized" tribes (the Choctaw, Cherokees, Chickasaws, Creeks, and Seminoles). In December 1886 Sixkiller was gunned down in the streets of Muskogee, an engagement in which Charles La Flore was also involved. Interestingly, a posse formed to pursue his murderers included U.S. Deputy Marshal Frank Dalton, elder brother of the outlaw Daltons. Among the hundreds of mourners at Sixkiller's funeral were the Adairs (Walter Adair had served with him in the Cherokee Rifles, and the town of Adair, Indian Territory, was named after him) and Dr. Leo Bennett, a prominent Indian agent who was both an Elk, as was Captain Jack, and a future Mason grand master. A eulogy that appeared in the *Indian Journal* (December 29, 1886) concluded, "The Captain has done probably more than any one person to free the railroad towns of this Territory of their dangerous and reckless elements, and to him the country owes in a great degree the comparative security to life and property that it now enjoys."

Kinney had many of the same credentials as La Flore and Sixkiller, if not comparable violent experience. On November 27, 1884, he was appointed deputy marshal of the United States for the Eastern District of Arkansas by U.S. Marshal D. B. Russell, who declared all Kinney's "official acts valid as if done by myself." Then in 1888 he became a Texas Ranger in one of the "Frontier Battalions," which had originally organized in 1874 to fight Indians and would continue until 1900, when a court ruling effectively disbanded the force by limiting arrest and criminal process powers only to commissioned officers.[18] One good reason for acquiring such affiliations was that, as only a railroad detective, Kinney had very little legal authority, perhaps no more than any other private citizen.[19] Credentials such as he had obtained were crucial to performing his job, which routinely required his travel far beyond any local jurisdiction. He was responsible for criminal investigations along the whole Katy route, which at that time stretched from St. Louis in the east to Omaha in the north, with two trunks winding south, one through Salina to Ft. Worth, the other from St. Louis through Sedalia, Parsons, Muskogee, Denison, and then to Dallas. A southern route from Dallas/ Ft. Worth branched off through Austin to San Antonio in the west and Galveston and Shreveport to the east. That segment of the Katy line just north of Muskogee to the Kansas border was, arguably, the most often robbed section of track at that time in the entire country.

As the No. 2 pulled into the Wagoner depot, Captain Jack would perhaps have first checked with Engineer Ewing about the condition of the track. One common method robbers used to stop trains was by piling obstructions across the tracks, or even separating the tracks from the ties in order to derail the whole train. Ewing would have been instructed, had he not already been, to watch for such impediments. Conductor Scales would have reported on the number and character of the passengers: another method robbers used was to have accomplices board the train as seemingly legitimate passengers, only to pull weapons at a predetermined place or time. Finally, Captain Jack would board the special car, if there was one, to inspect La Flore's guard and to review for the last time what was anticipated at Pryor Creek. Contingencies were certainly discussed, but the plan was probably no more complicated than to await the robbers' appearance, to order them to surrender, and, if they didn't, to shoot them down.

Immediately north of Wagoner was Leliaetta, where the Daltons struck ten months earlier, but through which the No. 2 now passed without incident. The train continued through Chouteau and finally, at approximately 9:00 P.M., reached Pryor Creek, where absolutely nothing happened.[20] Kinney and Captain La Flore would have had the train stopped there, receiving reports from the guards and deputies hidden about the station, wondering what to do next. In some ways, the Daltons' failure to show was the worst possible news. Most of the guards and deputies did not risk their lives for free, and so the Katy, already on financially shaky ground, was expending large sums with no return, a situation made even less tolerable given the knowledge that they would have to do so again upon receipt of the next rumor. Kinney decided that although it made no sense to keep the standing force deployed at Pryor Creek, because they had come this far with the mobile posse aboard the special car, they might as well go on a bit further and see what happened. This they decided to do, and the No. 2 proceeded north to the next stop: Adair.[21]

Here, on our vicarious journey to Adair, we must pause and get to know Captain Jack better. In this effort to understand the incident, the man, and the times, I have gained access to a number of historical sources not commonly available. In addition to various letters, mainly to his wife Elizabeth, written between 1875 and 1893, Captain Jack also kept a pocket "Excelsior" diary, costing $1.00, containing such useful information as a list of expected eclipses, a schedule of "Movable Feasts," tide tables for major eastern cities, and a valuation of foreign coins, including a helpful reminder that "Italian notes and silver are not current in France, Belgium, and Switzerland, but the silver of these countries passes current in Italy." Most of the entries are in an identical ink and, because the penmanship is consistent, one speculates that Captain Jack may have owned one of the new "hydraulic" or "fountain" pens perfected and marketed by Lewis E. Waterman in 1884. One would characterize this more as a business diary than a personal one, although it contains many personal details too. Unfortunately, I only have his diary for the year 1891. Because it seems unlikely to me that a man would keep a diary for just one year, other diaries probably exist, moldering away forgotten. Because he came from a large family (nine siblings) and had a large family of his own (eight children), many—indeed, too many—possible candidates exist who may have inherited his personal effects.

Thus, although most of Captain Jack's life is and will always remain a complete cipher to me, I can know, and in considerable detail, much of what he did during the year preceding the robbery at Adair. Opening the diary to Tuesday, January 20, 1891, I learn that the Katy hospital in Sedalia burned down, and it was his job, presumably after the fire was put out, to take charge of and guard the company safe that "contained over $400.00 and valuable papers." I know that Friday afternoon, February 20, Captain Jack left Sedalia for St. Louis in order to attend the funeral of General Sherman. And on Thursday, August 20, while attending the Sedalia State Fair with his family, Captain Jack "arrested Chas. Demming and J. F. Scott at Fair Grounds. Demming & Scott belong to Topeka. Demming is an all round crook." I know that on Thursday, December 17, while in Vinita to meet the legendary Heck Thomas,[22] Kinney also encountered "Indian Agent Bennett" who "was paying off the Shawnees."

Dr. Leo E. Bennett, like La Flore, Sixkiller, and Captain Jack himself, is no longer well remembered. Eventually appointed by President McKinley on September 21, 1897, as United States marshal, Bennett was (as historian Glen Shirley writes)

born in Kansas in November 1857, the son of Dr. James E. and Martha A. Bennett. Dr. James Bennett had relocated his family to Fort Smith, where Leo had attended public schools. Later Leo attended the prestigious Rugby Academy in Wilmington, Delaware, the University of Michigan at Ann Arbor, and finally graduated from medical school of the University of Tennessee at Nashville, to follow in the footsteps of his father. He began his practice in 1883 in the Creek Nation, at Eufaula, where he also engaged in stockraising, politics, and the newspaper business. In 1887 he was appointed federal agent for the Five Civilized Tribes at Muskogee, at the same time operating a store north of Muskogee on the Katy railroad. He made frequent trips to Washington and successfully obtained a post office at the growing little switchyard, Gibson Station. Seeing that Muskogee was destined to become the metropolis of the Territory, he resigned as Indian agent, sold his interest in the Eufaula *Indian Journal,* moved to Muskogee and launched the *Phoenix* on property he obtained by trading advertising space in his newspaper. The *Phoenix* became one of the Territory's leading newspapers, and in 1893, Bennett was named president of the newly formed Indian Territory Press Association.[23]

Returning to the diary I finally, and gruesomely, learn that on Friday, October 30, Captain Jack, while in Sedalia "remained at the jail all night with Sheriff Smith and the Death Watch for Tom Williamson who is to be hung tomorrow," an execution Captain Jack witnessed. This custom of the deathwatch, where legal officials keep the condemned company the night before his execution, evolved not just out of sympathy. The hope is that the prisoner will confess to other crimes. Although Kinney does not mention it, exactly that seems to have happened with Mr. Williamson, a laborer convicted of murder. The Albert Lea, Minnesota, *Freeborn County Standard* (November 4, 1891, 2) reported that "a confession was made by Murderer Williamson under sentence of death at Sedalia, Mo., for killing his wife, that in 1883 he butchered an entire family near Centralia, Ill., and also killed an old German named Koch." Other sources indicate that although Williamson was indeed suspected of killing his wife, the actual crimes for which he was executed were the murders (on May 26, 1890) of Jefferson and Thomas Moore, father and son, who had employed him as a hired hand.

Captain Jack was something of a public man, and like many in such a position, he kept a fairly extensive file of newspaper clippings to which I also have access. Although somebody went to great lengths to preserve these fading clippings, even to the point of having them laminated in plastic, such care was not always taken in recording their provenance, and so I have a considerable number of clippings to which I am unable to attribute a definitive source or date. But the important thing is why he clipped them, not from where he got them. And in many cases, the reason for his interest is obvious: they specifically detail his exploits. Although many people may still think that the primary duties of a railroad "bull" were largely limited to rousting vagrants and arresting fare cheaters, the clippings Kinney preserved show otherwise.[24] Train robbers were always his chief concern, but he became involved, if only peripherally, in cases involving murderers, rapists, swindlers, forgers, con artists, pickpockets, prostitutes, pimps, bootleggers, vandals, and thieves of everything from "a box of curry combs" to "25 lbs. of cinchona," the bark from which quinine was extracted.

Occasionally one clipping will explain the presence of another. The following, which must have pleased him, appeared in the *Dallas Times Herald* (date illegible):

John J. Kinney, chief of detectives of the M., K. & T. railroad, came in from the north this morning, and departed for Gainesville on the afternoon train. Kinney is one of the best known detectives in the country, and for six years was the lieutenant of Tom Furlong, of the Missouri Pacific until very recently, but now superintendent of one of Allen Pinkerton's agencies. He [Kinney] has been at work in the nation, ferreting out train robbers, and his visit to Gainesville means something.

Tom Furlong, a famous detective of the time, is still yet another once prominent person history has by now largely forgotten. A Union Civil War veteran (Company G., 1st Pennsylvania Rifles) wounded at the battle of Drainesville, Virginia, Furlong also served as the "Chief of the Secret Service" of the Allegheny Valley railroad and was the first chief of police of Oil City, Pennsylvania. During his long career, Furlong encountered every conceivable hue of criminal, from railroad wreckers to crazed Mexican revolutionaries, mad dynamiters, nefarious swindlers, and diabolical poisoners. In 1882 (probably the year Captain Jack was first hired as a detective), Furlong, with the help of Sam Sixkiller, arrested a train robber who had shot a conductor on the Katy line at Vinita, the next stop north of Adair. Later in his life he founded the Furlong Secret Service Company, among whose employees was William J. Burns, eventual founder of his own detective agency, which would grow to rival the Pinkertons in size and prestige.

Writing in 1912, Furlong asserted, "I am today, I believe, the oldest detective, in point of service, in this or any other country."[25] This is certainly the same Tom Furlong who, in 1889, published (source unknown) an open letter, which Kinney saved, to Terrence V. Powderly Esq., General Master Workman, Knights of Labor, challenging Powderly's opposition to Furlong's attempt to secure a federal appointment on the grounds that during the Southwestern railroad strike of 1886, Furlong's "prosecution, or persecution" of innocent workers rendered him unfit for office.

The great Southwestern strike of 1886, a huge event of the times, "began in Marshall, Texas," writes Robert C. McMath Jr., but "was not as well supported by Missouri unionists and their sympathizers as the one in 1885. Sensing the lack of unity, Gould's [Jay Gould, who also owned the Katy—see Chapter 3] agents moved to crush both the strike and the Knights [of Labor]. Less able to rely on mass community support than the year before, striking workers disrupted freight service by disabling engines and threatening non-strikers. . . . Eugene Debs of the Brotherhood of Locomotive Firemen said Irons' strike call was 'hasty and rash.' On 3 May Terrence Powderly officially called off the strike, but it had been already lost."[26] Still, as a contemporary writer in *Harper's Weekly* (April 3, 1886) observed, "the number of men out of employment is not less than 10,000, and the loss to the railroads and to owners of freight is incalculable. The effect of the blockade is felt from one side of the continent to the other."

Furlong was particularly incensed by Powderly's accusation that "there were some 600 arrests made by me during the strike, and that out of this number not a single conviction was obtained." To the contrary, Furlong asserts that "the number of arrests made during the strike was less than 200," and that of these "fully two thirds were punished by fines or imprisonment in jails and penitentiaries." The position for which Furlong was being considered was the chief of the Secret Service bureau of the Treasury Department, under President Harrison, but intense and widespread opposition by the Knights of Labor successfully "derailed" the appointment.

As Furlong's lieutenant, Kinney could hardly have escaped involvement in such labor difficulties, which in turn perhaps casts some light (although not much) on his visits, recorded in the diary, on Thursday, April 16, 1891, with Mr. J. C. Thompson of the infamous Thiel Detective Agency in St. Louis and on the very next day, in Chicago, with Mr. Pat K. Gray of the Pinkerton Agency. (Actually, Captain Jack probably had other reasons for these visits—see Chapter 5.) But a common strikebreaking tactic of the time was for management to hire operatives (some would say thugs) from the Thiel Agency to guard their property while simultaneously hiring agents (some would say spies) from the Pinkerton Agency to infiltrate the worker's ranks for the purpose of observing, or perhaps even instigating, violence.

The clippings also make it clear that Captain Jack was responsible for the railroad's internal security, ensuring that Katy employees were not aiding and abetting criminals and were in general of honest character, credits to their employers and their communities. Although such paternalism may strike us as sinister today, it was then an accepted, if not admired, aspect of labor relations, which may explain why Kinney clipped from the *Sedalia Gazette* (November 20, 1891) the following regarding the travails of a Mrs. Emma Tanner who, in the course of a nasty divorce,

> alleges that the defendant conducted himself in a brutal manner towards her, cursed and damned her, and said at a time when she was sick that he might as well buy a coffin and put her in it; and to show his contempt for her he took women of questionable character to the opera house and other places of public amusement, in Sedalia.
>
> The plaintiff is a most estimable lady and the defendant is an employee in the M. K. & T. offices at Parsons and is well known in this city. The suit brought by Mrs. Tanner will cause a sensation and some racy developments are anticipated if the case comes to trial.

Some of the clippings reveal Kinney's personal side. As a boy today would collect baseball cards, he snipped stories of regionally famous boxers. Prizefighting was then illegal in most states, although on a trip to New York (recorded in his diary) Kinney notes that accompanied by his father and his younger brother Henry, he "went to the Puritan Club House on L[ong] I[sland] to witness Boxing matches" (March 21, 1891). Often, to evade the law, such matches were called "exhibitions" or "demonstrations," or they were held on barges towed beyond the three-mile national boundary limit. Inland, matches were held at secret locations, often near state borders, so that the participants and spectators could flee arrest should the law appear. In 1890, New Orleans finally legalized boxing matches under the new "Queensbury" rules that mandated padded gloves, three-minute rounds, and a ten-count knockdown. But even as late as 1915 in Oklahoma, and on at least four separate occasions, authorities went so far as to mobilize the National Guard under the command of General Frank M. Canton to stop proposed bouts.

These "Knights of the Five," as the pugilists were then sometimes called, included such colorful figures as "Soap" McAlpine, Posh Price, Mr. Dublin Tricks, "Fiddler" Neary, "Gipsy" Miles ("the lightweight who attempted to face [John L.] Sullivan one night in East St. Louis, but was knocked into the middle of the audience"), and "Professor" William Clark, also known as the "Belfast Chicken." Speaking of chickens, the following clipping, source and date unknown, reveals both Kinney's interest in raising (and fighting?[27]) gamecocks and the sort of unapologetic racism then pervasive in society:

> The other day I met an old darkey limping up Lamine street and stopped to ask the cause and how he felt.
>
> "Pooly, pooly," he replied. "I'se suffering wid 'inflammatic rheumatics, or something like that."
>
> "Inflammatory rheumatism," I replied. "Why, what brought it on, Uncle Jim?"
>
> "Well, I'll tell you, confidentially. I'se been reading in de papers lately 'bout dat Marse Captain Kinney, of de railroad, owning some mighty fine chickens, some ob de fighting kind, an' some ob dem fly away pigeons, dem kind what flies off to New York wid a letter, gits answer and brings it back."
>
> "So de oder ebening I concluded to pay a visit to his chicken house, but de dog was awake and in gittin' ober de fence in somewhat of a hurry I hurt dis leg; but don't say nothing about it, coze I would like to have a good fighting rooster dat weighs bout seben pounds and one of them pigeons, and nobody aint got any of dat kind but Marse Kinney. Bit I'se afraid to perambulate around dare, as long as he owns dat dog."

Before continuing Captain Jack's narrative, I suppose I must emphasize that it *is* a narrative, a story that, perhaps like his ferocious dog, would romp freely into fiction except for a thin leash of fact—and a thin leash it is. Louis Menand observes "this is why historical research is an empirical enterprise and history writing an imaginative one."[28] One is entirely at the mercy of such documents and records that have survived, knowing all the while that most have not:

> You are almost completely cut off, by a wall of print, from the life you have set out to represent. You can't observe historical events; you can't question historical actors; you can't even know most of what has not been written about. What has been written about therefore takes on an importance that may be spurious. A few lines in a memoir, a snatch of recorded conversation, a letter fortuitously preserved, an event noted in a diary: all become luminous with significance—even though they are merely the bits that have floated to the surface. The historian clings to them, while, somewhere below, the huge submerged wreck of the past sinks silently out of sight. (Menand, 80)

Whatever else it may be, history is minimally a collection of narratives, providing a society or culture with a temporal context much as individuals share their family stories. Perhaps we feel compelled to tell such stories because, in a sense, we *are* stories, with birth, life, and death functioning as beginning, middle, and end. We turn our lives into narratives as compensation for the grim philosophical reality that our experiences are usually mediated by forces far beyond our control. If our own lives inevitably seem to unfold as stories, how can we possibly avoid turning the lives of others into narrative? The short answer is that we cannot, and there lies danger for anyone attempting historical resurrection, because all stories require details that, if not supplied by the past, will then necessarily be imported by the present.

An example will help illustrate this. Mr. Ben Townsend, writing in *Lost Treasure* magazine, describes the very events I have also presented:

> The hot night air off the Oklahoma countryside rushed past the engine cab of the Flyer, the Missouri-Kansas & Texas' crack passenger train speeding north out of Muskogee for the division point at Parsons, Kansas.
>
> His face glowing red from the fire in the boiler, fireman L. Brandenburg glanced at Glen Ewing, the engineer. "I ain't comfortable over that gold shipment back in the express car,"—he said. "I got a awful feeling we're going to lose it—the whole $27,000 of it."
>
> Ewing squirmed on the seat and tugged a red bandana from his overall's hip pocket. He wiped the coal grime off his face.
>
> "Naw, nothing to worry about tonight," he said. "We picked up 15 U.S. deputy marshals back in Muskogee, and got 'em scattered through the train. Up at Pryor Creek Station 50 armed men is staked out. An army couldn't stop the Flyer tonight."[29]

I'm not especially bothered by Mr. Townsend's (in my estimation false) claim that the express car contained $27,000 ($533,000 in 2005 dollars) in gold. I know the source of that claim, and exaggerated as it may be, I can understand his reasons for citing it, although he doesn't explicitly do so. He is, after all, writing a piece of interest to treasure seekers, and it would not suit his purpose to admit that better evidence indicates the Daltons got, if anything, far less.[30] Even

Emmett Dalton, writing many years after the incident, claims the Daltons only got $17,000. In another account written by Emmett, the amount is estimated to be "about nine thousand dollars."[31]

Nor am I all that bothered by his assertion that "15 U.S. deputy marshals" boarded at Muskogee and were "scattered" throughout the train, although the sources I think are more reliable indicate that there were fewer available guards who were initially confined to a special car, with at least one of them, Captain Jack, boarding at Wagoner. Similarly, the far-fetched idea that as many as fifty armed men were "staked out" in Pryor Creek is, I believe, attributable both to the unreliable source cited above and a misreading of another, usually more accurate source, historian Harold Preece, who does refer to "forty or fifty" men but makes it clear that the number included guards already aboard the train, those waiting at Pryor Creek, plus an indeterminate force available to Captain Jack for patrolling the entire Katy line.

No. What bothers me is Engineer Ewing's "red bandana." We know, to the extent we can know any of this, that train No. 2 pulled by engine 115 left from Muskogee to Parsons at about 7:35 P.M. the night of July 14, 1892. We know that Ewing and Brandenburg occupied the cab. We can reasonably speculate that if the express car carried a large gold shipment, and if the two men were told (or otherwise knew) about it, they may very well have had a conversation along the lines described. We know that burning coal produces soot, and that Ewing very probably carried, in his hip pocket or elsewhere, a bandana or handkerchief for the purpose of cleaning his face. But we can never *know* that it was red. This is exactly the level of detail a narrative demands but history can rarely supply.

I'm particularly bothered by this because I'm forced to write similarly. This chapter begins with Captain Jack pacing about the depot and checking for telegraph messages. But I don't *know* that Wagoner even had a telegraph office, or that it would be open that late in the evening. In theory, such information might be available. Even if I could ascertain that the depot had such an office (and they usually did), I have no basis whatsoever for asserting that Kinney spent any time checking it for messages. Even so early on the detail required for a story, the specific level of incident demanded by a narrative overreaches what is historically available. "One instinct you need in doing historical research," Menand explains, "is knowing when to keep dredging stuff up; another is knowing when to stop" (80). Perhaps the best we can do is to respect the boundary of the irretrievable even as we are forced to violate it.

In all that follows, then, I must weigh and evaluate often contradictory sources, sifting through the different stories while attempting to tell my own, hoping my version might more closely approximate events as they would have been recounted by those who actually experienced them (which may or may not be the same thing as what objectively happened). Further, I must do exactly what I deplore, consciously or otherwise inventing a level of detail that is saved from pure speculation, if indeed it is, only by the occasional waterlogged fact floating uneasily in the frothing chop above the past's submerging wreck. But although the dark of time will always far exceed its day, we may, even now, still be able to view the fast-fading embers trailed and scattered by the events of July 14, 1892, the night when Captain Jack, Winchester in hand, found himself on the train riding to Adair, the night when Captain Jack inspired the family story by briefly intersecting with historical forces whose momentum, however obscurely, continues to include him.

WRESTLING WITH WOLVES

In vain we compute our felicities by the advantage of our good names,
since bad have equal durations.
—Sir Thomas Browne

Any detailed account of the robbery at Adair, and the times during which it took place, must somewhere examine the exploits of the remarkable Mr. Alphonso J. "Al" Jennings (1863–1961), a talented and colorful man who achieved varying degrees of success in such not entirely dissimilar careers as prosecuting attorney, train robber, evangelist, chicken rancher, author, safe cracker, gubernatorial candidate, cattle rustler, and Hollywood movie director, actor, and technical expert. He was certainly known to Captain Jack, if not personally, and also has the distinction of being responsible for perhaps the most inaccurate account of the Adair train robbery ever written—indeed, he seems to be the source of the claim that $27,000 was stolen.

Al displayed both his sensitive nature and his quick temper at an early age, running away from home when his father, a prominent judge, killed his pet squirrel. Jennings was educated as a lawyer, became interested in politics, and was elected district attorney of Canadian County, Oklahoma Territory, serving in that position from 1892 to 1894. Al probably would have remained just another minor politician had not destiny, in the person of attorney Temple Lea Houston (son of Sam, the Hero of Texas), intervened in his life, catapulting him, at least in his mind, to the very peak of Oklahoma outlawry. Al's two brothers, Ed and John, were also lawyers, and on October 8, 1895, they found themselves opposing Houston in court. Tempers flared; the men had to be restrained from fighting in the courtroom. Later that evening, Ed and John encountered Temple in the Cabinet Saloon in downtown Woodward. Ed Jennings called Houston a "son of a bitch."

That was a big mistake, because Temple was an expert gunfighter. An often-repeated story (almost certainly apocryphal) is that in a friendly shooting contest Temple beat both Billy the Kid and Bat Masterson. Houston was also an excellent, although unorthodox, attorney. One anecdote is that during a trial, suspecting that a jury was prejudiced against his client, Temple pulled a gun loaded with blanks and began firing at the jury box, scattering the panicked jurors. He then successfully moved for a mistrial on the grounds that the jury was no longer sequestered. The exploits of Houston were later memorialized in a short-lived (1963–1964) TV serial starring Jeffrey Hunter. Temple also seems to have been the model for Yancey Cravat in Edna Ferber's novel *Cimarron*, despite Marshal Nix's (who we shall meet later) assertion that his own exploits inspired the character. Houston was certainly not the sort of man one might safely call a "son of a bitch."

The men pulled their pistols and began shooting at each other. Temple hit John in the arm, and a stray shot from John killed Ed.[1] Houston then immediately turned himself in, and after a quick trial, he was judged to have acted in self-defense. This verdict so angered Al that he decided to take revenge on the law itself, and so he embarked on what must be one of the most inept crime sprees ever recorded. The Jennings Gang, including Al and his brother Frank, the two O'Malley brothers (who also served as deputies under Marshal Nix), "Dynamite Dick" Clifton, and "Little Dick" West, among others, planned to rob their first train near Edmund, Oklahoma, on August 16, 1897. But the train's conductor, seeing them inspecting the express car door, sternly asked them their business, and they meekly slunk away. Three days later, Al attempted to stop a speeding train by standing on the tracks and frantically waving his arms. He was nearly run over. On August 23, the gang tried a new tactic, galloping their horses beside the train while firing pistols in the air. The engineer calmly advanced his throttle, waved goodbye, and left them behind.

Finally, on October 1, 1897, the gang managed to stop a Rock Island passenger train near Minco, Oklahoma. But they could not force open the express car door. Announcing that he had come prepared for just such an eventuality, Al pulled from his saddlebags a quantity of dynamite and proceeded to blow the entire car into splinters. No safe was found in the rubble. A search of the smoking wreckage yielded only, by one report, a miraculously unbroken two-gallon jug of whiskey and a bunch of—we would suppose—rather badly bruised bananas.[2] Enraged, the gang robbed the passengers of practically everything they had, even stripping a pair of new boots from a traveling salesman. Al later boasted they got $10,000 from this escapade, although more reliable evidence suggests their take was more on the order of $3, which would divide into the princely sum of 42 cents per outlaw. They then turned their attention to more stationary targets. On October 29, 1897, the Jennings Gang robbed the Crozier & Nutter general store of $15. Here, disgusted with risking their lives over literally pennies, the O'Malley brothers and "Little Dick" West quit the gang. The remaining members were eventually hunted down.

Wounded during his capture by a bullet in the leg, which doctors using ordinary probes could not locate, Jennings would add to his list of accomplishments the distinction of being the first person in the territory to undergo x-ray examination. Dr. Bennett's February 24, 1898, Muskogee *Phoenix* describes the procedure:

Jennings climbed upon the table and told Jailer Lubbes "if that thing electrocuted him, he (Lubbes) was to be held accountable." Jennings was as much interested in the scientific side of the question as of the purely personal feature of the test.

With drawn curtains the experiment began. The electrical apparatus kept up a terrific rattle, much like the click of a sewing machine, although much louder, and the glass bulb filled with a greenish, milky light. Jennings' leg was placed near the bulb and then the operator put a funnel-like box (called the fluoroscope) on the opposite side, put his eye at the spout and looked. The bullet was soon located and everybody in the room given the opportunity to see it for themselves. Later, a sensitized plate was placed where the fluoroscope had been and a good photograph made of the bullet and its location.[3]

In 1899, Al was sentenced to life in prison (or by some accounts 50 years) but was released on a legal technicality—remember, he was a lawyer, came from a family of lawyers, and his father was a judge—in 1902. In 1907 President Teddy Roosevelt, who perhaps had a soft spot in his heart for rough rider types gone bad, issued him a full pardon. Doubtlessly reasoning that his vast criminal expertise uniquely qualified him to prosecute others of that ilk, Jennings in 1912 ran for county attorney in Oklahoma City. "'When I was a train robber and outlaw,'" Glen Shirley reports him as saying, "'I was a good train robber and outlaw; if you choose me for prosecuting attorney I will be a good prosecuting attorney,' he said. Although voters questioned his sincerity, enough of them took his word to give him the Democratic nomination. He lost, however, to D. K. Pope in the general election."[4] That a convicted train robber would aspire to high political office may seem to us absurd, but in fact the good people of Oklahoma were a remarkably forgiving sort. In 1920 another convicted train robber, one even more inept than Jennings, was actually elected to the legislature despite, or perhaps because of, his belief that he was the reincarnation of Jesus Christ, a belief that earned him a stint in a lunatic asylum. The Honorable Manuel Herrick ("I may be a nut, but I'm a tough nut to crack") served a full term.

Jennings, who had an irrepressible disposition and was not easily discouraged, subsequently ran for governor of Oklahoma in 1914, finishing a respectable third in the Democratic primary. His campaign message, Zoe Tilghman scornfully recounts, was, "You know the worst of me. I have reformed. The other candidates are just as bad, but they have never been exposed."[5] But before then, and after a brief stint as an evangelist in Los Angeles, Al discovered Hollywood, where his tarnished reputation proved to be a considerable asset. One of the first successful commercial films was "Edwin S. Porter's *The Great Train Robbery* (1903), an eleven minute film often acclaimed as the first western—although it was shot in Dover, New Jersey. Telling the simple tale of a train robbery and the pursuit and capture of the robbers, Porter also pioneered several camera techniques, one being a close-up of a bandit firing directly at the camera, which caused people in the audience to duck, scream, or even faint."[6] Who could lend better verisimilitude to future productions than a real, although singularly inept, train robber?

Al eventually parlayed his reputation into a shot at directing his own film, *Beating Back,* which I've never seen. Films that old are hard to find, if copies still exist. Therefore, I leave the review to Zoe Tilghman:

It featured Jennings's conviction for train robbery, and was represented as "every word true." It contained such weird "facts" as the finding of a puff-ball by the roadside in *January,* and by it, the healing of his ankle shot through by a bullet from a Winchester, so that four days later the hero walked a long railroad bridge to try a train robbery. Such falsities as the government's offering a reward for the capture of whiskey sellers in the Indian Territory. Such discrepancies as, "We would scatter, after making an appointment for another robbery, often for months ahead"; and, "We never robbed a train unless we had a tip on a large shipment of money." In spite of such a prophetic gift that could foretell the date and train of a shipment "months ahead," the bandits came to grief after an actual career of four months.[7]

The movie is certainly memorable for its portrayal of various Oklahoma lawmen as fools and buffoons, which did not go unnoticed by them. Glen Shirley reproduces a friendly but teasing letter (dated January 1, 1915) on this matter from Emmett Dalton to Bud Ledbetter, the marshal who shot and captured Jennings:

My dear Mr. Ledbetter:

I have just witnessed the exhibition of *Beating Back* by Al Jennings, and I hasten to inquire, what's the chance to borrow the long-tailed Prince Albert coat, boots, star and heavy fierce black mustache you wear in the picture?

It's a good picture but I had one hell of a good laugh when I saw a party impersonating you dressed up as above mentioned, and then knowing you as I do, I could not help think while looking at it, how I would like to hear you express yourself, if only you could see it.

With kindest regards to yourself, family and any friends I may have there, I remain,

As ever, Your friend,
EMMETT DALTON[8]

In 1915 former Marshal E. D. Nix and Bill Tilghman tried to set the record straight, commissioning a film entitled *The Passing of the Oklahoma Outlaws* and casting real outlaws (Arkansas Tom, the last survivor of the Dalton-Doolin Gang) and lawmen (including Bud Ledbetter, Chris Madsen, and themselves) as characters. This film successfully toured the nation, accompanied by a sideshow where first Madsen and then later Tilghman would relate their law enforcement experiences to the attending audiences. Still, Jennings had the last cinematic word, receiving in the process the ultimate secular accolade: in 1951 a movie was made of his life, *Al Jennings of Oklahoma*, starring Dan Duryea as Al and Gale Storm as his new bride as they attempt to live the straight life but run afoul of plots hatched by an evil railroad detective.

Besides the films mentioned above, Jennings also appeared in such forgotten classics as *The Lady of the Dugout* (1918), *The Sea Hawk* (1924), *Fighting Fury* (1924), *The Demon* (1926), *The Riding Rascal* (1926), *Loco Luck* (1927), and *The Land of Missing Men* (1930). Later in his life (1945), believing he was a living icon of the western hero, Jennings sued the popular radio show *The Lone Ranger* for defamation of character. He was not especially bothered that the broadcast portrayed him as a train robber. Of that he was rather proud. But he resented the implication that he had induced a "callow, beardless youth" to join his gang. Train robbing, in his heartfelt opinion, was an occupation properly and strictly limited to adults. Then, too, after the broadcast, little schoolgirls would shyly approach him on the street, asking to join his train-robbing band. Such misguided admiration nearly brought tears to his eyes.

What seemed to anger him most was the radio drama's depiction of the Ranger capturing him by shooting a pistol out of his hand. Given his expertise in gunfighting, that could have never happened. In any real-life encounter between his younger self and someone like the Lone Ranger, he would surely have blown his opponent out of the saddle, and Tonto, too, had the faithful Indian companion been foolish enough to intervene. Although the jury appeared to be vastly entertained by Al's three days of testimony, they nevertheless dismissed his suit. This seemed a sad end for (as one newspaper charitably phrased it) "the little man whose blazing six-shooters and hard riding outlaw band terrorized the southwest 50 years ago" (Edwardsville, Illinois, *Edwardsville Intelligencier*, September 29, 1945, 1).

But it wasn't quite the end. Al's last bid for publicity occurred when, in 1950, a man calling himself "J. Frank Dalton" claimed to be the real Jesse James, and that James's death by the hand of cowardly Bob Ford was an elaborate hoax. In support of this assertion, Mr. "Dalton" enlisted the eager testimony of Jennings, who publicly swore the man actually was James. When he was later confronted by one of Jesse's biographers, Jennings readily admitted that he had indeed supplied such false testimony and then (as Dale Walker writes) "he added: 'Why not? They paid me a hundred dollars!'"[9]

Nobody seems to know who Mr. J. Frank Dalton really was, which is most unfortunate because, if words were deeds, then Mr. Dalton would certainly rank high among history's most remarkable people. In addition to being the real Jesse James, Mr. Dalton (so he said) served as a Texas Ranger and then as a colonel in the Brazilian Cavalry. He fought in both the Spanish-American and Boer wars, then stayed on in Africa battling unruly Hottentots. Later he rode with Pancho Villa and flew aircraft during World War I. He also claimed, having tired of civilization at one point, to have lived with a tribe of headhunters along the Amazon River. The headhunters, perhaps awed by so swollen an ego, respectfully refrained from harvesting it. Even more amazing than his life was that a considerable number of people seemed to believe his stories. He died while in the middle of a lawsuit attempting to establish his rightful claim to the identity of Jesse James.[10]

Curiously enough, *Oklahoma Outlaws* was not Tilghman's first experience with producing and directing films, nor was it even the first round in the cinematic battle with Jennings over how their shared history would be portrayed. Zoe Tilghman tells a wonderful story (I hope it is true) of how, in 1908, President Teddy Roosevelt attended a Rough Riders reunion in San Antonio where he witnessed a demonstration by cowboy John ("Catch 'Em Alive Jack") Abernathy, a close associate of Al Jennings, who had perfected the dubious skill of riding down wolves and wrestling them into submission with his bare hands, much as rodeo riders tackle and subdue errant cattle.[11] In awe, Roosevelt subsequently appointed Mr. Abernathy as United States Marshal, perhaps reasoning that wolf wrestling was a high qualification for territory taming.

As it turned out, and despite his incomparable proficiency in canine grappling, Abernathy did not make a very good U.S. Marshal and was eventually forced to resign. In addition to numerous financial irregularities, federal examiners investigating his tenure found evidence of repeated adultery, desertion, philandering, failure to support his children, bad debts, and seduction, including a statement by a janitor in the federal building who had discovered "Catch 'Em Alive Jack" engaged "in the act" with the wife of one of his best friends.[12] In another scandal, Marshal Abernathy eloped with the teenage daughter of a prominent Guthrie farmer, Mr. J. A. Pervaine, who swore to track down and chastise the libertine officer for the insult to his honor. The hastily wed couple prudently sought safe harbor in the house of Al Jennings, who was then living in Lawton (see the Ada, Oklahoma, *Evening News,* July 8, 1908, 1).

But all that disgrace lay ahead. Roosevelt returned to the east, extolling Abernathy's lupine prowess, deeds his friends there clearly did not believe. Such polite disbelief could only be quelled by pictures, and so Marshal Abernathy, in addition to his other duties, was instructed to have his stunt filmed. Knowing nothing about movies, Marshal Abernathy appealed for help to his friend Chris Madsen, who also didn't know anything about movies. But he did know Bill Tilghman, who, although not knowing anything about movies (who back then did?), had the reputation of a man able to get things done. At what we would now call a "script conference," the novice filmmakers, whose number grew to include both Heck Thomas and Bill's friend Comanche chief Quanah Parker, agreed that wolf tackling, although visually interesting, wouldn't by itself make a very good film. What they needed was a frame story, a western narrative, within which the wolf wrestling could be invested with thematic significance. And what better western theme than a bank robbery? And who better to portray the robber than Al Jennings, who happened to live nearby?

And so the film was shot, although not without incident. The bank robbery was staged, with permission, at a real bank, where a real customer, happening on the location, thought an actual robbery was in progress and jumped out the window to sound the alarm. Nor was the wolf wrestling as easy to film as one might have hoped, although eventually these furry stars were properly cowed into submission, but only by methods the ASPCA probably would not have approved. *The Bank Robbery* was completed in 1909, and Tilghman, Madsen, and the new Marshal Abernathy traveled to Washington to arrange a screening for President Roosevelt, who was so delighted with the result that he reserved the East Room of the White House for a showing to a large audience of doubting friends, obsequious high government officials, and puzzled foreign diplomats.[13]

As discussed above, one of the fledgling directors of and actors in this remarkable film was Quanah Parker, who certainly deserves some attention here. Quanah Parker, the son of Quahada Comanche chief Peta Nocona and Cynthia Ann Parker, captured by the band when she was nine years old, was among the most colorful figures of his time. He was a fierce warrior who led his band on bloody raids throughout the territory, culminating in the battle of the Adobe Walls trading post in 1874 and his successful escape from pursuing cavalry at Cañon Blanco. Finally, in June 1875, Quanah surrendered and was briefly imprisoned at Fort Sill, whereupon he came to realize that the survival of his people depended on accommodation with, if not complete acceptance of, the dominant white culture.

Befriended by many of the Texas cattle barons who had formerly numbered among his worst enemies (they saw him as a political ally in keeping open the ranges), Parker would frequently travel to Washington lobbying on Indian affairs. There he met and became friends with Teddy Roosevelt, who was later a guest at Parker's distinctive house, the roof of which was gaudily emblazoned with large white stars, each star supposedly representing one of his wives. Although he realized the need for political integration, Quanah also championed cultural independence, and he was instrumental in promoting the revival of traditional peyote religion. On another matter, while once in Washington, "Quanah was approached by an official who lectured him on the evils of polygamy [he had at one point seven wives]. When told to choose just one wife and tell the others to leave, Quanah thought for a moment and then told the official that he could pick the one to stay and tell the others they must leave. This reply ended the conversation."[14]

While jailed in the federal penitentiary in Columbus, Ohio, Al had the great fortune to have assigned as his cell mate a gentleman by the name of William Sidney Porter. Mr. Porter was born in North Carolina in 1862, and in 1884 he moved to Austin, Texas. Although he had no formal education to speak of, he worked as a sheep herder, a pharmacist, a draftsman, and, in 1891, as a bank teller for the First National Bank in Austin. But his first love was literature, and, gathering his courage, Porter left the bank to found *The Rolling Stone*, a humor weekly that failed dismally. Subsequently, bank examiners found shortages at the First National, and it was suspected that Mr. Porter may have gathered more than his courage on leaving the bank. Accused of embezzling funds, Porter fled, first to New Orleans and then to Honduras. But in 1898, hearing that the wife he left behind was in poor health, he returned, submitted to arrest, and was sentenced to five years in the Ohio penitentiary. Now he had plenty of time to pursue his literary ambitions, which he did under a pseudonym in an attempt to disguise his incarcerated status. One story is that his pen name was inspired by a friendly guard named Orrin Henry.

Another is that it derives from the author of a pharmacy textbook to which he had access in his work as a druggist in the jail hospital. The story I hope is true, because I like it best, is that as a boy he had a cat named "Henry," whom he would often call "Oh, Henry!" O. Henry of course went on to a remarkable literary career, publishing hundreds of short stories, but he died in an alcoholic stupor in 1910, almost dead broke, only 23 cents left in his pocket.

Al, who was never shy about cashing in on the fame of friends, would eventually write *Through the Shadows with O. Henry* (1921), but their relationship was certainly of reciprocal value: Al served as an inspiration for more than a few of O. Henry's celebrated characters and stories. Nor were all these accounts supposed to be fiction. In 1902, drawing on Al's expertise in the subject, the pair collaborated on a piece entitled "Holding Up a Train," which originally appeared in *Everybody's Magazine* under Henry's byline.[15] The article begins with a note: "the man who told me these things was for several years an outlaw in the Southwest and a follower of the pursuit he so frankly describes. His description of the *modus operandi* should prove interesting, his counsel of value to the potential passenger in some future 'hold-up,' while his estimate of the pleasures of train robbing will hardly induce any one to adopt it as a profession. I give the story in almost exactly his words."[16]

What follows is a ludicrous account of one who only in his wildest dreams "contributed some to the uneasiness of railroads and the insomnia of express companies." If periodicals could blush, *Everybody's Magazine* should appear scarlet red. Only once does Al refer to a robbery not completely embellished by his own fanciful imagination, and that is Adair (and worth quoting at length):

Along in '92 the Daltons were cutting out a hot trail for the officers down in the Cherokee Nation. Those were their lucky days, and they got so reckless and sandy, that they used to announce before hand what job they were going to undertake. Once they gave it out that they were going to hold up the M. K. &T. Flyer on a certain night at the station of Pryor Creek, in Indian Territory.

That night the railroad company got fifteen deputy marshals in Muskogee and put them on the train. Beside them they had fifty armed men hid in the depot at Pryor Creek.

When the Katy Flyer pulled in not a Dalton showed up. The next station was Adair, six miles away. When the train reached there, and the deputies were having a good time explaining what they would have done to the Dalton gang if they had turned up, all at once it sounded like an army firing outside. The conductor and brakeman came running into the car yelling, "Train robbers!"

Some of those deputies lit out the door, hit the ground, and kept on running. Some of them hid their Winchesters under the seats. Two of them made a fight and were both killed.

It took the Daltons just ten minutes to capture the train and whip the escort. In twenty minutes more they robbed the express car of twenty-seven thousand dollars and made a clean get-away.[17]

Although few knowledgeable readers would take Al seriously as a guide to train robbing, his views on the psychology of the event carry more authority and go some way toward answering the question, why did train robberies so often succeed? Not all did, of course—Al himself is ample proof of that—but enough did in spite of the many precautions used by the railroads and express companies. One of Captain Jack's colleagues was "Bill" Brady, described by a reporter from the *Washington Star* (date unknown) as "one of the shrewdest and most daring railroad detectives employed by any of the big railroad corporations." He poses the same question: "that two men should walk into a crowded car containing, say, forty men, two-thirds of whom, according to Western usage, are armed, and after 'holding up' each one separately escape unmolested is a tale that is almost beyond comprehension. But incidents of that sort, you know, were quite frequent."[18]

Jennings makes the good point that the element of surprise allows a small, organized group to dominate a far larger crowd of individuals, even individuals who would otherwise have experience reacting to just such situations:

As to the train crew, we never had any more trouble with them than if they had been so many sheep. I don't mean that they are cowards; I mean that they have got sense. They know they're not up against a bluff. It's the same way with officers. I've seen secret service men, marshals, and railroad detectives fork over their change as meek as Moses. I saw one of the bravest marshals I ever knew hide his gun under his seat and dig up along with the rest while I was taking toll. He wasn't afraid; he simply knew that we had the drop on the whole outfit. Besides, many of those officers have families and they feel that they oughtn't to take chances; whereas death has no terrors for the man who holds up a train. He expects to get killed some day, and he generally does. My advice to you, if you should ever be in a hold-up, is to line up with the cowards and save your bravery for an occasion when it may be of some benefit to you.[19]

"The attacking party has all the advantage," Jennings explains. "They have the outside and are protected by the darkness, while the others are in the light, hemmed into a small space, and exposed, the moment they show a head at a window or door, to the aim of a man who is a dead shot and won't hesitate to shoot."[20] Another advantage is that at least some train robbers were known to use a primitive, although effective, form of body armor. Detective Brady, in the clipping Kinney saved, recounts a robbery in which both he and his assistant were wounded by robbers who escaped unharmed. What puzzled him most "was the fact that he could 'down' none of the robbers. He carried a 48-caliber revolver of the best pattern, and when he had fired at them in both instances had stood only three yards apart. The mystery was cleared up the next day when two breast and head plates of steel were found alongside the track. The plates extended from the waist to the top of the head and were about three-quarters of an inch thick. Holes for eyes had been cut in them and straps were riveted on to hold them fast at the waist and neck." Ethical considerations can then arise, as shots glancing off the bulletproof robbers "become more dangerous to the other passengers than the robbers. Coupled with this a remarkable proficiency with the revolver, and it can easily be seen how great the odds are against anyone fighting a train robber when he has made his preparations of attack and defense."

Whether such armor was customarily or even occasionally worn by either outlaws or lawmen in the territories is not well documented. Bandit Dick Glass, later killed by Sixkiller and La Flore, reportedly wore such during a fight in 1885 when he shot Sheriff John Culp and Constable Rush Meadows. Historian Glen Shirley asserts that "Deacon" Jim Miller, notorious for killing Pat Garrett, invariably wore a long black duster, even in the hottest weather, inside of which was sewn a steel plate protecting his heart.[21] But it seems doubtful that such protective attire was commonly used, if for no other reasons than the cumbersome weight the armor would necessarily have and also the discomfort of wearing it in the summer heat.

By any calculation, train robberies in the 1890s reached epidemic proportions, prompting suggestions both imaginative and bizarre as to how this increasing criminal scourge might be combated. One editor recommended that train robbery be made a capital crime because "nothing short of hanging will check this growing evil." Others suggested that all trains include armored cars, fore and aft, with searchlights and Gatling guns. A pyrotechnic expert advised Wells Fargo that "express cars be equipped with tubes projecting through their roofs, enabling guards to fire off sky rockets and parachute flares. These, combined with bombs for noise, and white and blue lights and roman candles, would attract enough lawmen and citizens to discourage holdups." Another especially diabolical thinker may even have proposed (at least there's evidence some robbers thought so) what would have been a highly effective, although surely unethical, tactic of leaving about the express cars jugs of poisoned whiskey.[22] Despite such fanciful measures, most trains continued to depend on the protection of a posse of guards, sometimes carried in special cars that could also house horses and bloodhounds. Just such a train approached Adair.

Evening, July 14, 1892. Probably about 9:20 P.M. The sun had set that night at 7:39, with the official end of twilight at 8:09. A waning moon, three-quarters full, would not rise until 11:00. As Katy No. 2 left Pryor Creek into the fully dark night, the expectant mood among the train's guards naturally diminished. By now the guards had moved from the special car (if there ever was one) and were seated in the smoker, entertaining fellow passengers and each other with tall tales of what they would have done had the Daltons appeared. At least one of the guards, Deputy Marshal Sid Johnson, was disturbed by such bragging and is reported to have said, "You boys better start puttin' ammunition into your guns instead of your mouths. . . . There'll be plenty of shooting when the time comes, and with rifles."[23] But despite such good advice, a general feeling of euphoria spread: had they not scared off the Daltons without even firing a shot? A reporter for the *Sedalia Gazette*, interviewing Captain Jack three days later, notes that when they passed Pryor Creek without incident, "the guards on board of the train relaxed the vigilance of their watch and loosened their grip on their carbines."

One must here ask if such high spirits might not have been elevated by spirits of another kind. They were in the smoker car, after all, which also functioned as a bar. Thinking the danger had passed, those among them inclined to drink—and family lore states emphatically that Captain Jack was a lifelong teetotaler—may well have opened and passed around a bottle or two. But despite the "drunken, cowardly Indians" featured in the family story, it defies belief that, as Ben Townsend asserts, Engineer "Ewing couldn't know that in a dozen miles [north of Muskogee], the U.S. deputies would be roaring drunk, bragging to all on the train what they'd do to the outlaws if they tried to board the Flyer."[24] Still, another reputable source, Harry Sinclair Drago, wonders "why they were not riding in the express car, close to the money they were hired to protect, instead of drinking and lolling in the smoker."[25] Both Townsend and Drago are almost certainly depending on an account published shortly after the Coffeyville robbery by an anonymous author known as "Eye Witness," whose veracity, as we shall see, is in question.[26] None of the many other sources I have located says even a word about alcohol or drinking, but admittedly it's not the sort of activity that any participants would want publicly known. Had the guards been "roaring drunk," Captain Jack would have certainly noticed it at Wagoner, and it is highly unlikely he would have continued his mission with such men under his command.

Nor, strictly speaking, were they solely under his command, and Captain La Flore, who had accompanied and supervised them from Muskogee on, seems far too professional an officer to allow such conduct. There's an important distinction that many teetotalers fail to understand between "drinking" and "drunk," and although the best evidence indicates that some of the guards may have started drinking after leaving Pryor Creek, there is little evidence that they were drunk by the time they reached Adair. For one reason, there simply wasn't enough time. Adair is only about eight miles from Pryor Creek, a distance the train would cover in a little over fifteen minutes. The mechanics of human metabolism dictate that not even the thirstiest man, Indian or otherwise, could drink enough during that short interval to effect complete inebriation. And so on they went to Adair, where they were expected. The Daltons were already there.

Second only to Jesse James and his band, the Daltons remain arguably our culture's most celebrated outlaw gang. Although in most civilized societies a criminal record is considered a badge of shame, one is tempted to conclude that in America such a record, provided it is for the right sort of crime, acts instead as a springboard to lasting fame. As always, the popular film offers a barometer of cultural success. Al Jennings rated a movie, although a pretty bad one. Temple Houston only got, belatedly, a TV series.[27] Marshal Tilghman initially had to pay for the privilege of his own cinematic appearance, although many decades later his career was reprieved in *You Know My Name,* a made-for-cable movie starring Sam Elliot.[28]

The Daltons, in decided contrast, have spawned dozens of films, good and bad, from single reelers of the silent era to docudramas and made-for-TV movies as late as 1999 *(Gunfighters of the West: The Dalton Gang).* In the fall of 2004 the History Channel, a popular cable network, released a feature on the Daltons' Coffeyville raid. Part of this continuing legacy, particularly in the early days, is attributable to Emmett Dalton winding up in Hollywood as an "authenticity consultant," where he was involved in the production of *The Famous Dalton Raid on the Two Banks of Coffeyville* (1909), *The Last Stand of the Dalton Boys* (1912), and *Beyond the Law* (1918; "A Picture Historically Correct in Every Detail").[29]

After the hiatus of the Depression, the Dalton movies began to appear with regularity, beginning with—and this is not meant to be a definitive filmography—*When the Daltons Rode* (1940; "The Most Reckless Renegades in History!"), *The Daltons Ride Again* (1945), *Badman's Territory* (1946), *The Dalton Gang* (1950), *Jesse James vs. the Daltons* (1953), *The Dalton that Got Away* (1960),[30] and *The Last Ride of the Dalton Gang* (1979). After running out of original material, film directors also produced such forgettable spin-offs as *The Daltons' Women* (1950, starring Lash LaRue and Fuzzy St. John) and *The Dalton Girls* (1957). That's just a short list of films in which the Daltons principally figure. A listing of their occasional appearances in western genre movies might go on for pages. For example, one of the Daltons ("Rob") is featured, as are many other western characters, in the 1965 Three Stooges movie *The Outlaws Is Coming,* also notable for an early appearance by Adam West, who would later star as Batman. For another example, the lovely Jane Russell played the unlovely Belle Starr in *Montana Bell* (1952), the slender plot of which involves Bob Dalton rescuing Starr from a lynch mob and then hiding her in the Dalton cave, where she meets all the gang members, who vie for her romantic attention.

Nor can such abiding fame be confined to a single cultural expression, as powerful as it may be. Museums? The Daltons have at least two of them. The lesser known is in Meade, Kansas, where a sister of the Dalton clan lived and kept a house that supposedly also functioned as a Dalton hideout. A ninety-five-foot tunnel leads from a trap door in the parlor to a barn, which is now festooned with Dalton memorabilia. (Should visitors get bored with the outlaw displays they might also marvel at a two-headed calf, sensibly preserved in formaldehyde.)[31]

The main museum is in Coffeyville, Kansas, the site of their demise. Indeed, the entirety of the town acts as a display, and visitors are encouraged to take a walking tour past the sites where each body fell, the corpses' grim positions now commemorated by painted outlines and somber plaques. A life-sized mural recreates the famous picture of the Daltons lined up in death.[32] The museum gift store offers, wittily, Dalton shot glasses for only $4. Those on a more restricted budget must settle for a $3.75 refrigerator magnet. Visitors must also see a plaster replica of the "world's largest hailstone," which plummeted to the ground (at a speed, scientists have calculated, of 105 mph) on September 3, 1970. The hailstone is 17.5 inches in circumference and weighs an astonishing 1.67 pounds. I'm unsure whether that is the weight of the original ice or only the plaster.[33]

Music? The Dalton Gang is, or at least was, a popular music group. In 1973 the Eagles released their album *Desperado,* which included a specific tribute song to the Dalton-Doolin gang. Another of the songs is entitled "Bitter Creek," presumably a reference to gang member George "Bitter Creek" Newcomb. The back of the album shows the group in a pose resembling the famous picture of the dead Daltons. Memorabilia? Insignificant letters written and signed by Emmett Dalton are today offered by historical auction sites (minimum bid, $1,600). Games? A five-hundred-piece jigsaw puzzle entitled "The Dalton Gang" is widely offered for sale at $12.98. The puzzle depicts a group of cute kittens attired in western garb. The brothers are even, notes Robert Barr Smith, featured in a comic strip: "The Daltons— four of them—are the villains of a popular European comic strip called 'Lucky Luke,' in which Luke, with his faithful horse and dog, endlessly pursues the Daltons."[34] Popular literature, dime novels, and of course historical studies all bear witness to the Dalton phenomena.

Nor is this mania a recent occurrence. Captain Jack preserved a clipping from the *St. Louis Globe Democrat* (October 7, 1892) written two days after the Coffeyville raid, which notes that "hundreds of visitors arrive on every train to visit the scene of the Daltons' last raid, and the city is crowded with strangers." Some of the assembled spectators hoped to obtain more than fond memories of their visit, and "relic hunters took everything they could lay their hands on, even hair from the tails of the robbers' horses."

Many eminently worthy people from the past, now entirely forgotten except perhaps by their descendants, rise to the surface in our present only by some association, however tenuous, with the Dalton mystique. (Captain Jack is just such a figure.) Who has ever heard of Dr. W. W. McEwen? He was the mayor of Mound Valley, Kansas, and later Durango, Colorado, where he established a private hospital. During his long life, he must have treated thousands of patients. But he's now remembered only for treating one—Emmett Dalton—when the local Coffeyville physicians supposedly refused to help the dying outlaw.[35] An interview he gave to the *San Diego Union* on November 15, 1936, when he was eighty-six years old, recounts this experience and is preserved on the Internet by one of his granddaughters. Dr. McEwen is just one of nearly 33,000 hits an Internet search engine returns on the "Dalton Gang."

The Daltons' family history is one of those vexing subjects that seems to become more confused as more people write about it.[36] In what follows, I generally depend on an account provided by Ben Dalton himself. As best as can now be determined, the original Dalton family goes all the way back to France under the name "D'Alton." Later generations moved to the British Isles, then to Virginia and Kentucky, and finally to Missouri. James Lewis Dalton (1826–1890), father of the famous brood, served as a fifer under General Zachary Taylor in the Mexican War.

The Daltons also have a family story, one about the war heroics of their father. Ben Dalton recalled,

> Our family was from Kentucky, near Mount Sterling. Father was raised there and went through the Mexican war as a member of Col. Cleary's regiment. He was the fifer. At the battle of Buena Vista he

blew the long roll which aroused the American soldiers when the Mexicans were trying to surprise them. I heard him tell the story. The Sergeant came to the place where my father was sleeping, grabbed him by the foot and pulled him out. "The Mexicans are coming," he said, "blow the long roll." Without waiting a moment my father began to fife, the Americans fell into line and the surprise the Mexicans had planned fell through. (*St. Louis Globe Democrat*, October 16, 1892)

The battle of Buena Vista was fought on February 22 and 23, 1847, resulting in an American victory over Mexican troops (who greatly outnumbered them) commanded by General Antonio Lopez de Santa Anna.[37] Various Kentucky regiments served with distinction during the engagement, although I am unable to find one specifically commanded by a Colonel Cleary. Complicating the details of this family story is Dalton's application for a pension in which he lists his commander as "Col. Wm. R. McKee."[38] A number of officers who would later achieve prominence in the Civil War fought, including Colonel Jefferson Davis and Braxton Bragg.

By 1850, James had moved to Westport, a landing on the Missouri River (which later became Kansas City), where he found work as a horse trader and saloon keeper. On March 12, 1851, he married Adeline Lee Younger, of the Younger family whose sons rode with Jesse James, robbing the train at Adair, Iowa. Many of Captain Jack's contemporaries believed that the Dalton, Younger, and James families were closely interrelated, sharing "bad blood" responsible for their criminal inclinations.[39] A reporter for the *St. Louis Globe Democrat* asked Ben Dalton, shortly after the Coffeyville raid, this very question (in a clipping dated October 16, 1892, which Captain Jack saved):

"What is the truth about these stories of a relationship between your family and the James boys and Younger brothers?"

"There is no kinship whatever between our family and the James family," Ben said. "The Youngers and the Jameses were not related at all. That is all a mistake. We are distantly related to the Youngers in this way. The father of the Younger brothers and our mother were half brother and sister. Harry Younger, the grandfather of the Youngers, had two wives. The father of Cole Younger was a son of

Harry Younger by the first wife. My mother was a daughter of Harry Younger by the second wife. That is all there is in the relationship."

James and Adeline were a prolific couple, raising fifteen children, ten boys and five girls. After the Civil War, in which he did not serve, James moved the family to Cass County, Missouri, where they farmed 640 acres. But he became involved in speculating on cattle deals, which failed, and in the process, he lost the family farm, the mortgage of which he had pledged as collateral. The family then moved to a homestead in the Coffeyville area, which many of the younger sons came to consider their hometown.

The elder Dalton sons (Ben, Henry ["Cole"], Littleton, and Frank) were, by most accounts, honest and hardworking men. Frank Dalton served as a U.S. deputy marshal riding for "Hanging Judge" Parker's court and was acquainted with Heck Thomas. On November 27, 1887, he was killed in the line of duty while engaged in a shootout with a band of whiskey smugglers. Liquor law violations were by far and away the most common crimes in the territories, a situation not helped by the fact that federal law occasionally conflicted with Indian tribal codes determining what could be sold and to whom. For example, "uno beer," a supposedly 1 percent alcohol brew, could be legally sold in certain places but not to Indians, thus requiring that strict enforcement would necessarily involve training in both chemistry and genealogy. Attempting to uphold such laws was a largely futile but often dangerous matter. Perhaps Captain La Flore set a record when, during a series of raids, he single-handedly in only one short week "closed up twenty-eight beer saloons in the Chickasaw country—fourteen in Ardmore, eight in Purcell, three at Pauls Valley, two in Wynnwood, and one in Barywn. He not only closed them up but seized all the goods and houses and placed the same in custody of U.S. officers."[40] I am told by historians familiar with this area that even such heroic labors would have barely dented the trade.

The younger Dalton sons (Grat, Bill, Bob, and Emmett) initially followed Frank's example. As late as 1890, three of the Dalton boys were employed as law enforcement officers, either as deputy marshals or paid posse men. Many, but not all, of the Daltons' contemporaries remembered them fondly. Mrs. Katie (Whiteturkey) Day, for example, reported that "the Daltons boys used to camp near our place and have eaten with us many times. They were always very friendly and nice with our family."[41] Another view is presented by Ninnian Tannehill:

> But when the Dalton boys were United States Marshals they were cold and cruel. While I was in Fort Smith, the Dalton boys came to a place close to Fort Smith to arrest a boy. He was staying with his sister and her husband in a tent. As the Dalton boys approached, the woman came out of the front on the tent with her baby in her arms and they shot her through the breast; the ball passed through her body and for some time I helped care for her and she finally recovered. The men shot and killed her husband but the boy, her brother, escaped by leaving the thirty-foot tent by the rear.[42]

By some reports, Bob Dalton had even served a stint as chief of the Osage Indian Police, a position in which he must have been acquainted with Captain Charles La Flore, chief of the Union Indian Police.[43] But law enforcement was then a low-paying job. Perhaps even worse, pay was slow in arriving. Because Oklahoma was then a federal territory, salary vouchers and disbursements had to be approved not only by the head U.S. marshal but also the courts of jurisdiction and occasionally by bureaucrats far away in Washington, D.C. This led to situations, reports Ben Dalton, where his brothers Bob, Grat, and Emmett were broke despite being owed hundreds of dollars by the government.

Unable to support themselves on a deputy marshal's meager pay, the boys often supplemented their income by working as cowboys. Emmett was intermittently employed at the Bar X Bar Ranch, where he met Bill Doolin and Bill Power(s),[44] future members of the Dalton Gang. Working on nearby ranches were "Blackface" Charlie Bryant (named because his face was tattooed with black-powder burns), George "Bitter Creek" Newcomb ("I'm a she-wolf from Bitter Creek, and it's my night to howl-l-l!" —traditional cowboy drinking chant), Richard "Dick" Broadwell (whose honeymoon was interrupted when his new wife stole all his money and deserted him), and "Cockeyed" Charlie Pierce (a fugitive wanted on charges of peddling whiskey to Indians), all of whom would join the gang.

Nor did working as a deputy marshal ensure that one's colleagues and professional associates were necessarily of any better character than some of the cowboys mentioned above. The ever-delicate distinction between crooks and cops was then especially flexible. For example, on Monday, February 9, 1891, while at Ft. Smith working on the Alexander Lewis case, Captain Jack notes in his diary that he paid $2 for a "court transcript of convictions of James Yates Deputy U[nited] S[tates] M[arshal]."[45] Why he needed such a transcript is not known, but that he needed it, and that it even existed, support the point about the character of some deputy marshals. Legendary Oklahoma lawman Frank Canton provides another example, in the process writing one of the few negative things I've ever seen written about Heck Thomas. Canton recalls a dispute, the core of which is that he considered a certain gentleman—one of the Dunn brothers, who later killed Charlie Pierce and (so it was once widely believed) "Bitter Creek" Newcomb—an outlaw and wanted to arrest him, but was stopped by Thomas, who considered this same gentleman a valuable deputy marshal. He might have been, and probably was, both.

Canton is himself an excellent example of the often smudged line between lawbreaker and law enforcer. His amiable autobiography, *Frontier Trails,* somehow neglects to mention that under his true name, Joe Horner, Canton was both a murderer and a thief, and began his illustrious career in law enforcement only after escaping from the Hunstville penitentiary, where he was serving ten years imprisonment for robbery, on August 4, 1879.[46] Captain Jack's counterpart at Wells Fargo, Fred Dodge, similarly observes that "there was at that time a good many crooked Dep. U.S. Marshals in and through that Country."[47] Al Jennings, in "Holding Up a Train," further supports this point:

> But the outlaw carries one thought constantly in his mind—and that is what makes him so sore against life, more than anything else— he knows where the marshals get their recruits of deputies. He knows that the majority of these upholders of the law were once lawbreakers, horse thieves, rustlers, highwaymen, and outlaws like himself, and that they gained their positions and immunity by turning state's evidence, by turning traitor and delivering up their comrades to imprisonment and death.[48]

Combine legal authority with poverty, resentment, bad examples, temptation, and lack of close supervision, and the outcome is predictable, if not justifiable. When the Dalton boys arrested some whiskey runners in the Indian Territory, they were offered and accepted a bribe to turn the prisoners loose and not report the arrest.

"Worse offenders were treated in the same way for larger consideration," Ben Dalton recalls. "Such doings could not go on long without
discovery. Information reached superior officers. Complaints were
filed in court. The boys gave themselves up, agreed to stand trial and
were let out on bond. They repudiated their bonds and took to the
brush, in defiance of the Government" (*St. Louis Globe Democrat*, October 16, 1892).

From bribery, Bob and Emmett quickly graduated to selling Indians whiskey, and then perhaps horse thievery. One story has them
contracting with the owners of thirty horses to drive the herd to
Columbus, Kansas, where, representing that they owned the horses,
they sold them and pocketed the funds. By chance, the real owners
were in town and happened to meet with the man who bought the
horses, thereby exposing the theft. "Bob and Emmett Dalton had just
time to transfer their saddles to fresh horses when the angry crowd
started for them," Ben remembers;

> then ensued a great man hunt. Down through the Territory the out-
> laws fled, hard followed. The Daltons left the roads and went
> through pasture after pasture, jumping off their horses and snap-
> ping with nippers the wire fences as often as they came to them.
> Emmett's horse gave out, and he forced an exchange with the first
> farmer he met, but the pursuit was so hard that there was no time
> to saddle. Emmett went on bareback until he met another man on
> horseback. He offered him twice what his saddle was worth, trans-
> ferred it, and told him a party of friends would be along in a few
> minutes to pay for it. The chase lasted all day, and the Daltons es-
> caped. (*St. Louis Globe Democrat*, October 16, 1892)

Well, some of them did. Grat Dalton was accused of being an accomplice in this thievery and was for some months locked up in jail,
but he was released as a result of lack of evidence. First Bob and Emmett, then Grat, ran off to California, eventually joining their brother
Bill, then living—and reportedly doing quite well—in Tulare County.
About the time the four Dalton brothers were reunited, robbers attempted to stop a Southern Pacific train near Alila but were repulsed,
although not before the train's fireman was killed. Rightly or wrongly,
suspicion focused on the Daltons. Ben, as has already been reported,
emphatically denied that his brothers were involved:

When an express company gets after a man it has no mercy. . . . It may do injustice. I know it did in that case, for I have satisfied myself that all of my brothers were entirely innocent. Not one of them was at the Alila robbery. They had had trouble in the Indian Territory and they had gone to California to look for work and to begin their lives over again. That is the truth of it. William was living out there and was doing well. Grat and Bob and Emmett were on the way out there when this thing was laid on them. (*St. Louis Globe Democrat,* October 16, 1892)

Cole Dalton, who also happened to be in California, appeared before a grand jury for two days, pleading his brothers' case, but to no avail. "Boys," he advised his brothers, "you better take a couple of horses and get out of the country." Bob and Emmett fled back to the Indian Territory. Grat stayed and was arrested as an accessory.

Perhaps the brothers reasoned that if they were going to be accused of train robbery, they might as well become train robbers, if they were not already. Between May 1891 and June 1892 they robbed, virtually unopposed, trains at Wharton, Leliaetta, and Red Rock, but the take was small, perhaps as little as $3,500 for all three jobs.[49] On September 18, 1891, Grat escaped from jail and returned to Oklahoma to join his outlaw brothers and their accomplices. Had there been any doubt as to how dangerous these men could be, it was emphatically removed when Deputy Marshal Ed Short captured gang member "Blackface" Charlie Bryant in Hennessy, Indian Territory (August 1891). While confined in the express car, "Blackface" Charlie discovered a pistol left behind by a careless agent. In the ensuing fight, he and Marshal Short shot each other, each dying in pools of the other's blood.

Early evening, July 14, 1892. Perhaps about 8:45 P.M. A group of mounted, heavily armed men approaches Adair from the south. By some accounts, they had procured and were accompanied by a spring wagon. Exactly how many men rode toward Adair is in dispute, with estimates from only six to as many as fifteen. Nobody can now know with any certainty. Perhaps, as they neared the town, they split into smaller groups, so as not to arouse suspicion. E. D. Nix (himself a famous Oklahoma lawman[50]) writes, "They knew that a considerable shipment of money was being made on a Missouri, Kansas and Texas passenger train on this particular day, and they also knew that the train was being heavily guarded by a force, augmented by Indian police."[51] How they might have known this Nix does not say.

Writing many years after the event, Emmett Dalton provides at least one explanation for such prescience, telling the (probably tall) tale of one Eugenia Moore, brother Bob's girlfriend. She was "a valuable ally. She was a girl of unusual tact and quick wit and was a loyal member of our band. Riding up and down on the railroad from Parsons, Kansas, to Denison, Texas, she was constantly on the alert for bits of information which might prove of value to us. She being a telegraph operator, she frequently overheard messages in the depots telling of money shipments."[52] Most historians dismiss Emmett's story as nonsense, as do I. Few during that time rode the railroads from Parsons to Denison more frequently than Captain Jack, and he surely would have noticed a pretty girl who made it her habit to befriend and eavesdrop on the Katy telegraphers. Although the Daltons probably did have sources of inside information, it seems unlikely that so obvious a spy (under the name "Flo Quick," she had a notorious reputation as both a seductress and a horse thief) could have for long escaped scrutiny.[53]

Numerous outlaws of the time similarly claimed to have sources of inside information. Al Jennings boasted his band would never rob a train unless they first received a tip that it contained a large amount of cash. Again, given Al's track record as a train robber, skepticism is warranted. But many years after these events, in 1938, three old railroad men shared their memories on the NBC radio show *Interesting Neighbors*. Mr. E. C. Ott, a former express agent, remembered (inaccurately) that his train was held up twice during the 1890s by the Dalton Gang, at Pryor Creek and Gibson station. What disturbed Mr. Ott most about these robberies was that he had forgotten "the Dalton password to use in case his train was stopped by members of the gang."[54] This certainly suggests a level of collusion between some railroad workers and the outlaws who preyed on them.

In any event, as the gang approached Adair, the town would have been largely deserted. Most of the townspeople were farmers, accustomed to retiring early so they could arise before dawn. There just wasn't that much to do in so small a town. Skinner's general store may still have been open, as was Fishback's Pool Hall, where earlier in the week the Daltons were rumored to have visited. The town's physician, Dr. T. S. Youngblood, and his friend visiting from Fredrickstown, Missouri, Dr. W. L. Goff, were finishing up their rounds. After their day's work, they would often meet in the town's pharmacy and compare notes on patients, exchange medical gossip, and otherwise relax. They had planned to do so that night. Also sure to be open was a small ticket, telegraph, and freight office that the Katy maintained at the railroad depot, with a single station agent, a Mr. Heywood or Haywood, on duty. It was at this office that the Dalton gang converged, as a single body or as a collection of smaller groups. The station agent, facing multiple Winchesters, offered no resistance. The robbers broke open the cash drawer, which contained only three or four dollars. Before Haywood was bound and gagged, his watch was stolen. The thief was not so much interested in the watch as he was the time. It was, let us say, about 9:15 P.M. Katy No. 2 was due to arrive at 9:42.

BEGGARS AND BARONS

The greater part of men must be content to be as though they had not been.
—*Sir Thomas Browne*

Everything considered, Captain Jack had a pretty good year in 1891. He was happily married, and had been for fourteen years, to Elizabeth Jeffers, a woman from a prominent family in St. Louis. He would father eight children (his daughter Nellie died in infancy), and he had a job that enabled him to support them, if not see them as often as he might have wished. Not all families were so lucky. Thomas Schlereth notes that "in 1889 and 1890 a withering drought—coupled with declining prices for wheat and corn—ended the western land boom, destroyed the hope of profit and security on prairie farms, and left thousands of families facing bankruptcy and even starvation. On land that had recently produced twenty bushels of wheat to the acre, farmers were now lucky to grow four. By the end of the 1880s the price that one bushel would bring had dropped from $1.19 to $0.49."[1]

Railroads were both the motive and stress points of the economy, and prospered or failed as the financial cycles turned, which they did often with dizzying speed. It is fair to say, as Mark Svenvold does, that

never have things been so bad for so many, nor so good for so few. The period coincided with the most spectacular accumulation of capital in the fewest hands that the world is ever likely to see. By 1900, with a population of 76 million, a scant fraction of 1 percent—between 25,000 and 40,000 people in the United States—owned half of the country's wealth. It was the era of the booming industrialists of steel, railroads, and of coal—whose names we know from the marble columns, the grand estates, and the endowments they have left behind: Rockefeller, Carnegie, Frick, Morgan.[2]

One name missing from that distinguished list is Mr. Jay Gould (1836–1892). Gould, a distant relative of another much reviled historical figure, Aaron Burr, worked first as a clerk in a general store, a job from which he was fired. Learning that the store's owner was interested in an adjacent piece of land, Gould borrowed money and bought the property for himself. He later resold it to his boss at a price considerably above what that gentleman hoped to pay. In another curious episode, young Jay seems to have first visited New York for the purpose of touting the proverbial—although in this case literal—better mousetrap, a device invented by his grandfather. But the mousetrap, encased in an expensive-looking wooden box, was promptly snatched by a thief who Jay and his companion managed to catch and detain long enough for a policeman to arrive and escort the struggling threesome before a judge. "At the hearing," writes Maury Klein, "the magistrate ordered the box opened. When the mousetrap was revealed in all its brightly painted glory, the thief gasped in bewilderment. The justice burst out laughing and declared the prisoner to be the largest rat ever caught in a mousetrap. It was a good enough story to make the *New York Herald,* the first time Jay Gould's name appeared in the metropolitan dailies that were later to transform him into a legend."[3]

Gould's first real business success was as the general manager, then partner, and finally owner of a leather tannery, a success achieved despite the fact that, when he started, he had not the slightest idea of how to tan hides. But no matter. Gould quickly learned that although you could make money manufacturing goods people wanted, you could often make far more were you to gain control of such productive enterprises by arranging the financing they required. Why tan hides when you could instead print stock? Wall Street existed for just that purpose.

Companies, then as now (although it was a lot easier then), often supported their growth and operations by issuing stock, each share representing a claim upon the company's assets and revenue. But the price of stocks fluctuated considerably, both naturally and increasingly by design. An astute observer could determine a point where the value of the outstanding stock was less than the value of the assets of the issuing company. One could then, with sufficient capital, acquire the stock, sell the assets, and pocket the difference. More routinely, stock was "watered,"[4] or issued in amounts far exceeding the value of the assets, and propped up by rumor and speculation to a point where it was allowed to crash, the insiders first having sold it short. One might further note that insider trading, although illegal now, was then commonplace, and that accounting, if not an outright fiction, was rightly distrusted to the point where many publicly traded companies did not even bother to publish quarterly financial statements, because all parties were aware that such numbers were essentially meaningless.

Although issuing stock in theory would dilute ownership (though the company's original founder was usually allowed to remain in charge), in practice, the selling brokers would often retain and amass the proxies, enabling them to stack the board of directors, if not seize outright control, leaving the company under the mercenary direction of officers whose sole interest was in the price and fluctuation of the stock. Up or down didn't much matter, so long as they had advance knowledge. No one played this complicated game better than Gould: "Since Jay possessed large ambitions and meager resources, he cultivated the art of controlling huge enterprises with minimum holdings, utilizing not only equity control but funded debt, the proxy market, floating debt, contractual flaws, receiverships, and especially legal technicalities."[5]

The point is still debated whether or not the machinations of Gould, and others like him, ultimately helped or hurt the general economy. Take the rail industry, for one example. Before Gould and other speculators turned their attention to the railroads, the industry was largely fragmented into many dozens, if not hundreds, of small companies, each perhaps owning maybe a few hundred miles of track in a confusing patchwork of overlapping operations. Consider the cautionary fate of the Selma, Marion, and Memphis Railroad, a fairly typical start-up venture of the time. The railroad, which was incorporated in 1868, even if successfully completed, would have controlled only some 300 miles of track and connected markets of relatively minor importance. But only a few miles of track were actually laid, in part because of an acute shortage of labor, a situation the company's president attempted to remedy both by importing Japanese and Chinese workers and by contracting with the State of Alabama for convict labor. More seriously, the company did not have, nor could it raise, anywhere near the capital required for such a venture, despite the company's president signing and personally guaranteeing hundreds of thousands of dollars' worth of construction bonds (which are valuable collectibles today). Somehow, the company struggled until 1873, when the failure of Jay Cooke's bank in Philadelphia—a major railroad financier of the period—caused a financial panic resulting in many thousands of corporate and personal bankruptcies, including that of the Selma railroad company's president, Mr. Nathan Bedford Forrest. With exquisite historical irony, the general who had wrecked so many railroads during his Civil War raids was in turn ruined by one.

Of some interest here, at least to me, is that one of General Forrest's commands was the Second Missouri Cavalry led by Robert "Black Bob" McCollough. Enlisted as the "Forage Master" of the Second Regiment, Company A, was the son of a Welsh immigrant, a distant cousin of future English Prime Minister David Lloyd George, named Francis Marion George, my maternal great-grandfather. Private George seems to have participated in most of Forrest's campaigns, including—I am ashamed to say—the capture of Ft. Pillow, during which hundreds of black Union soldiers were killed, by many accounts after they had surrendered. The extent to which Forrest ordered this massacre, or allowed it to happen, is a still controversial topic. From what I've read, I don't think Forrest ordered the slaughter, but for reasons that do him little credit. A former slave owner and trader, he considered blacks not as people but as property, and his first concern upon their capture would be returning them to their rightful "owners."[6]

As a businessman, Forrest was strictly an amateur compared with the likes of Gould, who began forming his rail empire in 1867, successfully battling Cornelius Vanderbilt for the Erie Railroad. After achieving control in 1868, he immediately began buying competing lines and consolidating them into one enterprise. As that enterprise grew, it became apparent that the conglomerate value of the assets could become worth far more than their combined aggregate values. As consolidation inevitably reduced competition, the consolidator could begin to drive the market forces he was formerly forced to obey. Freight pricing structure could reflect not what the market would allow, but what it would bear.

That, at least, was the theory. The reality was that although consolidation cleared the ocean of minnows, the sharks were then left to devour each other. The prize in this increasingly savage struggle was control of the transcontinental railroad, a control that, if achieved, would yield unimaginable wealth. On May 10, 1869, the Union Pacific and Central Pacific railroads linked at Promontory, Utah, thus establishing a transcontinental connection, but it was by no means clear which lines would feed this connection, how the routes would evolve as a consequence, or who would control what. A feeding frenzy of epic proportions resulted to decide such questions, with railroad magnates and Wall Street speculators forming alliances in the morning that they would betray in the afternoon, pretending to buy this railroad while secretly acquiring that, expanding or threatening to expand existing routes for the sole purpose of undercutting rivals, and generally engaging in all manner of clever and vicious backstabbery.

Perhaps the most potent weapon in this protracted war was the rate cut. The railroads slashed freight rates (their primary source of operating income) beneath their own cost, sacrificing profit in an attempt to build market share, with each rail potentate betting the company that he had deeper pockets than his rivals. For the better part of two decades, at least in the railroad industry, the infamous "robber barons" seemed primarily intent upon robbing each other, subsidizing the cost of moving goods from producers to consumers. Still, a clever operator—and Jay Gould was certainly that—could occasionally turn even this bleak situation to his advantage. On one occasion, when Gould controlled the Erie and "Commodore" Vanderbilt the competing Central railroad,

the usual rate from Buffalo to New York was $125 a [cattle] carload. When Vanderbilt knocked the Central's rate down to $100, Gould put the Erie's at $75. The Commodore went to $50 only to have Gould drop to $25. Vanderbilt then decided to ruin the Erie's livestock traffic by setting his rate at the absurd figure of $1 per carload. At the same time hogs and sheep were being carried for a penny apiece. Sure enough, the Central filled up with cattle while the Erie's cars ran empty. Vanderbilt cackled with glee until he discovered the reason for his easy victory. Unbeknown to him, Gould and Fisk had bought every steer in Buffalo and shipped them into New York via the Central.

"When the Old Commodore found out that he was carrying the cattle of his enemies at great cost to himself and great profits to

Fisk & Gould, he very nearly lost his reason," Morosini [Gould's bodyguard, who wrote this in his memoirs] laughed. "I am told the air was very blue in Vanderbiltdom."[7]

Where Gould really excelled was in building synergistic relations between his railroad empire (which at its peak controlled over 10,000 miles of track) and his other ventures. Gould, expanding into communications, acquired Western Union and other telegraphy outfits, a handful of newspapers, and for a while monopolized the overseas cable business.[8] Even more lucrative was real estate "speculation," which bordered upon certainty. Eager municipalities and entire state governments would beg the railroad to expand in their direction, offering free land and rights of way. Because only the railroads knew exactly where they would go, and because the land adjacent to their route would increase in value many times, they were in the enviable position of being able to buy for pennies land the value of which their own presence would prodigiously multiply. A further benefit of such aggressive consolidation was the control of labor costs. Fewer and larger railroads meant less competitive opportunities for workers, who could be paid not what they wanted or even needed, but the lowest common denominator of what they would accept. Nor could unions flourish in such a climate. Gould only a little exaggerated the unenlightened spirit of monopoly capitalism when he reportedly said, "I can hire one half of the working class to kill the other half."[9]

Luckily for the working class, or at least half of them, those who nest in the very highest aeries of unrestricted capitalism at some point usually overreach themselves, often tempted by the thought that, instead of wasting their time by consolidating businesses that make money, why not attempt to consolidate, or corner, money itself? In principle, this seems easy to accomplish. Just start buying, say, gold. The more you buy, the shorter the circulating supply; the shorter the supply, the higher the price. And the higher the price, the greater the value of your own prior purchases. Eventually (in theory anyway), you own all the circulating gold, whose value has risen to approach infinity. The only problem with such a scheme is that holders of large gold reserves, like the United States government, may see the increasing prices as opportunities to sell, and depending on the quantity and timing of their sales, the price of gold could very well reverse from steadily and inevitably rising to precipitously and disastrously declining, eroding instead of augmenting the value of past acquisitions.

The obvious and simple way to avoid this danger was to bribe the political official responsible for making such decisions. However, one had to be careful, as the politician in question here happened to be the president of the United States, and although presidents were by no means immune to bribery, conventional wisdom had it they usually preferred more subtle and delicate methods than a sum of cash, however large, furtively passed over in nondescript bags. Although it may have been deemed unseemly for a president to sport a "For Sale" sign hanging from his neck, no such opprobrium attached to his relatives, and so Gould and his partner James Fisk contacted Mr. Abel R. Corbin, who was of interest to them because he had recently married Ulysses S. Grant's sister Virginia.

Grant, a gracious and cordial host, made every effort to welcome his new brother-in-law into the family, often inviting him and his sister to private dinners, after which the conversation always seemed to turn to fiscal policy and how a sound currency required that the treasury not diminish its hoard of gold. Corbin also arranged a number of private meetings between Grant, Gould, and Fisk, who used the opportunity to enlarge upon such views. Grant seemed quite receptive to such often repeated advice, but he was not a fool, and when the time came to act, he did just the opposite, authorizing the sale of $4 million in gold from the reserves. Had he timed the sale better, he could have ruined Gould, but Gould (perhaps warned by Corbin?) bailed out of the superheated market just in time. Many others did not. The ensuing financial panic, on September 24, 1869, became known as "Black Friday."

A lesson Gould learned from this misadventure (aside from the shocking revelation that not all men could be bribed[10]), as he turned his attention back to the railroads, was that, after a certain point, it didn't really matter that much if one of his companies was forced into bankruptcy. Indeed, bankruptcy could be a positive tool, as a railroad in receivership was excused from paying interest on its bonds. While amassing capital for his run at the gold market, Gould stripped the railroads bare, leaving them to survive, if they could, only on their own operating revenue. Although in principle it was a fine thing to put oneself in a position where one could charge everything the market could bear, the reality was that in times of drought and depression, the market simply couldn't bear that much. The reality was further that until the sharks stopped savaging each other, income from operations would be at best sporadic. The real money in railroads initially came from the expansion and land speculation, money that could be easily skimmed off for other purposes. As a consequence, nearly every one of Gould's railroads at some point was forced into bankruptcy, including a company that was once a southern branch of the Union Pacific, but that organized itself independently as the Missouri, Kansas, and Texas Railroad. Receivers were appointed by the courts for the Katy (Mr. George Eddy and Mr. Harrison C. Cross), and finally in 1888 Jay Gould was forced out. 1888 also seems to be the year the Katy hired railroad detective John J. Kinney Jr.[11]

Phytophthora infestans. Have you ever seen one? No? Admittedly, these critters are pretty small, although they do present a distinctive appearance: "*P. infestans* is an obligate biotroph that produces no macerating enzymes. The thallus consists of coenocytic, diploid hyphae for most of its life. The sporangiophore is characterized by unrestricted growth and lemon-shaped, detachable, papillate sporangia."[12] Clear? The lemon-shaped sporangia should be a dead giveaway. If you are Irish, as many of the people in this account are, *P. infestans* has at least significantly influenced your very life, and also probably caused the death of many of your ancestors. *Phytophthora infestans* is scientifically classified as belonging to the phylum Oomycestes, which is, as best I can tell, sort of like a fungus but in some ways not. It seems to occupy an odd biological niche between athlete's foot and toadstools. This weird organism is of interest here because it is the cause, in potatoes, of a disease known as "Late Blight," and is thus responsible for the great famine Ireland suffered from 1845 to 1848.

Famine was nothing new in Ireland, even before much of the population became dependent upon a single crop. One author, writing to Alexander Pope in 1729, observed that "As to this country [Ireland], there have been three terrible years dearth of corn, and every place strowed with beggars."[13] That same year, that same author wrote an essay to address the problem, which begins,

It is a melancholy Object to those, who walk through this great town [Dublin], or travel in Country, when they see the *Streets*, the *Roads*, and *Cabbin-Doors,* crowded with *Beggars* of the female sex, followed by three, four, or six Children, *all in Rags,* and importuning every Passenger for an Alms. These *Mothers* instead of being able to work for their honest livelyhood, are forced to employ all their time in Strolling, to beg Sustenance for their *helpless Infants,* who, as they grow up either turn *Thieves* for want of work, or leave their *dear native Country to fight for the Pretender in Spain,* or sell themselves to the *Barbadoes.*[14]

The rational solution to this continuing problem, so proposes the author, is that the Irish eat their young, as he is informed (by a "very knowing American") that "a young healthy Child well Nursed is at a year Old a most delicious, nourishing, and wholesome Food, whether *Stewed, Roasted, Baked,* or *Boyled,* and I make no doubt that it will equally serve in a *Fricasie,* or *Ragoust."*[15]

Ireland's long history of misery, of course, has its continuing roots not in potatoes but politics, which the Irish characteristically pursue by means high and low, peaceful and violent, the best and worst among them equally gripped by passionate intensity. One of the best among them—the man for whom Grat Dalton perhaps was named[16]—was Henry Grattan (1746–1820), a remarkably successful parliamentarian who confronted, peacefully, many of Ireland's most difficult issues. Presciently realizing that "'the Irish Protestant could never be free till the Irish Catholic had ceased to be a slave,' he saw that Ireland would never be free of control by the British parliament so long as there was a division into two nations, the Protestant and the Catholic."[17] Backed by huge popular support, Grattan demanded free trade, forcing the British to lift restrictions on the woolen industry and allowing free trade of exports. Finally, he fought for and won equal representation of the Irish parliament in the Commonwealth: "The Irish parliament had regained its ancient position as the sole legislator for Ireland and the Irish House of Lords was, once again, Ireland's supreme court. The passage of bills via the Irish privy council to the English privy council was scrapped. From henceforth, all Irish bills were to be sent direct, for approval or veto, to the king."[18] In one of his last speeches before the parliament he had liberated, he declared, "I am now to address a free people. Ireland is now a nation; in that new character I hail her and, bowing to her August presence, I say, *Esto perpetua."*[19]

But the worst are rarely satisfied by the efforts of the best. Just three years after Grattan's triumph, Mr. Robert Emmet—after whom Emmett Dalton was named—decided that what Ireland needed was yet another rebellion. Why he thought he might succeed when so many others before him had failed is not completely known, although perhaps it may have had something to do with the meetings he had arranged in Paris (1802) with both Napoleon and Talleyrand, importuning them to aid the Irish cause. So patriotism courts treachery. While in Paris, he happened to meet an American inventor who had developed a crude land mine that Emmet thought might be especially deadly against the hated British. So Emmet began his career as a revolutionary, a career whose bungling would nearly match Al Jenning's exploits as an outlaw. After the obligatory proclamation was published (in July 1803), calling the Irish to arms, Emmet must have been disappointed when, at the appointed time and place, only eighty or so fellow rebels showed up. But his troubles were just beginning: "the fuses for hand grenades were lost, the man who was to have made fuses for the land mines had forgotten to do it, the scaling ladders for the attack upon Dublin castle were not ready, and the horses pulling the coaches, which were to take the rebels to the castle, had mysteriously bolted!"[20]

Panicking, Emmet had his followers distribute his cache of arms to passersby on the streets, his generosity indeed attracting a large crowd, but a crowd whose subsequent actions predictably resembled less an army of patriots and more a mob of thugs. In the following riot, which lasted all night, at least two people were killed, including the Lord Chief Justice, whose coach was surrounded by a mob, a member of which ran him through with one of Emmet's pikes. After evading the law for only a month, Emmet was captured, then tried, and finally hanged on September 20, 1803. In a moving speech before his execution, Emmet asked to be buried in an unmarked grave: "When my country takes her place among the nations of earth," he concluded, "then and not till then let my epitaph be written."[21] Like the Daltons many years after him, Robert Emmet was to become a legend, suitable for the naming of young boys. His final words struck deep chords on Eire's fabled harp, whose lasting melody somehow charmed the hangman's noose into a martyr's necklace, and by whose resonant tune the gallows became a portal not to ignominious death but to enduring fame.

Under the theory that any country is only three meals away from revolution, some of the more radical of Ireland's fallen martyrs may have even welcomed—although surely only briefly—what many contemporaries described as a "queer mist" that wafted in from the ocean just before the 1845 potato harvest. "The potato," writes one historian,

> had been the staple diet of a continuously growing proportion of the Irish people for well over a century (and by the 1840s it had become the sole diet for three million out of a total population of about 8,000,000). The diet, particularly when it was combined with buttermilk, was highly nutritional, and in the view of some authorities it made a contribution to Ireland's relatively low infant mortality rate in the eighteenth and earlier nineteenth century which, in turn, was a key factor in Ireland's rapid population rise. . . . A potato crop grown on one acre of land was enough to feed a family of five or six for the best part of a year. It was easy to plant and easy to harvest: all you needed was a spade.[22]

But that "queer mist" harbored *P. infestans,* which had somehow traveled all the way from Mexico. At first the harvest proceeded without incident, with the gathered potatoes nestled in their customary bins. But inspecting those bins a few days later, horrified farmers discovered that their contents had been reduced to a black, stinking slush. "This happened without warning," the histories tell us, "in big fields and small gardens alike, in barns, shops, kitchens of houses great and small. In front of his eyes, a laborer's or a cotter's entire stock of food for the coming year would disintegrate."[23] All told, about half the 1845 crop was blighted. The next year, it all was. The crop recovered some in 1847, but it failed again completely in 1848. Even the relatively healthy harvests were small, for the farmers had eaten their seed crop and had given up hope. The Great Hunger had begun.

At the very outset panels of experts, both secular and religious, hurriedly convened in an effort to understand and cure the blight. Was God punishing the wicked? Was the Devil tormenting the good? Secular explanations ranged from static electricity to the poisonous smoke emitted from railroad locomotives to "mortiferous vapours" rising from hitherto unseen underground volcanoes. One theory neatly combined a number of such causes, advancing the view that the blight resulted from "puffing, hooting locomotives, that thundered up and down the countryside at the unholy speed of 20 miles per hour . . .

discharging electricity into the air."[24] No proposed cure worked. Famine disperses populations; dispersing populations were ideal vectors for disease, including plagues of cholera, typhus, and dysentery, all of which swept a hungry and now sick Ireland. A magistrate from Cork traveling to Skibbereen witnessed a family which illustrated in small what Ireland suffered at large: "I entered some of the hovels . . . and the scenes that presented themselves were such as no tongue or pen can convey the slightest idea of. In the first, six famished and ghastly skeletons, to all appearance dead, were huddled in a corner on some filthy straw, their sole covering what seemed a ragged horse-cloth, and their wretched legs hanging about, naked above the knees. I approached in horror, and found by a low moaning they were alive, they were in fever—four children, a woman, and what had once been a man."[25]

At least the family described above was afforded the dubious luxury of dying in their home. Almost certainly, it wasn't "their" home but instead belonged to an absentee landlord, many of whom would evict for nonpayment of rent tenants equally afflicted, which perhaps was a cruel mercy in that it hastened their deaths. By 1850, more than a million Irish had died. Another million and a half decided to leave.

One of the enduring myths of the Irish diaspora, responsible for much of the prejudice they later encountered, was that only the lowest classes of the Irish population emigrated. The "lowest classes" were, in fact, the people most likely to die. Moving required money. In any event, class distinctions virtually collapsed as the Irish economy disintegrated. Famine, pestilence, and poverty are great levelers. As if such misery were not enough, in 1848 a group calling itself the "Young Irelanders"[26] staged yet another failed rebellion. (Ireland—or a part of it—would not achieve independence until early in the morning of December 6, 1921, when its representatives signed a treaty offered by my distant relative Prime Minister David Lloyd George.[27]) For many, it was time to leave. Nor would such a trip be easy: "Greedy and unscrupulous middlemen—and to their shame, some ships' captains and owners, too—took their money and put to sea in old and decrepit ships carrying two, three or four times the number of passengers considered safe for voyaging across the Atlantic, ships in which more than one-fifth of the starving and debilitated emigrants perished before they even saw the New World. Coffin ships they were aptly called."[28] Among those million and a half emigrants was a young "iron worker" named John Kinney, also spelled "Kenny" and "Kiney."

Virtually nothing is now known about this Mr. Kinney, other than he somehow turned up in Glasgow, Scotland, where, early in 1850, he met and married Ms. Annie McGuigan (also spelled "McGonghan" and "McGough"). They remained in Glasgow long enough to have two sons, Peter (in 1851) and John Jr.—Captain Jack—in 1852. Sometime thereafter, they arrived in the United States, probably through the port of New York, and initially settled at Troy, New York, where Captain Jack's little brother Henry was born in 1854. The family later moved to Yonkers, New York, and by the time of the 1880 census, the mother and the father were living in Philadelphia. Along the way, they had six other children. Mother and Father Kinney were still alive in 1891, still living in Philadelphia. All that now remains of Captain Jack's parents is a single, fading letter, undated, consoling them over the death of their infant daughter Nellie:

> Dear Eliza,
>
> I received a letter from Johnny telling me of Nellie's death. I am very sorry for I thought of all the pleasant days we spent here with her and many a time I longed to hear her coming on to Philadelphia again with you.
>
> But we all know that she is better off. I know that you must feel grief over her so believe me we all feel sorrow for you.
>
> Accept our love to you and Johnny and the children.
>
> John and Annie Kinney

What collection of causes could be responsible for a famine immigrant's second son one day to find himself, on July 14, 1892, carrying a Winchester and riding the train to Adair? We must depend on pure conjecture. As Tom Furlong's "lieutenant," Captain Jack worked for another of Jay Gould's railroads, the Missouri Pacific. The MoPac, as it was called, was based in St. Louis, which is where, before moving to Sedalia, Kinney lived for many years, involving himself in, among other pursuits, ward politics.[29] Curiously, when the MoPac was about to start actual operations in the early to mid-1850s, the original Kinney family had just settled in Troy. A Web site history of the MoPac mentions that the line's first passenger cars (which seated sixty and cost $2,300) were manufactured in Troy, New York. Might Father Kinney, the iron worker, have been involved in their manufacture? If he was, did he establish connections leading to his son's eventual railroad employment?

Probably around 1873, young Captain Jack drifted to St. Louis and met and later married (in 1877) Elizabeth Jeffers, who in due course gave birth to their eldest daughter Mamie. But he was evidently unable to find suitable employment, so, leaving his wife and daughter with the Jeffers, he returned to New York City, hoping to reunite his family as his economic situation improved. That didn't happen. At first the only work he could find was tending bar and cooking stews and oysters for a saloon. He lived in a small, bug-infested rooming house with six other gentlemen so poor that between the seven of them, they owned exactly one good shirt, which they would exchange as necessary for job interviews. His letters from that period reveal an intensely lonely man desperately missing his wife and daughter. At one point, probably through his father's influence, he obtained a job at nearby Hunter's Point in a foundry, but he quickly discovered that entry-level jobs in foundries were hot, dirty, dangerous, and physically exhausting.

Here's a typical letter from him (silently corrected for spelling errors) to Elizabeth, dated August 10, 1881:

My dear wife,

You will have to excuse me for not writing to you before now but to tell you the truth I expected to be in St. Louis before now and take you by surprise. The boiler in our shop collapsed and we have been idle 8 days and I was going to pack up and go to you but when I counted everything up I thought it would be better to wait for a while yet. We started to work this morning and I will work three weeks and then I will start for St. Louis. You ask me how I like this life and I must say that it has been the sorest trial of my life. Just a moment ago Mrs. Con [?] waited on me for the rent—we have a new landlord and he is in a hurry for the rent. . . .

[S]o you see I have made up my mind to be with you soon. I will pack up the bedding and one bedstead and spring and the pictures and the looking glass and the bed clothes and the iron ware and sewing machine and wringer and I will sell the rest for what I can get. I will be in St. Louis by the 1st of September or shortly after. Eliza you must know that I felt down hearted at being locked [?] out of work at this time but it may be for the best. . . .

From your Husband,
John J. Kinney

And if you are in want of money let me know. Good night and God Bless you all and give my love to all.

Because events had not worked out in New York, it seemed best to return to St. Louis, where he would at least be able to be with his family. This he did, and by 1882, he had somehow managed to secure employment as a detective for the Missouri Pacific Railroad.[30] One knows this because on October 21, 1882, Captain Jack is writing a letter to Elizabeth from Lenora, Kansas, and he notes that "there is great excitement in this place." One of the men he is "after"—indicating he is now working as a detective—is sitting shackled in the very lobby he is writing from, already under arrest. There has been, so he writes, some sort of a fight in which "four officers" were killed. Captain Jack is under the impression that the felon, who is watching him even as he writes the letter, is a horse thief. As best I can now tell, there was in that part of Kansas and on that very date a "great excitement," although it didn't have anything to do with horse thieves. A large mob of drunken cowboys, led by a character known as "Texas Jack," had decided, apparently just for the hell of it, that it would be great fun to shoot up a train. This they did, inflicting considerable damage but not actually hurting any passengers. News of this outrage quickly reached Dodge City, and a special train was loaded with deputies, who soon confronted the cowboy mob, the leaders of which were captured after a wild shootout in which nobody was wounded. The accounts make clear that some of the shackled prisoners were lodged in hotel lobbies until their transport could be arranged.[31]

Thus much of Captain Jack's life, his childhood, his maturity, and his early middle age, now rests on history's deep bottom, never likely to resurface. Although no one expects history to be fair, it is nevertheless disconcerting that the outlaw Kinneys of the time ("Kinney" and its variants are common Irish surnames) have achieved some measure of notoriety, and thus remembrance, even as Captain Jack languishes in obscurity. Consider a gentleman known only as "Yank" Kinney. In the summer of 1860, a prospector found gold in an alluvial sand bar on the presciently named Orofino Creek, Idaho (or what would become Idaho), causing yet another of the gold and silver rushes that so characterized western history. By the middle of the

1860s, perhaps 40,000 people occupied the Boise Basin, scattered among dozens of towns and encampments. Law enforcement for the most part simply didn't exist, except as sporadically administered by that peculiarly American institution known as the lynch mob. One of the mob's organizers, Big Bill McConnell, is quoted as follows: "Disorder was in fact better organized than order. It was impossible to impanel a jury that was not composed of thugs and gamblers. Prior to 1865, about sixty deaths by violence had occurred without a single conviction for murder."[32]

In July 1867 a group of prospectors working the Thomas Gulch foolishly allowed the *Idaho World* to report that they were about to transport some $13,000 in gold from their camp to town for safekeeping. This announcement presented an open invitation to any nearby outlaws, including "Yank" Kinney, who had drifted into the area two years before, formed a gang of thugs, and was widely believed to be responsible for a number of robberies and killings. When the Kinney Gang ambushed the miners, they encountered more resistance than they had expected, with Kinney himself wounded during the fight, as was a Mr. Stuart, one of the prospectors. The vigilante committee held a mass meeting that night."'You know who the leaders are,' Big Bill McConnell cried. 'Round them up and show them no more mercy than they have shown their innocent victims!'"[33]

That was what [as Harry Sinclair Drago writes] the angry crowd wanted to hear. Men were appointed to various tasks, and the roundup began. They worked quickly, but the news of what was under way ran ahead of them and enabled a score of undesirables to make a hasty exit from Idaho City. Even so, ten blacklegs, including Yank Kinney, were dragged out of the saloons and marched up the gulch to the cottonwoods. Yank did not cringe when his turn came and the noose was dropped over his head. Hands tied, he was lifted to the back of a horse. "To hell with you!" he snarled as the animal was driven out from under him and he was left dangling in the air.[34]

Not all the outlaw Kinneys were victims of vigilante justice. At least one was a prominent instigator of it. Meet "Captain" Nathaniel ("Nat") Kinney who, just as Captain Jack, immigrated to the United States from Ireland by way of Scotland and who was, at one point in his life, employed as a railroad detective. He also claimed to have worked as a prizefighter, a Pinkerton agent, an army scout, and a shotgun rider for stagecoaches, killing four bandits during attempted robberies.[35] Captain Jack must have known of him, as did surely everybody then living in Missouri, for it was there, in Taney County in 1881, that this Captain Kinney founded and led the Law and Order League, better known as the Bald Knobbers, a vigilante group named after a rocky prominence where they held their first meeting. Then a saloon keeper turned preacher,[36] Captain Kinney was a huge, strong man, standing six feet seven inches and weighing some 300 pounds, easily combining the moral authority of the pulpit with the physical stature of a noted barroom brawler, although upon one occasion as he engaged in the latter pursuit, "he was laid out with a billiard cue in the hands of a gentleman who now occupies a prominent place in Kansas politics."[37]

In the decades after the Civil War, southwestern Missouri was generally a lawless place, and it is fair to say that the Bald Knobbers, an organization that would eventually boast of over a thousand members, originally enjoyed considerable popular support. First, they would deliver a warning—a bundle of hickory sticks left at night on the front porch of someone whose behavior they felt needed improvement. If that didn't work (and it usually did), then the night riders, wearing terrifying horned masks,[38] would return and drag the offender from his home, strip him naked, and then beat his back to a bloody pulp with the same hickory sticks he had foolishly ignored. This would reform all but the hardest cases, and for those who nevertheless persisted in their errant ways, a final visit, with a rope, would end the matter. Exactly that happened to Frank and Tubal Taylor on April 15, 1885, lynched by a mob led by Captain Kinney, his huge size preventing effective disguise.

Although never legally codified, a popular defense then against murder, by the vigilante's rope or otherwise, was that the victim deserved it. This must have seemed the case to the citizens of Taney City, who had long been terrorized by the Taylor brothers. Mr. John T. Dickenson, who owned a small store, swore out a complaint against Frank Taylor on April 8, 1885, for theft. Enraged, the Taylor brothers returned to the store, where (as one account describes it),

Frank grabbed the merchant by the throat with his left hand. With his right, he drew a .32-caliber revolver and jammed its barrel against the struggling storekeeper's mouth. Frank pulled the trigger. The ball knocked out four of Dickenson's teeth and passed out through his neck. Then Frank pushed his victim to the floor and fired another ball into his right shoulder. Dickenson fainted.

During the fracas, Tubal and Elijah [Sublett] fired five shots at Mrs. Dickenson. One ball cut off the end of her finger and another grazed her neck, drawing blood. She also fell in a faint.[39]

The next year Kinney enlivened one of his sermons by murdering (or shooting in self-defense), outside his own church, an occasional parishioner who had an annoying habit of interrupting Kinney's homilies with wry comments about the propriety of both preaching the Gospel and leading the lynch mob.

Predictably, what began as an effort to curb lawlessness instead created far more of it, various factions forming to oppose the Bald Knobbers with terror campaigns of their own. In an effort to end the increasing cycle of violence, the governor of Missouri himself prevailed on Kinney to disband the group, which he did, but to little effect, as the forces unleashed were by then too powerful for any one man to control. The Knobbers merely shifted the focus of their activities to adjacent Christian County and continued until three of their leaders were caught, tried, and themselves hanged. Before then, on August 20, 1888, Captain Kinney was himself murdered, or killed in self-defense, by William Mills Jr., a young man (he was twenty-three; Kinney was then sixty) with whom he had been feuding for years. "From 1881 to the breaking up of the Bald Knob gang," reported the *Atchison Daily Globe* (August 22, 1888, 1), "Kinney was the king of the boldest band of outlaws that ever disgraced the Southwest. His first individual murder was the killing of Andrew Cogburn at a church near Ozark on Sunday, March 19, 1886. After this numerous outrages were charged to him and his death is hailed with as much joy by the anti-Knobbers as it is with frenzied sorrow by the members of the old band."

Middle initials deserve our unstinting praise, as they enable one to distinguish between Mr. John J. Kinney and Mr. John W. Kinney, an almost exact contemporary of Captain Jack, and certainly known to him, at least by reputation, for Mr. John W. Kinney was then popularly crowned "King of the Rustlers," a signal achievement when so many rival pretenders to this cattled throne plied their felonious skills. Born in Hampshire, Massachusetts, around 1848 (some sources say 1853), the young Mr. W. Kinney traveled to Chicago, where, in April 1867, he enlisted in the army, doing well enough to muster out as a sergeant in 1873. For reasons only known to himself, he then decided to become a cattle rustler, and he concluded that the territory of New Mexico would offer fine opportunities for such a career. "By 1875," one source notes, "the John Kinney Gang was the most feared band of rustlers in the territory."[40] No steer, horse, or mule—stray or not—was safe from his criminal rope. Sheep were exempted only because few could fatten upon New Mexico's arid, sandy soil.

While celebrating the 1875 New Year's Eve in Las Cruces, Kinney and some of his band got involved in a saloon brawl with a number of soldiers, were soundly beaten, and were unceremoniously pitched into the street. Crowned outlawry could not bear such shame, and so the Kinney Gang returned armed and shot up the bar, killing three soldiers and one civilian, wounding another two soldiers and one bystander. Nothing much seems to have been done about so deadly a spree. Kinney, perhaps enjoying this taste of blood, on November 22, 1877, and for no good reason that can now be remembered, shot and killed Mr. Ysabel Barela. After this, the authorities could no longer ignore Kinney, so they did the logical thing and deputized him as a lieutenant in the Silver City Volunteers to fight in what was known as the El Paso "Salt War," where he and his gang reportedly murdered several men and raped at least one woman.

That men would kill each other over gold, although deplorable, is at least on some level understandable. But salt? Other factors were involved, including rival politicians, competing property rights, lingering animosities over the Civil War, and racial hatred between Anglos and Hispanics. Still, incredible as it may now seem, men killed each other (at least twelve died, and over fifty were wounded) over the contents of salt shakers. This bizarre "war," which is also known as the San Elizario Salt War of 1877, was ostensibly fought over ownership of salt deposits located at the foot of Guadalupe Peak, 100 miles west of El Paso. Mexican nationals and other area residents had for generations been accustomed to mining the salt for free. In 1872, after some preliminary violence in which Judge Gaylord Clarke was killed on December 7, 1870, a Missouri lawyer named Charles Howard moved to the area and was appointed district judge in 1884. Asserting legal claim over the salt flats, Howard attempted to have some men arrested who were gathering the salt, leading to a riot. The Texas Rangers were called in, but the situation quickly overwhelmed their "One riot? One ranger!" reputation, and they were forced, along with Howard and his associates, to take refuge in an adobe hut, where a five-day battle and standoff ensued. After falsely being promised leniency, Howard and the Rangers surrendered, whereupon a Mexican firing squad executed Howard and his two friends, mutilated their bodies with machetes, and dumped them down a well. Chico Barela and other leaders of the mob fled to Mexico. Order in the area was not completely restored until nearby Ft. Bliss, which had been evacuated in 1872 as a cost-cutting measure, was regarrisoned.

Kinney, a fine example of the faint line between outlaw and lawman, was hired by district attorney William Rynerson in June 1878 to fight in yet another "war," this one the famous Lincoln County War, a confusing and bloody episode in which most of the participants could offer résumés in crime at least equal to Kinney's own. By this time, Kinney boasted that he had killed fourteen men. During one memorable skirmish in this "war" (July 19, 1878), Kinney and his band—now a legal posse—tracked down, surprised, and attempted to capture an adversarial group including Mr. Henry McCarty, also known as Henry Atrim, also known as Mr. William Bonney, who, as he managed to escape, shot Kinney in the cheek.[41] The young Mr. McCarty is of course better known as Billy the Kid.

Finally, Kinney was arrested for the murder of Barela but was acquitted, enabling him to continue his dual occupations as enforcer and breaker of the law. In 1881 he was deputized to serve as a guard for prisoner Billy the Kid, fueling speculation that some authorities wished to spare Mr. Kid from fulfilling his fated and fatal appointment with Pat Garret, expecting instead his convenient execution by a vengeful guard. Mr. Kinney failed to oblige, thereby ending his legal usefulness, after which in April 1883 he was arrested and convicted, not for murder or rape, but for cattle rustling, fined $500, and sentenced to five years in the Kansas State Penitentiary. After his release on February 19, 1886, Kinney by all appearances went straight, rejoined the army, and served in Cuba during the Spanish-American War. He spent his later years as a miner and died in Prescott, Arizona, on August 25, 1919.

Disturbing as some of the antics of those sharing his surname might have been, Captain Jack certainly had no reason to feel embarrassed, and was indeed doing his part to redress the balance between shame and honor in the family tree. Other notable Kinneys of the era included Abbot Kinney, an Indian agent to various California tribes, who acted as a guide to the poet and novelist Helen Hunt Jackson, author of *Ramona,* a novel that attempted to do for Indians what her friend Harriet Beecher Stowe's work did for blacks. Abbot Kinney also founded the city of Venice, California. A John F. Kinney served as a chief justice of the Utah supreme court during a time when federal officials in Utah were frequently the target of death threats by the Mormons. Another John F. Kinney served first as an official interpreter to the plains Indians and later as head of the Yankton Indian Agency. Nor should one overlook George (no middle initial) Kinney, a distinguished representative of the extended family's equine branch, who as a three-year-old finished second in the Monmouth Stakes in August 1883 and thereafter numbered among the top racehorses of his time.

Captain Jack was, as the clipping put it, "one of the best known detectives in the country." When the Katy finally escaped receivership on June 30, 1891, his continuing employment prospects must have seemed considerably more secure, and he was invited to participate in various conferences with the new management, Katy vice president J. Waldo even occasionally making available for Kinney's travel Waldo's own private car. His beloved wife Elizabeth had completely recovered from a life-threatening illness that had left her bedridden for over a week. Mamie, his eldest daughter, had reached her fourteenth birthday (he bought her a pair of diamond earrings, perhaps from Sedalia jeweler Charles Taylor, who will later figure in this book), requiring that he spend increasing amounts of time in the task—surely dreaded by every father—of scouting out the best school where she might complete her education and so be presented to the admiring world as "finished." One school he had in mind was the North Texas Female College in Sherman, Texas, where three of Captain La Flore's daughters had graduated in June 1891. He was even lucky in cards, and he gleefully notes in his diary entry for January 30, 1891, that he won $5 playing Casino with his good friend Ellis Smith, Sheriff of Pettis County, Missouri, with whom he would later that year attend the "death watch" over Thomas Williamson. He seemed to be naturally popular, just the sort of man a community would select to be a judge in the county fair. In fact, on September 30, 1891, the town of

Muskogee appointed him to judge the "Best Lady Rider" competition at the fairgrounds, where from a select field of three finalists—Mrs. J. N. Cole, Mrs. Laura West, and Mrs. Dora Tittle—the latter was deemed most graceful horsewoman.

Most of all, his extensive travels enabled him to establish a large network of friends, associates, and colleagues wherever the western railroads went. Mr. J. L. Dunn, in an undated article that appeared in the *Sedalia Gazette,* observed that "the genial Capt. 'Jack' Kinney, of the M., K., & T. secret service, has a host of admiring friends. It is impossible for him to visit any city, town, or flag station in the United States without meeting some of them." This probably overstates the case, although Dunn should be considered a reliable source for such information, as he had accompanied Captain Jack on a number of long rail trips—as Captain Jack's prisoner (see Chapter 5).

Fraternal organizations, in which Kinney was an active member, also provided a fertile source of friends and acquaintances. In *Victorian America,* Schlereth notes that such groups were something of a national mania: "Everyone seemed to be joining some temple, clan, castle, conclave, hive, or lodge. Some participated for the sake of the sickness and death benefits many orders provided. Others took out membership to maintain business contacts. But such reasons only partially explain the stampede to become members of the Ancient Arabic Order of Nobles of the Mystic Shrine, the United Order of Druids, the Tribes of Ben Hur, the Independent Order of Gophers, the Prudent Patricians of Pompeii, or the Concatenated Order of Hoo-Hoo" (213).

With perhaps one exception, Captain Jack's affiliations were far more conservative and traditional than any of those groups listed above. For many years he was an Elk, serving in various capacities as an officer of the Benevolent and Protective Order of Elks Sedalia Lodge No. 125. Later in his life he joined the Knights of Columbus, becoming the grand knight of the Topeka, Kansas, council, from 1902 to 1904.

One of the newest and fastest-growing fraternal groups in late 1890—a year that also gave birth to the Independent Order of Owls, the Social Order of the Beauceant, and the Woodmen of the World— was a mysterious and ephemeral organization called the Knights of Reciprocity, to which the Sedalia Lodge elected Kinney as vice president in 1891. "At first," reports the *Kansas City Journal* (September

10, 1891), "the old time politicians looked askance at this new organization. It was thought not to have any place among the various orders and societies of the day." But within a year of its founding, it attracted over 25,000 members in many hundreds of lodges distributed throughout Kansas, Missouri (which itself had 263 lodges), Louisiana, Nebraska, Iowa, and a scattering of eastern states. The Knights' announced mission was both laudable (I think) and obscure: "this organization is in favor of reciprocity between all nations on the American continent and between all interests in the nation" (*Kansas City Journal*, September 10, 1891).

So innocuous and obvious a mission is probably a cloak for something else, and as best I can tell, the real purpose of the Knights was a stealth effort by the Republican Party to siphon off some of the dangerous political energy generated by the Populist movement, which was by then threatening much of the established political order.[42] Certainly Kinney was active in Republican politics and successfully campaigned for the chair of the Pettis County Republican Party: "The election of John J. Kinney as chairman of the republican county central committee means that we are to have a continuation of the aggressive campaign. . . . Mr. Kinney is no novice in the political arena. Naturally shrewd, he has in addition the experience of thorough training for years of campaigning in St. Louis" (*Sedalia Gazette*, no date).

Despite so busy a schedule, Captain Jack found opportunities for fun and games. As something of a sports enthusiast, Kinney could not have lived in his time without an awareness and appreciation of baseball, which the *New York Clipper* had declared way back in 1856 to be "generally considered the National game amongst Americans" (December 13). On Saturday, May 30, 1891, Captain Jack notes that he attended a game at the Sedalia Fair Grounds, where the MK&T team beat a group of rivals from the St. Louis Clothing House. These were interesting years in baseball's history.[43] By the 1890 season, most, although by no means all, of the players were using padded gloves, a practice that had hitherto seemed to some "unmanly." Sunday games were becoming more popular, although players still ran the risk of arrest for violating blue laws. Scores were generally high, occasionally leading to forfeiture by the home team as they ran out of balls. A popular challenge, daring anybody to catch a ball released from the top of the Washington Monument (555 feet and 5-1/8 inches tall), was canceled for reasons of safety, as "natural scientists" had calculated that a ball falling from so great a height would impact any below with a fired cannonball's force.

In February 1891, a dispute involving control of players' contracts was settled in favor of the Pittsburgh team. However, the settlement was deemed by some a "piratical" move, eventually resulting in the team being named the Pittsburgh Pirates. In April, the Brooklyn Bridegrooms opened their season at the new Eastern Park, which was located in a maze of streetcar lines. Arriving spectators were forced to dodge trolleys and became popularly known as Trolley Dodgers—hence the Brooklyn Dodgers. On March 12, 1892, the New York State Assembly distinguished itself by passing a law prohibiting the employment of women as baseball players. Not to be outdone by such madness, in which he took a professional interest, Dr. S. B. Talcott, superintendent of the State Lunatic Asylum of New York, opined in April that baseball was a promising cure for lunacy, in that a strong interest in baseball would form an "external" mania capable of replacing the internal fantasies and delusions by which lunatics were consumed.

But the best day of 1891, at least insofar as the Kinney children were concerned, was surely Thursday, May 28, when the whole Kinney family attended the famous Sells Brothers Circus. The Sells brothers (Ephraim, Allen, Lewis, and, later, Peter), based in Columbus, Ohio, organized their first show in 1871, with cast-off equipment consisting of little more than a patched tent and a few elderly and mangy animals. But they could offer at least one first-class attraction: a "percussive aerialist" (that is, a human cannonball) named Mr. George Richards. By 1890, the Sells Brothers had grown into the second largest circus in the United States, advertising themselves, as announced on the many posters distributed by their advance teams, as the "Sells Brothers World Conquering and All Overshadowing Three Ring Circus, Real Roman Hippodrome, Indian Village, and Pawnee Bill's Famous Original Wild West Show."[44]

By 1891, the year the circus became the first to tour Australia, the originally pitiful menagerie now featured "18 elephants, pumas, black panthers, antelope, lions, tigers, leopards, zebras, bears, rhinoceroses, sea lions, monkeys, hippopotamuses and around 250 horses."[45] One newspaper admiringly reported that "such features as the pair of Liliputian Cattle, the flock of Ostriches, the Hairless Horse and the pair of giant Hippopotami are not to be found elsewhere" (*Chillicothe Constitution,* May 8, 1891, 2). Mrs. Jane Devere, a "hirsute lady," had joined that year, amazing audiences with a beard that in 1884 measured at fourteen inches, a record for a woman. Other sideshows featured a "Hindoo Giant and his Many Wives," an American Giant with only one, but Giant, wife, man-and-wife midgets, snake charmers, tattooed people, magicians, and two geeks (who each earned $5 a week and, presumably, all the chicken heads they could eat), one specializing in having rocks broken on his head, the other noted for his realistic impersonation of a cannibal. One act, to which I hope Captain Jack paid particular attention, showcased the talents of a husband-and-wife rifle marksmanship team, a position at Sells once occupied (although not in 1891) by Mr. and Mrs. Frank Butler. Mrs. Butler was more commonly known under her stage name, Annie Oakley.[46] In little more than a year, Captain Jack would have good reason to appreciate such skill.

DEATH OF A CROW

Sorrows destroy us or themselves.
—Sir Thomas Browne

Early July 1888. Three men, Mr. J. T. Holloman, his cousin Mr. R. T. Rodgers, and Mr. Kelp Queen (a "notorious desperado," as one might guess given his unusual name) are riding toward Coffeyville, Kansas, hoping to arrive in time for the town's Independence Day celebration, believing this would be a good place to steal horses. Had they completed their journey, the three men undoubtedly would have witnessed one of the holiday's main ceremonial events, the firing of the Coffeyville courthouse square cannon, a rusty but apparently still functioning Civil War relic. The cannon is of interest because—according to some sources—it would later prominently figure in a battle (November 2, 1892) between a large group of lawmen, including Paden Tolbert, Deputy Marshal Barney Connelly (later killed by former deputy marshal turned outlaw Shep Busby), Captain G. S. "Cap" White, and outlaw Ned Christie, considered by many the most dangerous outlaw ever to inhabit the territory.

Christie, a full-blooded Cherokee, presented a distinctive appearance, having been shot in the face by a posse commanded by Heck Thomas. "The Winchester slug," one historian informs us, "had struck Christie on the bridge of his nose, angling in such a manner that it destroyed his right eyeball."[1] Later, while exchanging gunfire with Deputy Marshal Isabell, Christie wounded him in the shoulder, crippling him for life. Near Tahlequah, Indian Territory, the large posse finally trapped Christie, who took refuge with some of his followers in a stout wooden fort they had earlier constructed as a hideout. The fort was so strong that the lawmen decided they needed a cannon, which they borrowed from the courthouse square at Coffeyville.[2] During the ensuing fight, in which over two thousand rounds were fired by the posse, the cannon—wherever it was from—was shot perhaps thirty times, the three-pound balls not having much effect. (This incident is sometimes claimed to be the only time law enforcement officials have ever used artillery against a private citizen.) Finally, two lawmen got close enough to Christie's fort to blow it up with six-inch sticks of dynamite. Emerging from the splintered, smoking ruin, Christie, defiantly still shooting back, was riddled by Winchesters. His corpse was later taken to Ft. Smith and photographed propped up on a board in front of Judge Parker's courthouse.

Coffeyville on the Fourth of July would certainly have been a good place to steal horses, which were required because Holloman, Rodgers, and Queen planned to rob a bank in Seneca, Missouri, and would need fresh mounts to escape posses. The men had recent experience with being pursued by posses, and in fact then were, in a haphazard fashion, being pursued by one, an experience that at least one of them, Mr. Rodgers, did not find enjoyable. He, along with the young Mr. Holloman, is having second thoughts about continuing a life of crime. Mr. Queen, by then too far entangled in the outlaw life, knows himself well enough to doubt he will ever change, but he does not object to his colleagues' desires. Spying a crow perched on a branch, Mr. Rodgers pulls out his Winchester and shoots it clean through. He retrieves the tattered body and sprinkles its blood over his saddle. The plan is for Mr. Queen to return one of the horses and the bloody saddle to Mr. John Barber (their accomplice and the horses' owner) with a story about how Rodgers and Holloman were killed by pursuing marshals. The hope is that the story will allow Rodgers and Holloman to plausibly disappear and begin new lives.

Two weeks earlier, on June 15, 1888, these three men had been part of a group that robbed the Katy No. 507 train at the Verdigris water tank. Historian Glen Shirley gives one version of what happened:

> At 10:30 p.m., when the train stopped at the tank for water, a man who called himself [I hope this is a coincidence] "Captain Jack" and had his face blackened with mud, crawled over the tender and covered the foreman and the engineer with a six-shooter. At the same moment, four other men appeared, wearing bandanna masks

and carrying Winchesters. They seized mail agent W. S. Colton and forced him to lead the way to the express car, where they surprised Messenger A. B. Codding and looted the safe of $8,000.

While they were looting the safe, Colton attempted to escape through the door, and one of the robbers, who had been left on the ground, shot him through the left forearm. The train boy, Harry Ryan, ran out on the steps of the smoker to see what was happening, and the same robber shot his left arm to splinters. The bullet, passing through the open door, struck B. F. Tarver under the left jaw and broke his neck. Tarver, a Marlin, Texas, cowman who was returning from Chicago, fell forward on the steps in front of Ryan.

The wounded and dead were brought to Muskogee, and the Indian police notified. Captain LeFlore and his men left in direct pursuit of the bandits.[3]

At first, the train robbers were suspected to be members of Belle Starr's gang, probably because her notoriety, much like the Daltons' afterward, attracted official attention after any crime of note. This was unfair to Starr, as the only crime she was ever convicted of was stealing cattle, for which she served six months in prison. But what appears to be the transcription of a telegram, probably sent by U.S. Deputy Marshal Gant Owens the next day after the robbery, asks for reports on her whereabouts and notes that when questioned, "she denies being there near scene of robbery and murder."[4]

The Verdigris robbery, incidentally, provides an excellent example of how the sources differ on the details. Roughly half those I found state the robbery occurred on June 16, whereas the others cite June 15. And the exact date will become important in the trial to follow. In his diary, Kinney, referring to the robbery in numerous entries, lists June 15. Stockman B. F. (or B. C.) Tarver is from, variously, Rose, Rosebud, or Marlin, Texas. The train boy is either Harry Ryan or Harry Fan. The mail agent is W. S. Colton or Willis P. Colton. "Holloman" is in some accounts spelled "Holleman." Tarver is killed either by the bullet striking his jaw and breaking his neck or by the ball entering "at the base of the left ear and coming out just over the right eye" (*Sedalia Gazette,* n.d.). Rather than the $8,000 cited by Shirley as the robbers' take, other sources note the proceeds were "$8.75 and a lady's gold watch." The location is alternatively "Verdigris," "Verdi Gris," or Gibson Station.

The events leading to the robbery were set in motion by a Mr. Jim Johnson, who, in March 1888, visited Rodgers and Holloman, both then living in Leon County, Texas. Johnson convinced the pair to accompany him to the Indian Territory, where (so he said) they might each earn as much as $50 a month by herding cattle. In May 1888 the group by various routes arrived at the home—five miles southeast of Tulsa—of Alexander S. Lewis, where they were joined by Kelp Queen. Not finding employment, their money almost exhausted, the group passed their time by playing cards. During one of these games, Johnson suggested that they might profitably rob the Katy train when it stopped for water at the Verdigris tank. Overhearing their plans, Mr. Lewis decided this was a fine idea and asked to accompany them. They had no objections. But then Lewis—perhaps something of a henpecked husband?—decided, amazingly, that he had better first ask his wife for permission ("Honey? The boys want to rob a train. Is it all right with you if I go along?"). Mrs. Lewis ("Just don't get caught. But slop the hawgs first.") raised no objection. The card games resumed, but now for stakes of who would perform what function during the robbery.

On July 14, the gang left on their larcenous mission, carrying a picnic lunch of bread and meat prepared and thoughtfully packed for them by the formidable Mrs. Lewis. The next day, by luck of the cards, Holloman and Queen hid themselves near the Gibson station (last stop before the tank), as it was their job to hop the train as it left. But the train's conductor, Hugh Hagan, and the porter, Dan Moffet, noticed a man (Holloman) attempting to jump aboard, and with the assistance of Mr. I. N. Bishop, a pump repairer, they together threw him off, and not gently. Holloman thus remained behind at Gibson. During this confusion, the other man, Kelp Queen, was able, unobserved, to hop on the front end of the mail car. He crawled over the tender and pulled his revolver on the engineer, commanding him to stop the train at Verdigris, where the other members of the gang were concealed. Johnson and Queen then robbed the express car, and it was during this time that another member of the gang shot and killed Tarver and wounded Ryan and Colton. The robbers escaped on horseback and returned to Lewis's home on July 16, where they were soon joined by the bruised and dusty Mr. Holloman.

The card games resumed, but Holloman must have noticed that his fellow robbers, who had told him that the take from the train was only

$8.75 and a gold watch, were using as poker chips $20 gold coins which they claimed were proceeds from a bank they had recently robbed at Cisco, Texas. His natural suspicion here may have been a factor in his subsequent decision to quit the criminal life. Also during these games Lewis admitted, or perhaps boasted, that he was the one responsible for killing Tarver. The card games would alternate between Lewis's house and that of his neighbor Wilburn Dawson, and at the home of the latter, Mr. Chaula Gunta, a visiting "cow boy," observed the game and the high stakes, facts he reported on July 18 at a dance in Clairmore to Deputy Marshal Heck Thomas. Thomas seems to have already had a posse in the area, seeking other criminals, and so was immediately able to begin his pursuit, but Dawson, who happened to be gathering provisions in town, learned of the posse and was able to warn most of the gang before Thomas arrived.[5] For reasons known only to themselves, both Lewis and Dawson chose not to run and were duly arrested at their respective houses.

Because the other members of the gang had fled with the loot, however much of it there actually was, little hard evidence remained on which a case against Lewis or Dawson could be charged, and so the two were eventually set free, after spending six months in jail. Holloman, Queen, and Rodgers, now on the run, made their plans to rob the bank at Seneca, but before doing so, as described, Holloman and Rodgers changed their minds, the decision costing the life of an innocent crow. The gang went their separate ways, most of them meeting with bad ends. Shortly after arriving back home, Rodgers was killed in a street brawl. Jim Johnson was arrested in Fayetteville, Arkansas, for horse stealing and sentenced to twenty-five years in the penitentiary at Rusk, Texas. In 1889 Kelp Queen was killed in a shootout by Sheriff Ed Saunders. A final member of the gang, Mr. John Barber, died in an encounter with Deputies Barney Connelly and G. S. "Cap" White (the same deputies later involved in the battle with Ned Christie).

Holloman safely made it to his home at Rodger's Prairie, got married, settled on a farm, and began living the straight life. There matters stood for some two years. But a blessing, or maybe a curse, of the straight life is that one is apt to develop a conscience. Holloman had developed one, and it began to bother him. Advised by relatives that confession was the only cure for an uneasy conscience, Holloman decided to do just that, whereupon a meeting was arranged on December 13, 1890, at Marquez, Texas, between Holloman and the chief detective of the MK&T Railroad, Mr. John J. Kinney. Holloman confessed in full, agreed to testify, and implicated Alexander Lewis in the killing of Benjamin Tarver. After summoning Charles La Flore to accompany him, Captain Jack immediately rode to Tulsa, arrested Lewis, and took him to the infamous jail at Ft. Smith, Arkansas.

By 1890, the Ft. Smith jail was not nearly as foul as it had once been. During the early 1870s, the jail's crowded and filthy condition rivaled that of the Black Hole of Calcutta, or so asserted one knowledgeable observer.[6] Scandal was once narrowly averted when an imperious member of a sitting grand jury, hearing terrible rumors about the dungeon located beneath the courtroom, insisted on conducting an impromptu inspection. He retrieved from the jail's kitchen a meal of maggot-infested meat and stale bread, which he contemptuously threw on the judge's high panel cherrywood desk, threatening to inform Washington about the facility's deplorable state. Partially to address such conditions, a new jail, built in 1877 (at a cost of $75,000), was designed to contain

> a large three story steel cage, with a seven foot open space between it and the walls of the building at the two sides and the southwest end, while at the other end, adjoining the old court house, is sufficient space for stairways and an area way. The cells are in size five by eight feet, each supplied with two iron cots, one above the other; each cell closes with an iron door, which opens into a four foot aisle that extends along the entire length of both sides of the cage, inside the steel lattice and across the southwest end.
>
> On each floor are twenty-four cells, twelve on each side. . . . The lower twenty-four cells—being those on the first floor—were designated "Murderers' Row," and were used to confine persons charged with murder while awaiting trial, sentence or execution, as well as for the detention of the more desperate class of men charged with various severe crimes.[7]

New or not, a jail is an unpleasant place to hang about, filled as it is with unsavory and scary characters on both sides of the bars. Should one's "hanging about" move from the figurative to the literal, courtesy of Judge Parker's pronouncement, one would then be afforded the privilege of meeting, if only briefly, the acknowledged Prince of Hangmen, Mr. George Isaac Maledon (1830–1911). Although photographs seldom do people justice, the exception must be Mr. Maledon, whose surviving portraits show him to be a most frightening individual. Invariably dressed in a black suit, black vest, and dark trousers, with a brace of pistols (handles reversed[8]) cinching his waist, his attire is completed by a black necktie (tied with a Windsor, not a hangman's knot) standing out against a starched white shirt. The tie and the shirt peek from beneath an enormous and scraggly gray beard that, joined with a thick mustache, shrouds his thin, wan face. His high forehead, with a receding hairline, is often hooded beneath a sinister black bowler hat. Huge, staring eyes dominate his narrow face, eyes spaced too closely together, and set too far back in his skull, each unblinking eye half ringed by ominous dark circles that further accent a pair of wrinkled, cadaverous, hollow cheeks. He has seen Death too often and has become its human image, and during his tenure of twenty-two years working for Parker's court, he would officiate at over sixty executions. Nor were the pistols just for show: he shot five prisoners attempting to escape, killing two. Somehow, this grim Bavarian man managed to father eleven children by his loving wife Elizabeth.

One might have thought, given so scary a prospective father-in-law, that suitors for Maledon's daughters would take care to always be on their best behavior. Sadly, that turned out not to be the case. Maledon's daughter Annie "was beautiful of face and figure, possessed of a wealth of long, heavy black hair and soft, dark brown eyes."[9] Unfortunately, she was "an unchaste woman" who fell in with bad company: she became the mistress of Frank Carver, an adulterer, gambler, and alcoholic who (on March 25, 1895) murdered her during a drunken quarrel. Before the killing, Carver had consumed four bottles of Jamaica Ginger, popularly known as "jake," an intoxicant containing as much as 85 percent spirits, often contaminated by methyl (wood) alcohol and organophosphate neurotoxins. Carver was convicted and sentenced to hang, but the sentence was reversed by the Supreme Court. At a new trial, Carver was instead sentenced to life in prison, cheating Maledon of the pleasure of legally killing his own daughter's murderer.[10]

Hanging was then, and still is now in the two states that permit it (Delaware and Washington), both a science and an art. If arranged properly, the hangman's knot will dislocate the spine (that is, break the neck) between the third and fourth cervical vertebrae, upon which the condemned prisoner will lapse almost immediately into shock and unconsciousness. Brain death will follow in approximately six minutes. In eight minutes, typically the heart will stop beating, after which, once the attending physician has verified death, the body can be cut down for burial. A successful hanging requires rope of the finest Manila hemp, of a diameter between ¾ and 1¼ inches. The rope should be boiled for at least an hour, then repeatedly stretched and allowed to dry completely, in order to resist coiling. The knot must be expertly tied, with its interior surface generously lubricated by a paraffin wax to facilitate smooth travel. One must properly position the knot between the left jaw and ear, with the slack of the rope draped over the right shoulder, so that torquing force can augment pressure on the vertebrae. The prisoner must be weighed and measured before the execution in order to calculate the proper "drop," or the distance the condemned must fall to generate a force sufficient to snap his neck. Generally, the heavier the person, the shorter the required drop. If the hangman calculates too long a drop, the likely result is that the head will be ripped off the body, exactly the fate of train robber "Black Jack" Ketchum at his execution in New Mexico on April 26, 1901. Too short a drop ensures a protracted and gruesome strangulation, which by some accounts can last for at least fifteen minutes and as long as an hour.

The professional hangman is responsible for the care and correct functioning of the many accouterments of his trade. Black hoods are customarily provided to both the condemned and the executioner, but because only one hood has eyeholes cut into it, great caution must be taken to prevent the two from being mixed up. Because some prisoners do not greet their fate enthusiastically, the hangman must have available suitable arm and leg restraints, the latter also serving, should the drop take place in a visible area, to minimize any unseemly kicking and twitching. Given that an occasional prisoner will refuse even to climb the gallows steps—which should be well oiled and secured to prevent creaking—the hangman should have available a sturdy stretcher upon which the condemned can be fastened and carried to the trap. Once standing upon the trap, most prisoners will remain erect under their own power, paralyzed by fear and futility. But as a last resort, the stretcher bearing the recalcitrant prisoner can itself be stood on the trap, which a wise gallows builder has designed with a width sufficient to accommodate such an unlikely situation. Gags may become necessary, to prevent screaming and cursing or to quiet a condemned who thinks to use the opportunity for his last words as an occasion to recite the entirety of the *Iliad*. After the trap has been released (and of course the trap will have been thoroughly tested with appropriately weighted sandbags before its penultimate use), the hangman is then responsible for securing in a respectful manner from the dangling body all the utensils he has used, most especially the rope, a highly coveted object among souvenir hunters.

In its later years, the Ft. Smith gallows was enclosed by a high fence, and between executions it functioned as a cow pen (or horse corral—accounts vary). One contemporary writer noted that it was "about as foul, muddy, and disreputable a place as one could find." Maledon regarded his gallows affectionately and would "pat its beams with his hands as one has seen an engineer fondly stroke the burnished metal of his machinery."[11] He seemed to conduct his macabre duties in an almost cheerful manner: "There was nothing hardhearted in the way the work was done. A favorite remark of his to a doomed man was: 'Oh, come on, now; it's nothing at all. You won't feel it and I'll have it all over in a jiffy.' He never failed to offer the prisoner a chew of tobacco just before the clergyman began the customary prayer."[12]

Despite his fastidious attention to the details of demise, not all of Maledon's executions resulted in quick deaths. Roger Tuller writes, "although George Maledon prided himself on his expertise as a hangman, later boasting that he had dispatched sixty men who 'never even twitched,' he botched this job [a quintuple hanging on April 21, 1876] badly. Of the five men executed, only Orpheus McGee was still after the drop. Even though his hands and arms were bound, Aaron Wilson struggled for eight minutes, convulsing so violently that the crucifix he wore around his neck was torn from the ribbon that secured it. Isham Seely moaned audibly for several minutes; the knot had slipped under his chin, strangling him slowly. Gibson Ishtonubee lingered for nine minutes, and the penitent William Leach for ten. Despite Maledon's skillful preparation and technique, hanging remained an inexact 'science.'"[13] In 1882, condemned prisoner Edward Fulsom strangled for over an hour before his death.

If the Prince of Hangmen could so bungle a hanging, one cringes to imagine the fate of condemned prisoners entrusted to less regal executioners. Even veteran lawmen could be disgusted by an incompetent hanging. Tom Furlong tells of a time he was asked to assist a sheriff at an execution, an experience almost comedic were the outcome not so gruesome. Both he and the sheriff—large, burly men—were standing on the trap next to the condemned, keeping the man still while the executioner adjusted the noose. But shortly after the rope was adjusted, the prisoner fainted, and in the confusion that followed, the executioner prematurely sprung the trap while all three men were still on top of it. They all plunged through, but not far, as their combined bulk stuck fast in the opening. After much struggle, Furlong and the sheriff managed to extricate themselves, but what about the prisoner, who had by now revived? Should they haul him back up and try again? Nobody seemed to know what to do, and so nothing was done. The prisoner slowly strangled to death while the flustered lawmen debated the correct protocol. From this point on, Furlong was a staunch opponent of capital punishment by means of hanging.[14]

Botched hangings in fact were commonplace, so much so that in 1888, the New York state legislature abolished hanging as a method of capital punishment and formed a commission to study alternatives. Thomas Alva Edison, testifying before the commission, although he was opposed to capital punishment, shrewdly and cynically recommended the invention (alternating current) promoted by rival George Westinghouse, thereby hoping to associate in the public's mind this competing technology (to Edison's direct current) with danger and death.[15]

It was a tough job, being a hangman, requiring the mechanical proficiency of a skilled engineer, the rope expertise of an Eagle Scout, the emotional distance of a slaughterhouse butcher, and a flair for macabre ceremony and spectacle that would do credit to the most unctuous undertaker. For all this Mr. Maledon received, in addition to his regular court deputy's salary, the trifling sum of $5 each for attending to the death needs of his special customers. While inspecting his prospective clients, Maledon would often prowl the jail's narrow aisles, silently estimating with a practiced, dead eye the strength and resiliency of their necks. And now, housed in the lower tier on Murderers' Row, was Mr. Alexander S. Lewis, only a verdict away from undergoing Mr. Maledon's professional services. One must wonder how they regarded each other.

In a lengthy interview provided to the *Sedalia Gazette,* Captain Jack details the trial's preliminary stages: "On February 5th, 1891, Lewis was indicted for murder. Holloman was a witness before the grand jury. Lewis' case was set for trial May 20th, 1891, but was continued by the government on account of the absence of important witnesses until October 15th, 1891. On that date all the witnesses were present at Ft. Smith, but the trial did not commence until October 20th." A number of points here deserve emphasis; trials then were in some respects quite different from those we see today. First is the enormous area over which the court had jurisdiction. "Never in the history of the United States," observe the editors of *Hell on the Border*, "was there a court to match the United States District Court for the Western District of Arkansas and Indian Territory. The geographic boundaries of the court were almost as broad as the entirety of the New England states, an area later divided into courts of seventy-two separate judicial districts" (13). As for the Indian Territory itself, explains C. H. McKennon, it

> was a stepchild born of the famed 1803 Louisiana Purchase, which had wedded the fledgling United States to a gigantic western acreage. An act of Congress created the new home for the Cherokee, Choctaw, Seminole, Creek, and Chickasaw Indian Tribes then dwelling in the southern states east of the surging Mississippi River. The "Great Removal" of these, the "Five Civilized Tribes," was practically completed by the early 1870s. The old tribal governments worked well in governing the new "Nations," but, these governments had no provisions for prosecuting a white man who was wanted for a felony in the "States."[16]

As a rule, the larger the court's jurisdiction, the more difficult the logistics of any trial, for both the prosecutors and defendants, can become. Consider the usually routine matter of serving subpoenas upon potential witnesses. Over fifty witnesses would be compelled to testify during the Lewis trial, including (for the prosecution) Heck Thomas, Charles La Flore, Bud Kell, Willis P. Colton, Harry Ryan, and of course Captain Jack himself. An officer of the court, often traveling hundreds of miles, must first find and notify them, not always an easy task when people didn't necessarily live in houses with addresses helpfully painted on the curb. Some not insignificant percentage of witnesses would not want to be found, and had been attracted to live in the Indian Territory precisely because it was so easy to disappear.

Being subpoenaed as a witness could often involve more than minor inconveniences. Mr. Ninnian Tannehill remembers,

> There were no courts here in those days except that the Cherokee had courts for their own people but if one of the persons involved was a white person it meant a trip to Fort Smith, Arkansas. Once I was called there to be a witness against a boy for selling whiskey. They allowed you 10 cents per mile for going and $1.50 per day while there. I had to stay there two months before the case came for trial. I could not leave. Out of the money paid you, you had to keep yourself and it was a costly matter to most people and for that reason many things were never reported because nobody wanted to have to go to Fort Smith and perhaps have to stay there for months.[17]

If any of the witnesses were, or could plausibly claim to be, Indians, then the court's jurisdiction did not necessarily apply—at least not until after complicated and special hearings resembling extradition actions between sovereign nations. Having served a particular witness was no guarantee he or she would actually show up. The court's crowded docket had little or no room for vigorous prosecution of those who ignored subpoenas, a situation well known by most. Given such circumstances, I'm not sure if it is more difficult to understand the staggering volume of cases the court tried, or the fact it was able to try any at all.[18]

Many of the same difficulties attendant on subpoenaing witnesses could also complicate a trial's official beginning, concerned with gathering, selecting, and impaneling a jury. For reasons now not known, Judge Parker allowed, or ordered (over the objection of the defense), the prosecution and defense attorneys to conduct portions of their voir dire separately, an irregularity that would bear consequence. But a jury was in due course selected, before which Alexander Lewis, "a man perhaps forty-five or fifty years of age, with long sandy whiskers and good appearance," stood accused of both train robbery and murder.

A modern observer of Lewis's trial, and others like it, would be struck by the almost complete absence of forensic evidence. Why was not the bullet that killed Tarver compared with one fired from Lewis's gun? As far back as 1822, Francois-Eugene Vidocq, founder of the *Surete*, "solved the case of a murdered Comtesse with the bullet he removed from her head. He proved that it was too big to have been fired from her husband's gun, but just the right size to have come from her lover's."[19] In 1835 Henry Goddard, of Scotland Yard, identified a murderer on the basis of a groove in the bullet caused by a faulty casting mold found in the suspect's possession. But legal interest in these promising techniques stagnated until 1889, when Alexandre Lacassagne, of the University of Lyons, began a systematic attempt to identify individual bullets on the basis of the marks imparted to them by the barrels from which they were fired. His work was advanced in 1898 by Paul Jestich in Berlin, who developed a comparison microscope enabling two bullets to be thoroughly examined and evaluated side by side. It would not be until 1924 that August Vollmer, the Los Angeles chief of police, established what we would now recognize as a crime laboratory.

Similarly with fingerprints. Why weren't those of Lewis matched to any at the scene of the crime? Some authorities date the use of fingerprints for purposes of identification all the way back to the ancient Chinese. In 1880, Henry Faulds, a Scottish missionary doctor, first advocated fingerprints as a means of criminal identification in an article he had published in *Nature*. Eight months to the day after the conclusion of Lewis's initial trial, June 29, 1892, marks the first recorded criminal case solved by fingerprint evidence, although it was solved because its threatened use elicited a confession, not because a court or jury was convinced by its actual evidentiary presentation.[20] The first actual criminal convicted in a British courtroom on the basis of fingerprints was Harry Jackson, a burglar, in 1902. The first United States conviction, by similar means, occurred in 1911, when Thomas Jennings was tried for murder.

Cruder forms of physical and circumstantial evidence, of course, had long been featured in trials, but such evidence was widely distrusted.[21] Much was made, for example, of a distinctive spotted "iron gray horse" ridden by one of the Verdigris train robbers. And it was proven that Mr. Lewis also owned an "iron gray horse." But was it the same horse? And even if it was, does that prove Mr. Lewis was riding it? One can imagine the fun a clever defense attorney would have had with such evidence. Can you tell us, exactly, which precise shade of gray defined the horse's appearance? Because the robbery took place at night, how could you see the horse at all? Because you only saw the horse in dim light, how can you know it is exactly the same color as that Mr. Lewis now owns? And by the way, how good is your eyesight? Do you know, even approximately, how many horses there are in the Indian Territory? Do you further know how many of them are gray? Physical evidence, of whatever sophistication, could seem to become persuasive only if solidly grounded in science, and it was not until 1891 that Hans Gross, of the University of Graz, Austria, published *Criminal Investigations,* one of the first attempts to integrate the legal use of physical evidence with the scientific methods and procedures. Colin Beavan observes that

> It didn't help, either, that science didn't have the foothold in the courtrooms that it does today. For most of history, the only evidence allowed at trial was the testimony of eyewitnesses. The use of physical evidence to reconstruct events had been considered too vulnerable to manipulation. The legal process had since been dragged slowly forward, but juries were still more used to hearing what people had seen with their own eyes than what experts said they could deduce by other means. Unlike the rest of society during the industrial revolution, the judiciary had not yet been won over by science.[22]

Although the modern court, at least in capital trials, would evolve into something resembling a science classroom, where attorneys function as professors instructing the juror-students in ever more arcane and recondite forensic subjects, the court Lewis faced was a theater of character, the lawyers both principal actors and stage directors, hoping the juror-audience would find their carefully studied performances superior to those of their opponents. And without question, the very best defense attorney available at Ft. Smith—whom Lewis had the good sense to hire—was J. Warren Reed, of the firm Barnes & Reed, popularly known (with justifiable hyperbole) as "The Lawyer Who Never Loses His Cases."[23]

Historian Glenn Shirley gives a good account of Reed's background:

> Reed had been born December 9, 1849, in Parkersburg, West Virginia. Like Judge Parker, he spent his childhood on a farm and early in life chose law as a profession. . . . In 1886 he was admitted to practice in the Supreme Court and in the United States District and Circuit Courts of West Virginia. In April of the same year he

went to California, and was admitted to the bar there by the Supreme Court, in full session at San Francisco. For a while he successfully handled many important mining, land, and criminal cases, then became interested in criminal law and decided to specialize in it. He made a tour of Mexico, the United States, and Canada, and returned to his native state to settle down to permanent practice; but he was called to Fort Smith to defend a prominent case and, noting the volume of business being transacted in the famous court, decided to stay.[24]

Perhaps Reed's most famous case, although one that he eventually lost, was his 1895 defense of Mr. Crawford Goldsby, better known as "Cherokee Bill," who murdered at least seven people and was guilty of multiple robberies of everything from post offices to trains to country stores. During the robbery of Schufelt & Son's store in Lenapah, on November 8, 1894, Cherokee Bill killed bystander Ernest Melton, and it was for this specific crime he was tried. Despite Reed's best efforts, Bill was found guilty and Judge Parker sentenced him to death, whereupon Reed, who specialized in appeals, sent off a flurry of correspondence, including a direct petition to President Grover Cleveland for pardon and/or clemency. Reed writes of his own efforts that "the petition was ineffectual, but it proved the relentless and tenacious spirit of the persistent attorney to save the neck of his client from the deadly noose."[25] While awaiting the outcome of Reed's appeals in the Ft. Smith jail, Bill somehow managed, during an attempted escape, to secure a pistol, with which he killed guard Lawrence Keating. Reed came to feel guilty that his many appeals, staying the execution, indirectly caused Keating's death. On March 17, 1896, Cherokee Bill was marched up the gallows. Asked if he had any last words, Bill, with admirable brevity, replied, "I came here to die, not to make a speech."[26]

Finally, on Tuesday morning, October 20, 1891, the Lewis trial began as follows, the official transcript stating,

On this day come the United States of America, by Wm. H. H. Clayton, Esq., attorney for the western district of Arkansas, and come the said defendant in custody of the marshal and by his attorneys, Mess. Barnes & Reed, and it appearing from the returns of the marshal that the said defendant has been served with a duly-certified copy of the indictment in this cause, and a full and complete list of the witnesses in this cause, and that he has also been served with a full and complete list of the petit jury, as selected and drawn by the jury commissioners for the present term of this court, more than two entire days heretofore, and having heretofore had hearing of said indictment, and pleaded not guilty thereto, it is, on motion of the plaintiff by its attorney, ordered that a jury come to try the issue joined (146 U.S. 370).

The heart of prosecutor Clayton's case was J. T. Holloman's testimony, in which he implicated Lewis in both the train robbery and the murder. This testimony, notes one modern source, "was supported by a mass of evidence assembled by railroad detective J. J. Kinney, who brought the felon to justice at Ft. Smith (Ark.)."[27] However, most of that "mass of evidence" was circumstantial and suggestive, like the "iron gray horse"—certainly not conclusive. The case would stand or fall on whether the jury believed Holloman.

Against this, Reed offered an alibi defense. Scores of witnesses were paraded before the court, each swearing to have seen Lewis in Tulsa on the day of the robbery, June 15, 1888, Tulsa being far away enough from the Verdigris tank that had he actually been in Tulsa, he could not have possibly participated in the robbery, much less the murder. And how, the witnesses were asked, could they be certain they saw Lewis in Tulsa on that exact day? Some of them produced business records, purporting to show Lewis had then patronized their shops. Many others testified they remembered the precise date because a well-known resident of Tulsa, one Thomas Claywell, was arrested that very day by Deputy Marshal Isabell, Lewis's presence in Tulsa thus linked in their recollections with the news of Claywell's arrest. Again and again the various witnesses, sounding a little too like a well-rehearsed orchestra, repeated the theme that Claywell's arrest on June 15 proved Lewis's presence in Tulsa.

As the defense concluded, it looked as though the trial would be decided, as so many were and still are, on the issue of character. The prosecution, in addition to a "mass" of corroborating evidence, had just one strong eyewitness, Holloman, a confessed robber, against whom it might be plausibly inferred that his testimony was tailored in the direction of self-preservation. Would the jury believe him? Or would the jury believe the long string of alibi witnesses produced in favor of Lewis? Was their character, singly or collectively, reputable enough to brand their words with truth?[28] At this point, it certainly looked like the defense had a very strong case. Why would all these witnesses run the risk of perjuring themselves, particularly in front of Judge Parker, a man who could be expected to take a dim view of such behavior? Although it was not unheard of during these times for testimony to be bought and sold, the sheer number of alibi witnesses argued against this possibility. That all these perfect strangers would vouch for Lewis surely must have impressed the jury.

However, given how matters unfolded, there may be some reason to suspect that all these alibi witnesses were by no means strangers to each other. At that time, and primarily in the Creek Nation where Lewis farmed his land, there existed a large clan of families, interrelated by birth and marriage, a clan in fact known as the "Lewis" clan. Whether Alexander was a member cannot now be definitively known, and admittedly, "Lewis" was a common surname.[29] But many of this clan were known to associate—as did Alexander himself—with the outlaw elements in the territories and had a reputation for supplying perjured testimony as circumstances warranted, although usually for liquor-law violations. Daniel Littlefield writes that "when law enforcement officers attempted to build a case against one of their members, the Lewis clan closed ranks, testifying to one another's innocence and swearing at times that the whiskey belonged to another member of the family who was not in custody or lived in some other jurisdiction and would be difficult to find."[30]

Still, somebody had made a big mistake. Whether acting on his own initiative or at the direction of prosecutor Clayton,[31] Captain Jack decided to check the paperwork on the Claywell case, which included a writ of arrest executed by Deputy Marshal L. P. "Bones" Isabell (also spelled Isbel), a writ clearly dated not June 15, but June 17. This devastating fact was brought out in the rebuttal phase of the trial, blowing the defense completely out of the water. The alibi witnesses were obviously lying, whether because of perceived family loyalty, dishonest coaching by the defense attorney, or (despite their numbers) simple bribery. The defense rested, its case a complete shambles. Even Judge Parker seemed to acknowledge the disaster, for he issued the jury instructions that emphasized that the alibi defense was "often resorted to, and often attempted to be sustained and made effective by fraud, subornation, and perjury" (146 U.S. 370). Curiously, and perhaps strategically, Reed offered no objection to the Judge's phrasing. Lewis was found guilty.

Parker then, in due course, delivered one of the lengthy and scary sentencing orations for which he was famous. Only a portion (from one of Captain Jack's undated newspaper clippings) is reproduced here:

> Listen now to the sentence of the law as pronounced by the court. That sentence is, that you, Alexander Lewis, for the crime of murder, in willfully and with malice aforethought killing Benjamin C. Tarver, in the Indian Country, and within the jurisdiction of this court of which crime you stand convicted by the verdict of the jury in your case be deemed, taken and adjudged guilty of murder, and that, you be therefore for the said crime against the laws of the United States, be hanged by the neck until you are dead; that the marshal of the Western District of Arkansas by himself or deputy or deputies do, in peril of what may befall them at some convenient place in the Western District of Arkansas, cause execution to be done in the premises on Wednesday, April 17, a.d. 1892, between the hours of nine o'clock in the forenoon and five o'clock in the afternoon of the same day; and that you be now taken to the jail from whence you came, there to be closely and securely kept until the day of the execution, and from thence on the day of the execution as aforesaid, there to be hanged by the neck aforesaid until you are dead.
>
> And may God, whose law you have broken, and before whose dread tribunal you must then appear, have mercy on your soul.

Reed then did what he did best, which was appeal, an appeal that reached the United States Supreme Court and was decided, by a split decision, on December 5, 1892.[32] One of the points of the appeal was the prejudicial language of the judge in his jury instructions. Justice Shiras, writing the majority opinion, dismissed the issue on procedural grounds, noting "the only other error assigned which calls for notice is the one objecting to the language used by the court when cautioning the jury in respect to the testimony bearing on the defense of an alibi. Whether the language of the learned judge went beyond the verge of propriety, we are not called upon to consider, as no due exception was taken at the trial, and no opportunity was, therefore, given the court to modify the charge" (146 U.S. 370). This is precisely why attorneys, then and now, object so often during trials: failing to do so may allow an appellate court to ignore a substantive issue on the grounds that no exception was made at the time the alleged error occurred. Object in a timely fashion, or forever hold your peace.

Reed then raised the issue of "contemporaneous challenging." Both sides in a trial, during jury selection, are allowed an unlimited number of challenges to excuse potential jurors for cause and a limited number of peremptory challenges by which jurors can be excused for no reason at all. But Judge Parker, over the defense objection, allowed portions of the selection, including the challenges, to occur simultaneously and separately, resulting in the defense not always knowing what jurors the government had challenged. As it so happened, the prosecution and the defense, independently of each other, challenged the same three jurors, a situation that resulted, so Reed argued, in depriving the defense of three challenges, as they would have never exercised and wasted challenges on jurors already excused by the government. Justice Brewer, writing the minority opinion (concurred with by Justice Brown), neatly skewers this argument: "So far as respects the matter of contemporaneous challenging, at common law, and generally where no order is prescribed by statute, the defendant is required to make all his challenges before the government is called upon for any. In that aspect of the law, contemporaneous challenging works to the injury of the government, rather than to that of the defendant" (146 U.S. 370).

The final, and successful, point of Reed's appeal was that the independent jury selection process not only led to a result detrimental to the rights of the defendant, but was prejudicial prima facie, on its face, to the defendant. This argument convinced a majority of the court. Justice Shiras observed that "a leading principle that pervades the entire law of criminal procedure is that, after indictment found, nothing shall be done in the absence of the prisoner. Although this rule has at times, and in the cases of misdemeanors, been somewhat relaxed, yet in felonies it is not in the power of the prisoner, either by himself or his counsel, to waive the right to be personally present during trial" (146 U.S. 370). And further: "Thus reading the record, and holding, as we do, that the making of challenges was an essential part of the trial, and that it was one of the substantial rights of the prisoner to be brought face to face with the jurors at the time when the challenges were made, we are brought to the conclusion that the record discloses an error for which the judgment of the court must be reversed" (146 U.S. 370). The case was remanded for a new trial.

Reed changed his tactics for Lewis's second trial. Instead of attempting to prove, by means of alibi, that Lewis could not have been at the murder and robbery, he forced the government to attempt to prove he was. Maybe his horse was, or a horse that looked like his was, but was he? The only offered proof of that was the testimony of a felon. "Reed was . . . brilliant in the second Lewis murder trial," writes Jay Nash. "He assailed the integrity of the government witnesses under cross-examination, and his unvarnished courtroom theatrics helped win his client a verdict of Not Guilty. At no time, he maintained, could anyone place Lewis at the murder scene. It was an argument the jury found difficult to refute; Lewis was acquitted."[33] Perhaps Lewis really was innocent. Perhaps Reed trained his witnesses to lie more skillfully. Perhaps even both. We can never know now. We might never have known even then.

"Hanging Judge" Isaac Parker died on November 17, 1896. "'I never hanged a man,' he said when lying on his death bed, 'I never hanged a man. It is the law.'"[34] Parker's ferocious reputation obscured his real personality. He was active in civic affairs with a particular interest in educational reform, and for many years he served on the Ft. Smith school board. Parker also seems to have had a sense of humor. Tom Furlong tells a story about some fun-loving Katy railroad conductors who were called as witnesses to Ft. Smith for the trial of accused murderer and train robber William Sweeney in the early 1880s. Knowing of Parker's habit of enjoying a Sunday ride, one brave soul among them decided to surreptitiously tether a beer barrel to the buggy's axle: "As the Judge's abstemious habits were known to all the citizens of the town, the sight of the beer keg under his buggy created a great deal of amusement on the part of the citizens when they saw it as the carriage was drawn through the streets. The Judge did not discover the trick that had been played on him until after the ride was over, but he seemed to enjoy the joke as much as did the jokers."[35]

Shortly before Parker's death, the enormous jurisdiction of his court, the District and Circuit Court of the United States for the Western District of Arkansas and the Indian Territory, was sharply curtailed by the legislature, beginning a process that would establish in its place courts of lesser jurisdiction but presumably of greater focus. By 1897, the court's reduced function was symbolized by the removal of its gallows, leaving Mr. George Maledon temporarily without work. But not for long. Attorney Reed was by then contemplating writing a book about his legal experiences in Parker's court, and he decided to perform what we would now call "test marketing" to see whether his exploits in particular, and the affairs on the court in general, would interest the public. To that end, he hired George Maledon, and "after securing from him some of the ropes and other gruesome relics of his late vocation," he exhibited him around the territory in a carnival tent. "The success of the venture," Reed reports,

> far exceeded my most sanguine expectations. At every stopping place people of all classes flocked to the show ground, stood about the tent entrance to listen to the lecturer (who never failed, in addition to detailing and describing what was to be seen within, to make a statement concerning the book then in contemplation), and eagerly crowded the interior to look upon the famed executioner and view the evidences of his craft, while he told of the various criminals whose lives had, in the name of the law, been strangled out by this and that of the various ropes, the instruments in his hands of an avenging people.[36]

The demise of Parker's court mirrored the eclipse of J. Warren Reed's career. "His practice," the editors of *Hell on the Border* relate, "was intimately associated with the outlaws of the Indian Territory and he was never able to adjust to the simpler civil practice before the Arkansas and Oklahoma courts. Reed moved to Oklahoma and was forced to sell his book on the streets of Muskogee. The great attorney who had won so many judgments against Judge Parker became a book drummer pushing his works at cut rate from door to door" (17).

Supreme Court Justice Brewer wrote a dissenting opinion to the Lewis decision, and there is evidence that later he and Captain Jack would meet in person. In the spring of 1898, Mr. James Collins, a wealthy and popular Topeka citizen, was discovered murdered in his own bed by means of his own shotgun. A group of leading Topeka citizens, many of them lodge brothers of the victim, dissatisfied with the way the local police were handling the case, hired an independent detective to investigate. Given that Kinney was prominent in Topeka at the time and very active in lodge affairs, one may reasonably suppose that he was a member of this group, particularly because the detective they hired was his old boss at the Missouri Pacific, Mr. Thomas J. Furlong. Furlong (or more accurately his assistant D. F. Harbaugh and others) uncovered strong evidence suggesting that Collins's son was culpable, and after a week-long trial —which "attracted great attention throughout the entire country"—John Collins was found guilty and sentenced to hang, although everybody understood such would never happen, because Kansas then had a de facto, if not de jure, policy against capital punishment. Collins was eventually pardoned after serving ten years in the penitentiary. An avid spectator at the trial (which Captain Jack probably also attended) was Justice Brewer, whose daughter had married prosecuting attorney Jetmore. Brewer made a point of complimenting Furlong "very highly for my work in solving the mystery."[37] Curiously, Furlong does not mention Kinney anywhere in his book, which is odd given that in another account of the Collins murder (by Aaron Green, "Riddle of the Phony Footprints," *Master Detective* [December 1941], 41 ff.), Captain Jack is described as playing a significant role in solving the crime, and indeed was hired by Furlong's assistant to aid in the investigation.

As for Captain Jack? He must have been disappointed by the eventual outcome of the Lewis matter, particularly as he certainly would have been one of the government witnesses whose integrity was "assailed" by Reed during the second trial. But one moves on. Even during the first trial, which consumed much of his time, he had other cases to investigate. One involved Mr. E. Ellis Godlove. Or maybe his name was Thomas F. Sibley. Then again, he identified himself as James L. Dunn. And also Mr. J. Stewart Crockett, J. D. Evans, and John F. Ray, agent for the MKT Railroad—that surely caught Captain Jack's attention. A gentleman so variously self-named has little or no respect for the sacredness of identity attached to either persons or things. Precisely this attitude encourages forgery. Mr. Dunn (let us call him) was a forger.

DUNN DEALS

Mummy is become merchandise . . . and Pharaoh is sold for balsams.
—*Sir Thomas Browne*

Missouri State University, Columbia, Missouri. Sometime in 1875. At the campus, early on a night lit by a full, red moon. Tree branches stir and groan, rustled by a chill wind. Scattered low clouds, swiftly moving, first occlude, then release and focus the moon's red-silver light, turning the ground below into a dim chessboard of shifting shadows. An elderly black gentleman tiredly walks across the deserted quadrangle, having finally finished with his duties as a porter or a janitor (or, for all I know, having just taught a late class in advanced trigonometry). Behind him, rising above the distant calls of night birds and the wind's low moan, he hears muted, maniacal laughter, then a distinct, ominous whirring and clattering. Spinning about in alarm, he turns, and OH MY GOD! Diving right out of the blood red moon, swooping down through the shadows at frightening speed, a ghastly HUMAN SKELETON, bony arms outstretched, evilly grinning, is racing right toward him. This would scare the hell out of anybody, professor or janitor, black or white. Of course, that was the point. For this prank, Missouri State University would expel Mr. James ("Jimmy") L. Dunn, a student who—so he said—in 1873 had also been kicked out of Transylvania College for locking a calf into the room of a vacationing professor.

"I was born," Jimmy tells a reporter for the *Sedalia Gazette* (May 28, 1891), "at Centralia, Boone county, this state, August 15, 1857, and my father was Col. James L. Dunn, for whom I was named. There were only two children, and my sister is now living in Paris, she having married a distinguished Frenchman. I could be released on bond very soon if I was to cable her regarding my condition, but I would rather remain in jail than to let her know of my disgrace." Colonel Dunn moved after his son's birth to Mississippi, where he became a wealthy plantation owner, the plantation somewhat incongruously named "Poverty Point," consisting of 10,680 acres of cotton-bearing land and 1,250 slaves who did the work of planting and picking it. Colonel Dunn then served with great distinction under General Lee for the duration of the Civil War (during which his wife died), his bravery remembered long after his death in 1884.[1] When he returned to his burnt-out plantation after Lee's defeat, Dunn began the arduous work of rebuilding his house and fortune, but, as Jimmy tells the story, he somehow managed to get into a quarrel with, arguably, the very last man on the planet with whom it was wise to argue: Colonel Alexander Keith McClung, also known as the "Black Knight," a notorious duelist. Challenges were issued, and during the encounter, Colonel Dunn's left arm was shattered, requiring amputation, crippling his reconstructive efforts, and leaving him to live the remainder of his life further burdened by an increasingly wayward son.

At this point in Jimmy's recitation, a listener knowledgeable about the history of dueling would have reason to pause. Dueling, or what amounted to quasi-legalized murder, was an unfortunate but widespread practice for much of the nation's history, and although it was generally outlawed, it was a common feature of life until well after the Civil War.[2] President Andrew Jackson, a noted duelist, participated (as charged by his detractors) in some capacity in over 103 duels. What particularly outraged his critics was not so much that he killed a man— which he did, Mr. Charles Dickson, in 1806—but that the manner of his killing was a clear violation of the Code Duello, formalized in 1777, another of Ireland's contributions to world culture. Men could be, and were, killed over the slightest of trifles. Once two gentlemen shot it out over a passionate argument about the correct way to bake potatoes. Francis Scott Key's ("The Star-Spangled Banner") son Daniel was slain in a dispute regarding the speed of a steamboat.

Another of Key's sons, Philip Barton Key, was murdered in February 1859 within sight of the White House by his former friend Daniel Sickles, who correctly suspected that Philip and Sickles's wife Teresa were having an affair, although the murder was not precisely a duel. Something really needs to be said here about Sickles, who was by far one of the most interesting men of the times. Sickles, a notorious womanizer himself, could not tolerate such behavior in others. At his trial, one of the most scandalous affairs of the age, Sickles was principally defended by Edward Stanton, later Lincoln's Secretary of War, who invented the promising legal defense of "temporary insanity," thereby convincing the jury to acquit his client.

Also of interest here is that another member of the Sickles's defense team was Thomas Francis Meagher, one of the leaders of the "Young Irelanders'" failed rebellion in the midst of the Irish potato famine in 1848. Meagher, convicted of treason and sentenced to be drawn and quartered (although a wise parliament commuted the punishment to transportation), eventually escaped from Australia to America, read law, and helped defend Sickles, whom he knew because they had long been involved together in Tammany Hall politics. Meagher would later serve as a Union general in the Civil War alongside Sickles, both of whom were at one time under the command of "Fighting Joe" Hooker, whose headquarters, so detractors charged, featured the combined charms of a bar and a brothel, the latter activity resulting in prostitutes being commonly referred to as "hookers."

Sickles also figured in the affairs of Jay Gould. Although he was then ambassador to Spain, a position in which he distinguished himself by seducing and conducting a torrid affair with Spain's deposed queen, Isabella II, Sickles temporarily abandoned his post upon receipt of a large sum to secure his services provided by allies of the Vanderbilt faction in the battle for control over the Erie Railroad. In March 1872, Sickles tricked Gould into scheduling a board meeting, which he was able to pack with Vanderbilt directors, who promptly voted out the Gould supporters. Sickles wished himself to convey such good news to Gould, and, finding that the latter had prudently locked himself in his office adjacent to the rebellious boardroom, he smashed the door open with a crowbar and pitched Gould out on the street. This was remarkably spry behavior for a man whose leg was crushed by a nearly spent cannon ball on the second day of Gettysburg, a battle where Sickles's unauthorized troop movements either, depending on who is telling the story, won the day and saved the Union, or should have resulted in his court-martial. (Sickles's amputated leg, comfortably nestled in a plush velvet case, was for many years put on display at Walter Reed hospital, where he would regularly visit accompanied by lady friends, the sight of his crushed and orphaned tibia evoking amorous sympathy.)

By all accounts, Sickles was a most unusual diplomat.[3] In 1853, appointed as the first secretary to the United States Embassy in England, "Devil" Dan arrived at his new post in London openly accompanied by Fanny White, a notorious prostitute, having left his young wife Teresa and his infant daughter behind. He then, audaciously, managed to introduce his companion as a "lady of quality" to the grim and prim Queen Victoria and wittily compounded the outrage by introducing her as "Miss Bennett," an insult to his sometimes friend, sometimes enemy, James Gordon Bennett Senior, founder of the *New York Herald,* a man who friends of Dan once publicly horsewhipped (then a common occupational hazard for newspaper editors), and a man whose son Jamie should never be allowed into a parlor containing a grand piano, lest his lack of visual acuity provoke yet another duel.

And so back to dueling. The prevalence of dueling reflected the then enormous social pressure upon men to defend what they perceived to be their honor, and those who declined a challenge would be "posted," or publicly declared cowards. But because the Code Duello allowed the challenged the choice of weapons, one could by means of ridicule sometimes avoid an actual engagement. Abraham Lincoln did just that when, challenged by another lawyer, he specified as his weapon cow excrement. (On another occasion, Lincoln narrowly avoided a duel involving swords.) Then there was the time when the challenged, whaler captain S. M. Harvey, selected harpoons at twenty paces, completely unnerving his unseaworthy opponent.

The undisputed king of duelists was Alexander Keith McClung, "who once killed an opponent at over 100 feet with a smoothbore pistol. This remarkable shot—and subsequent killings at shorter distances—honed McClung's fearful reputation."[4] Nobody seems to know how many men McClung killed. One account has him killing, in separate duels, seven brothers of one Kentucky family (the Menifees). The point to be noted here is that Dunn, in the interview provided to the *Sedalia Gazette,* clearly implies that his father fought McClung in a duel after the Civil War. But most sources agree that McClung committed suicide with his own dueling pistol in 1855.[5] Is the Dunn family story occasionally less than accurate (as are most)? Is Jimmy making the whole thing up? Is this man really J. L. Dunn?

Young Dunn's biggest problem, as he continued his story—a problem many of us would like to share—was that he had too much money: his father provided him with an annual allowance of $5,000 (over

$100,000 in today's money), far more, as he himself recognized, than he could "judiciously spend." Having so much money at so young an age usually kills the ambition required to achieve independence, financial and otherwise. After his expulsion from Missouri State, Dunn drifted to St. Louis with the idea, but not really the desire, to enroll in medical school, and for several months he stayed at the Southern Hotel, "during which time I heard of and afterwards knew Mr. Kinney, who was a prominent ward politician" (*Sedalia Gazette*, May 28, 1891). He returned to Mississippi and the plantation, where for awhile Dunn assisted in the family business. Jimmy also found sporadic work in building roads and constructing levees. "I made some money," he confessed, "but spent it freely." It seems obvious that he was just marking time, waiting until his father died and he would receive his inheritance (the plantation was by one estimate valued at over $400,000, then an enormous sum, but was encumbered by debt).

After the death of Colonel Dunn, but with his inheritance tied up in litigation, Jimmy began wandering about the country, apparently in an aimless fashion, moving to Dallas and then to Wichita, Kansas, "where I remained sixty days, it being a better city then than it is now." From there he moved on through, among other places, Galveston, Houston, and San Antonio before finally settling in Austin, where he began speculating in real estate options. Jimmy, styling himself a capitalist, although the bulk of his capital was unavailable, soon exhausted his available money through high living and a number of abortive business deals, including an attempt to buy a newspaper. A *Saint Louis Globe-Democrat* article, dated April 30, 1891, reports that "before Mr. Dunn left the city he contracted for a controlling interest in the Austin *Daily Statesman,* and made a cash payment either to bind the trade or secure the option, but which we are unable to learn. Mr. Dunn had been very honest in his transaction with the people of this city, so far as has yet been learned, but he has made no substantial investments here, as he only seemed to be dealing in options."

With an admirable civic spirit entirely befitting a prospective newspaper publisher, Jimmy secured an option to one centrally located lot upon which, he announced, he intended to build a brick five-story opera house, thereby endearing him to Austin's society set. Accompanied by a local architect, Jimmy then left on a tour of the East Coast for the purpose of inspecting established and famous opera houses and of learning all the intricacies of their construction, as he intended that his new Austin opera house would be the rival of any. So seemingly wealthy a young man on so noble a cultural mission is bound to attract female attention, and in New York City, Dunn became enamored of a lady known only as Miss Maurice, employed as a "skirt dancer,"[6] whom he persuaded to join him on his aesthetic quest.

This attractive trio—architect Watson (expecting a large commission), the voluptuous Miss Maurice (willing to decorate Dunn's arm so long as the hand thereto attached had access to a fat and generous wallet), and above all Jimmy Dunn himself, now a self-styled expert on operatic acoustics—must have presented quite a spectacle, dining in the finest restaurants on only the most expensive dishes, staying only in the most elegant hotels, generally living the high life, spending money as if it were so much paper. And in a sense it was, particularly a form of paper known as a "bill of lading." Jimmy Dunn had somehow become an expert at forging both them and the signatures they required. When Dunn returned to Austin through Atlanta, he was there, on April 30, 1891, recognized by the victim of one of his scams. The police were summoned, and they promptly threw him in jail.[7] As the case developed, it became apparent that Dunn's "aimless wandering" about the country was hardly that at all, for the scheme he devised would probably only work once in any given location, thus explaining his frequent travels. And each time he worked the fraud, Dunn had to assume a series of new identities, because those damaged by his prior crimes would be sure to warn their colleagues.

Let us suppose, in 1891, you wanted to sell some cattle. (In principle, any commodity could be substituted. Dunn's arrest in Atlanta was for a shipment of cotton valued at $12,500.) You would go to any of the major railhead cities, establish a local bank account, and then visit the offices of a livestock commission merchant. There, if the agent was buying and you could agree on the price, the agent would give you a "sight draft," instructing your bank to pay or credit your account from their funds the agreed-upon price. At this point, by itself, the sight draft is worthless; it serves only to record a contract to be paid out after certain conditions have been met. Then, in a legitimate transaction, you would approach by prior arrangement a shipper, usually a railroad, and board your livestock on the appropriate date. The sight draft is proffered to the shipper as evidence of the contract. The railroad agent then prepares a "bill of lading" itemizing what you have actually delivered, and should your delivery match the terms stipulated on the draft, the railroad forwards to your bank both the original sight draft and the bill of lading, which now approves it for payment. After your bank has paid or credited your account, often less 10 percent of the face value, which is held as escrow, the bill of lading is forwarded to the buyer's bank and then delivered to the buyer, and this document is required to be presented when receiving the contracted shipment.

The railroad acts as an escrow agent in this transaction. The protection for the shipper is that from the very outset, he has a draft recording the transaction, a draft that can be cashed the moment the cattle complete their boarding (as they then legally become the property of the buyer), assuming a proper bill of lading is executed and delivered. The protection for the buyer is that if the seller doesn't deliver, or the delivery does not exactly match that specified by the draft, a corresponding bill of lading will not be executed, without which the sight draft is worthless. Complicated as it may now seem, this was the financial mechanism by which billions of dollars' worth of commodities, usually sight unseen, were moved about the nation from sellers to distant buyers. The weak point, as Dunn recognized, was the bill of lading.

Dunn was by no means the first—or the last—crook to work such a scam, but he carried it off better than most.[8] The key was to convince the commission agents to issue a legitimate sight draft, something they didn't just hand out, particularly to new sellers with whom they lacked a sustained, continuous business relationship. During the initial negotiations, the seller would be asked many pointed questions by agents experienced and expert in the proposed commodity, questions designed to test the seller's knowledge of what he offered to supply. Precisely what grade of cotton do you wish to sell, and by what method have you established its grade? What number bailing wire do you use, and are you sure it is strong enough to guarantee the shipment arrives intact and compressed? Say, we heard there was a weevil plague in your area. How did you eradicate them? If the seller lacked convincing answers to such questions, he would be shown, politely or not, the door.

Letters of introduction would be of help here—or better yet, personal introductions. The former were no problem to a forger. As for the latter, here is where Dunn excelled. Jimmy was the kind of guy—probably everybody knows someone like him—who could show up completely unknown in any town, and by patronizing the best restaurants, appearing at the most fashionable night spots, drinking at the right sort of bars, and buying the whole house drinks, he would within an amazingly short time have made many new friends. Naturally gregarious and extroverted, Dunn was eminently likeable, funny, witty, and amusing, a great companion with whom to share a beer or invite to a friendly game of cards. He had a dangerous ability to inspire trust in others, and if, say, during that friendly card game Dunn casually mentioned he had some business to transact, business that would be helped by a personal introduction, this would seem to his new friends to be but a small matter to arrange.

Dunn was also clever in determining the amount of his frauds. The $12,500 fake cotton shipment, for which he was eventually arrested in Atlanta, would have been pushing the envelope, given that the larger the proposed shipment, the more careful scrutiny it would receive, particularly from a new seller, but Dunn was somehow, probably on the strength of his cotton knowledge obtained (so he said) from working on the family plantation, able, at least temporarily, to successfully deceive the buyers. Jimmy's downfall here was that he forged a letter of introduction from a Mr. Crocket, a real and respected cotton dealer in Jonesboro, Georgia, but who had been dead for over two years, a fact unknown to the particular agent with whom he was negotiating but well known to others, leading to the investigation.

For the scam he was to run at Sedalia, bringing him to the attention of Captain Jack, Dunn proposed the much more reasonable sum of $5,250 for the promised delivery of thirteen cars of cattle and hogs, a large enough amount to make the transaction worthwhile, but not so large as to attract undue notice. Jimmy also gave some thought to the aftermath of his crimes, knowing that most criminals are caught because they suddenly begin living beyond their perceived means. Bartenders, shopkeepers, and waitresses all gossip about the habits of their customers, and such gossip eventually reaches the police. A clever part of Dunn's act was that from the outset, he had established the persona of a wealthy playboy, thereby allaying suspicions about his subsequent conduct.

In any event, sometime early in March 1891, a gentleman who identified himself as Mr. Thomas F. Sibley, but who was really Jimmy Dunn, arrived in Sedalia and visited the local offices of the Wood Brothers, Livestock Commission Merchants. Wood Brothers was an old and prosperous firm, established in 1867, with headquarters at the Chicago stockyards, district offices at Omaha and Sioux City, and local offices, like the one in Sedalia, in many of the smaller rail towns. Sedalia had once been, but by 1891 was no longer, one of the major railheads for transporting cattle. Dee Brown writes,

> the Longhorns were there [in Texas, shortly after the Civil War] for the taking, unfenced and unbranded. All a man needed were horses, saddles, a few supplies, and some good drivers working on shares. The goals were the nearest railheads, and these were in Missouri. . . . Sedalia, Missouri, was the nearest railroad point for Texans, and in the warm days of early spring, thousands of cattle from south Texas were driven north along the Sedalia trail, passing Fort Worth and heading for the crossing of the Red River.[9]

Sibley was able to present the agent with the very best kind of introductory letter, from the headquarters office itself, as he offered in prior correspondence to them Mr. John Swasher as a reference, a gentleman whom they knew well and respected. In return, they had written a letter on behalf of Mr. Sibley. Dunn had gambled, correctly, that most people didn't actually bother to check such references. On the strength of this correspondence, and impressed by the manner and bearing of Mr. Sibley, the agent issued him a sight draft for the amount described. Dunn then took this draft, which would have been itself an impressive credential to any local banker, and established an account at the Sedalia First National Bank.

The next step would be a visit to the MK&T freight office, where again, a sight draft from the Wood Brothers—a major Katy customer— would command attention. There Dunn would meet with Mr. John F. Ray, the chief rail shipping agent and also the man responsible for preparing the bill of lading that would convert the sight draft to ready cash. Mr. Ray would naturally be eager to please someone doing business with one of his most important customers, and Dunn would be at his most charming. Perhaps we could discuss the shipping details over lunch? Can I buy you a beer? Dunn's goal was to learn everything he could about Ray and the procedures in his office, a task surprisingly easy to begin over lunch and a beer or two, as most people are eager to talk about their work, some few unable to talk about much of anything else. Ray would very likely have arranged for the curious and affable Mr. Sibley a tour of his office, from which Dunn could learn much. Where do you keep the bills of lading? Can I see one?

Dunn would similarly arrange lunches with his new bankers, seeking to know how they worked things at their end. For his scheme to work, he needed four items. First, he needed a specimen of Ray's handwriting and signature, probably easily obtained from the office trash. Second, an actual, blank bill of lading needed to be procured—if possible, one with plausible sequential numbering, but at the very least, Dunn needed to know (if he did not already) how they appeared. Third, he required a canceled or expired bill of lading recording a transaction similar to what he proposed, enabling him to mimic the particulars in the form the bank was accustomed to seeing. Again, this was in the days before paper shredders, and people threw out a lot of stuff they perhaps should not have. Finally, perhaps the most difficult of all, Dunn needed to know the customary "batching" procedures followed by the bank and the railroad office. A safeguard in this type of transaction, established to prevent precisely what Dunn was attempting to do, was that the seller was supposed, at the time of shipment, to surrender the draft to the shipper, who, if everything was correct, would "batch" the draft with the bill of lading and deliver both documents to the bank. Because the bank received the documents from the shipper, not the seller, the bank could presume the documents to be authentic. Was this procedure always strictly followed? Would any exceptions be allowed?

Exactly how Dunn accomplished all this cannot now be known. But on Thursday, March 19, 1891, the date of the proposed livestock shipment, there appeared at the appropriate desk of the Sedalia First National Bank, whether properly batched or not by some prior arrangement, both a legitimate sight draft and an entirely fake bill of lading, to all appearances genuinely executed and signed by Mr. Ray, instructing the bank to release for payment the sum of $5,250 from the Wood Brothers account to Mr. Thomas F. Sibley. Mr. Sibley then promptly cashed out his account and disappeared. If the correct procedures were followed, as I'm sure they were, the bill of lading would then have been forwarded to the Wood Brothers in Chicago. But the cattle and hogs, having never existed, never arrived. The Wood Brothers would have been displeased by this outcome. The Katy railroad would have been made aware of their displeasure. Someone would have brought the matter, in a more or less urgent manner, to the attention of Chief Detective John J. Kinney.

But first, that someone would have to wait until Captain Jack returned from a well-deserved vacation. Accompanied by his daughter Mamie, Kinney had left Sedalia on March 16 for a two-week trip, swinging first through Chicago and then to Philadelphia, staying with his father and mother, and then, accompanied by his parents, on to New York City, where (on March 21) he was met by his younger brother Henry. That night, as has been discussed, Captain Jack indulged in his passion for observing boxing matches. Returning by roughly the same route, visiting relatives and friends along the way, Kinney did not return to Sedalia until April 1, there to find a desk piled high with work, including the priority matter of a forgery by Mr. Thomas F. Sibley. Probably because it was necessary to clear away some of the backlog, Kinney does not mention the forgery case in his diary until April 15, when he notes that he is to leave for St. Louis on that very matter.

But how, exactly, does one go about finding a forger? Presumably, Captain Jack would begin by interviewing everybody who had any contact with Dunn, finding out what he could about the man, compiling a detailed description of his appearance—although there was no guarantee his appearance would not change. Because Dunn's fraud was a relatively sophisticated operation, the odds would be that Sedalia was not the only place Dunn had operated, as criminal success tends to tip the psychological balance away from fear and toward greed. The more times Dunn worked his scam, the greater were the chances he would soon be caught. And the surest way to find a criminal is to look in a jail. Perhaps Dunn, or Sibley (as Captain Jack then thought of him), had already been caught. The time had come for an extensive, and initially somewhat unfocused, investigative search, handing out wanted circulars to conductors and porters, talking to station agents up and down the line, crisscrossing the Midwest to gather information, contacting his extensive network of law enforcement friends and associates—exactly the kind of detective work at which Captain Jack excelled.

Kinney stopped over in St. Louis the next day and stayed at the Southern Hotel,[10] the very hotel Dunn lived in while contemplating a medical career. He met with representatives of the Thiel Detective Agency, hoping to learn of active forgers that may have come to their attention. That afternoon, for the same purpose, he was off to Chicago to confer with the Wood Brothers and also Pat Gray of the Pinkerton Agency and William Welett, Assistant United States District Attorney. Perhaps following leads they had provided, he next traveled that Sunday back down to Kansas City, then on to Topeka (during the ride to which he spotted, and noted in his diary, the presence of Mr. Thatch Grady, a notorious confidence man, accompanied by two of his accomplices). Then it was off to Denver on April 21 for a meeting with James McParland,[11] who was in charge of Denver's Pinkerton regional headquarters, where the first solid lead developed, requiring him to travel to Cheyenne, Wyoming, to interview Mr. Harry Bates, who was in the jail there charged with forging a bill of lading for cattle consigned to, but never received by, the Brown Brothers firm of Chicago.

Mr. Bates, predictably, denied any involvement and did not much resemble the description witnesses provided of Sibley, but Captain Jack learned he was arrested in the company of a lady known variously as "Minnie Woods" or "Minnie Murphy," who was being held in a separate jail back in Denver, and that at the time of her arrest, she possessed a trunk also containing many of Mr. Bates's personal effects. This information was worth a trip back to Denver, where, having secured search warrants, and accompanied by Detective Reno[12] of the Denver Police Department, Captain Jack opened the trunk and examined its contents. Nothing of any importance was found. But in another conversation that afternoon (April 24) with McParland, the Pinkerton agent, Kinney got a good lead, this one requiring that he travel to Adrian, Michigan, for the purpose of interviewing prisoner Tom Fiox, who had recently been arrested in nearby Manitou Springs but who was now being held by Michigan authorities. To get to Adrian, one first had to connect back in Kansas City with the Wabash Railway, and finally (on April 27), after delays en route, Captain Jack was able to meet prisoner Fiox, who indeed resembled far more closely than did Bates the described appearance of Thomas Sibley. Kinney directed that Fiox be taken from jail to a photographic studio, where his picture was taken.[13] Then on Tuesday, April 28, Captain Jack traveled back to the Midwest, where, stopping in St. Louis, by chance he noticed in the *Globe-Democrat* a story reported from Atlanta, detailing the arrest of Mr. James L. Dunn for forgery.

This was certainly worth a telegram and letter of inquiry, and be-cause the Dunn case was generating considerable publicity in Atlanta, Captain Jack's letter was published in the *Atlanta Journal* on May 2:

Sedalia, Mo.
Chief of Police, Atlanta, Ga.
Dear Sir:—On March the 19th, one Thos. F. Sibley received from the first national bank, of this city, $5,250, upon forged drafts on Wood Bros., live stock commission merchants, union stock yards, Chicago. Attached to said forged drafts was a forged bill of lading to cover a shipment of cattle and hogs. I notice by the morning pa-pers one J. L. Dunn, of the brokerage firm of Dunn & Perkins at Austin, in your city, is charged with forging a draft to the amount of $12,500. I believe this is the same party. I will consider it a per-sonal favor if you will send me a picture of this party and woman, and any other information that you may obtain from papers in his possession. I have just returned from the west where I have been trying to locate the party who forged the drafts here. One of the party named Harry Bates is now under arrest at Cheyenne, Wyoming. I have requested the sheriff to get his picture and send same to me. If I receive the picture of Bates I will forward you a copy. Any information you can give me relative to this matter will be thankfully received. Please let me know how much money, if any, was found in his possession.
Yours respectfully,
J. J. Kenney [*sic*], Special Agent

Captain Jack's letter is puzzling to me in a number of respects. His diary clearly indicates that it was prisoner Fiox, precisely because of his resemblance "somewhat" to the witness descriptions, who was photographed. Nothing is said about Bates in this regard, although it is possible the Cheyenne police had offered to have him pho-tographed as well. It may be that Kinney had reason to suspect that the forgery was committed by two people, with a confidence-type per-sonality like Dunn to set the stage and a technical expert like Bates to actually produce the forgeries. It may be that he simply confused the two—understandable given his hectic and tiring schedule.

Also puzzling is that Kinney in his letter clearly states that *both* the sight draft and the bill of lading were forged. This simply doesn't square with my understanding of how Dunn operated. Although there is not anything particularly difficult about forging a sight draft, the point is that because it initiates the whole financial process, people's natural suspicions, particularly in a transaction involving a relative stranger, will be at their highest. The cleverness of Dunn's scam depended on procuring a legitimate sight draft and slipping in the forgery later, after people's natural wariness lessened. Because Sedalia is further a relatively small town, and because this financial transaction depended on the coordinated cooperation of parties who had extensive experience with each other in just these matters, it seems inconceivable to me that a double forgery of the sort Kinney describes could have succeeded. Another point is that in every diary reference to the matter (and there are many), Kinney describes the case as one involving a forged "bill of lading"—nowhere are forged "drafts" mentioned. I strongly suspect that the Wood Brothers, who were one of the driving forces behind the investigation, asked, or ordered, Kinney not to mention that it was their negligence, in not checking Dunn's reference, that was in some large portion responsible for the issuing of a genuine sight draft. Perhaps such misinformation—if it was—was a calculated strategy, a trap for potential forgers, encouraging them to believe that the established financial safeguards could be easily circumvented, when in fact, were they to operate in the manner here ascribed to Dunn, they would probably be subject to immediate arrest.

Before the above letter was published, Atlanta Police Chief Connolly had assigned the Dunn case to Chief Detective Couch, who, in response to the telegram, invited Captain Jack to visit Atlanta and interview and perhaps identify the prisoner for himself. Thus, on Thursday, April 30, Captain Jack was off to Atlanta, accompanied by Mr. Fountaine ("Font") Merriweather, head cashier for the Sedalia First National Bank, the witness who had the most contact with Dunn and who cashed out his account. When he arrived in Atlanta on Saturday, May 2, Captain Jack noted in his diary that "Fountaine Merriweather and myself called at Police Headquarters at Atlanta Georgia today and identified J. L. Dunn as Thos. F. Sibley, party who on April 19th forged a bill of lading and drew fifty two hundred dollars out of the 1st National Bank of Sedalia."

The question then became, who wanted to prosecute Dunn more, Georgia or Missouri? The Georgia forgery was considerably larger, but I suspect the Missouri forgery had better witnesses and was therefore more probable to end in conviction. To that end, the governor of Missouri signed and forwarded to Captain Jack extradition papers requesting transfer of the prisoner's custody, a process that somehow required that Captain Jack pay Chief Connolly the suspiciously round-numbered sum of $500, perhaps as a reimbursement for expenses already incurred by the Atlanta Police Department. Finally, on Tuesday, May 5, Merriweather and Kinney, now in charge of prisoner Dunn, left Atlanta and headed back to Sedalia, where they arrived on May 7. There, Mr. James L. Dunn, or Mr. Thomas F. Sibley, was escorted to his new address at the Pettis County jail.

Not until after three weeks in jail would Dunn admit, or rather assert, in an interview to the *Sedalia Gazette* (May 28, 1891) conducted by reporter Ed Burris, and at which Captain Jack was present, that his name was actually "Dunn." "There is no use of my endeavoring to longer conceal anything regarding my identity," said the alleged criminal, "for it is bound to come out some time, and I now propose to give it to you straight, as you can easily corroborate." Then we hear the tale of Mother and Father Dunn, both conveniently dead, and the duel between Colonel Dunn and a man who had also been dead for some ten years, and a sister suspiciously far off in France whom "Dunn" will not contact due to embarrassment over his present circumstances:

The statement was made in the presence of only Mr. Kinney and the Gazette reporter, in the parlor of Sheriff Smith's residence, and only once did the prisoner refuse to answer a question, and that was when Mr. Kinney said:

"Tell me, Jimmy, when you first conceived the idea of this forged bill of lading racket?"

"Now, you are getting on to something that I know nothing about," replied the prisoner, and he gave a light laugh as he puffed away on a fragrant La Pluma.

He has never admitted that he turned the Sedalia trick, it will be remembered, nor that he ever went under the name of Sibley, but what he will do later along, when confronted with the evidence already accumulated, remains to be seen.

This was the prisoner's life story as it came from his own lips, and Detective Kinney feels pretty well satisfied that it is the truth. Dunn thinks considerable of Kinney, and has presented him with a handsome oil painting, "A Hungarian Scene," the value of which, he says, is $500. . . . Other things have developed that may cause him trouble hereafter, but he [Dunn] is not of the kind to worry over what cannot be helped, and is one of the most cheerful prisoners ever confined in the Pettis county jail.

A point of note is that many of the supposed details of Dunn's life surfaced only in interviews he provided weeks after his arrest in Atlanta. An important part of Captain Jack's job (as it had been in the Lewis case, where he uncovered a "mass" of corroborating detail) was to gather further relevant evidence, so that the case did not depend solely on the testimony of a single eyewitness, as compelling as such testimony might be. During his initial investigation, Kinney had discovered that the last people in Sedalia to see "Sibley," on March 19 as he fled town, were two local merchants, a clerk at Van Wagner Brothers who sold him a distinctive pair of boots, and gun dealer A. B. Dempsey, from whom Dunn purchased a Colt revolver. While searching through Dunn's personal effects confiscated by the Atlanta police, Captain Jack found a claim check to a trunk stored in Austin, thereby enabling him to focus the preliminary investigation more narrowly.

Before he had even left Atlanta, Dunn in his custody, Kinney had telegraphed his very capable assistant, Detective Edward Taylor, based at the Katy office at Denison, Texas, with the particulars of his discovery, instructing Taylor to investigate further. An undated article in the *Sedalia Gazette* describes the outcome: "It will also be shown at the trial [originally scheduled for November 1891] that Thomas F. Sibley left here with $5,250 in his possession on the evening train on the 19th of March, and that he arrived in Austin on the morning of the 21st, when he registered under his own name, J. L. Dunn, at the hotel where he had previously stopped, and a couple of days later he presented two of his friends with the revolver and pair of boots he had purchased in Sedalia." One might suspect that Dunn's contrite admission that he was, in fact, "Dunn" was less motivated by a newly cooperative attitude and more influenced by the knowledge that Captain Jack and Taylor had already discovered his true identity—if indeed it was. But although Dunn freely confessed to being Dunn, he adamantly denied posing as Sibley, a matter of significance because the state of Georgia had dropped charges against Dunn for the Atlanta forgery in order to facilitate his extradition to Missouri. If he could plausibly deny any connection to Sibley, perhaps by proving that as

Dunn he was elsewhere at the time of the fraud (and he tried to do just this), then he stood to be cleared on both charges.

But the question still lingers: was "Dunn" his true identity? It's hard for us to understand the import of this question, living as we do in a time when the state has developed sophisticated techniques and technologies establishing beyond doubt the precise identity of any given individual. One of our very first experiences, shortly after birth, is having our footprints inked on a hospital certificate. Later we must acquire driver's licenses, social security cards, draft cards, credit cards, worker's identification badges, and passports, to itemize only some of the means of identification required by modern life. If you've ever joined the military, held a security-sensitive job, been arrested, or even used certain forms of check-cashing verification systems, then your fingerprints are somewhere on file—or more accurately, because of computer technology, potentially everywhere on file. Identification is now possible from DNA genotyping, retinal scanning, voice printing, and—at the time of this writing—a new type of video computer analysis promising to identify us by our gait. The very idea that someone could conceal his identity for long seems preposterous to us.

Not so in Captain Jack's time. If a man claimed to be James Dunn, or Tom Sibley, the tendency would be to believe him, not because people back then were more naive and trusting than they now are, but because the means to verify independently such information largely did not exist. You were who you said you were because other people recognized you as such, family members could vouch for you, and you had ties in a community—exactly the relationships Dunn appeared to lack. Police officials had long recognized the need for reliable techniques of identification, and not just for the purpose of apprehending criminals. For most of history, the criminal courts had focused strictly on the crime. If you stole a loaf of bread, in the eyes of the law, it didn't matter whether you were poor and stealing it to feed your starving children, or rich and stealing it simply for a thrill. In theory, both crimes would merit the same—usually harsh—punishment. But the focus of the law was in the process of shifting from the crime to the criminal. Colin Beavan (in *Fingerprints*) dates this change to 1869, when

Parliament passed the Habitual Criminals Act, providing longer sentences for more hardened criminals. A first-time offender, the rationale went, might merely be a weak character faced with desperate circumstances—the type of criminal who . . . was the victim of societal conditions. To this otherwise decent citizen the judicial system delivered a short, sharp shock, deterring him from offending again.

Habitual offenders, on the other hand, were "a criminal class distinct from other civilized and criminal men," wrote the Scottish prison surgeon J. Bruce Thompson in 1870. (54)

Because the law was beginning to recognize the character of the man, apart from the particulars of his crime, it became important to know who the man was. Jimmy Dunn, wealthy son of a Civil War hero, a fun-loving playboy whose only confessed crimes were "affrighting Negroes" with skeletons on wires and afflicting his professor with four-legged houseguests, might deserve, upon conviction, the minimum penalty allowed by the law. That same Mr. Dunn, if it could be demonstrated that he was in addition to a forger a serial impostor and a habitual criminal, might receive a far harsher sentence.

The difficulty would be to prove the latter. If he had been arrested and convicted in the past for a similar crime, presumably under a different name, and if the court could be persuaded to admit such evidence, how could it be shown (other than by eyewitness testimony, which demonstrably fades as it ages) that he was the same man? By 1891, forensic systems capable of making such determinations were just beginning to be adopted, although they were more prevalent in Europe than in the United States. One of the most promising was that devised by Alphonse Bertillon (1853–1913). Bertillon, the son and grandson of famous anthropologists, after a dissolute youth, in March 1879 got a job as an assistant clerk with the identification bureau of the Paris Prefecture of Police. His duties were by turn tedious and ineffectual, shuffling through files that, although occasionally including mug shots, more often simply had physical descriptions of criminals written down by the arresting officer. A criminal might have his appearance listed as "ordinary." Or that he was "shorter than average," his face given to "horrible and hideous expressions." Recognizing that such subjective commentary was useless, Bertillon remembered the anthropomorphic measurements used by his father and grandfather, measurements premised on the assumption that no two bodies could be identical, and he wondered whether such a system could be adopted to conclusively identify criminals, regardless of how they identified themselves. This he proceeded to do, designing a method based on eleven separate body measurements (such as length of middle finger, exact size of ear, and measurement of arm and forearm) and by 1883 had recorded his first success, identifying a criminal as habitual entirely by means of his system.[14]

But that was no help to Captain Jack. He was hoping for, and needed, a full confession. During the latter stages of his confinement, Dunn and Captain Jack were playing some sort of an elaborate game with each other. Kinney seemingly befriended Dunn, extending him courtesies not normally afforded prisoners (such as allowing reporters to interview him in Sheriff Smith's comfortable parlor), presumably angling for a confession, while Dunn—always able to provide good press copy—would shamelessly flatter Captain Jack, entertaining reporters with amusing anecdotes about his capture. So reports the *Sedalia Gazette* in an undated piece:

> Dunn thinks a good deal of Detective Kinney and yesterday gave the *Gazette* the following paragraphs in regard to his friend:
>
> "The genial Capt. 'Jack' Kinney, of the M. K. & T. secret service, has a host of admiring friends. It is impossible for him to visit any city, town, or flag station in the United States without meeting some of them."
>
> Say, have you heard the latest? It's "General Kinney" now. This title was acquired a few weeks ago, at Atlanta, Ga. Col. Font Merriwether [*sic*] introduced the genial Jack to one of his friends in that city—one of those old fighting colonels, who shook his hand warmly and said:
>
> "General Kinney, I am very glad to meet you, sah! How do you come on, sah!" This title could not have fallen on shoulders better adapted for it than those of J. J. Kinney.

Such mutual admiration—don't forget Dunn's gift of the valuable oil painting—must have abruptly ended shortly before Jimmy's trial, when Captain Jack somehow managed to discover that Mr. Thomas F. Sibley, also known as James L. Dunn, was in fact Mr. E. Ellis Godlove. "For nearly a year," reads an undated article in the *Saint Louis Globe-Democrat,* "it transpires, young Ellis has been carrying on operations similar to that for which he is now under lock and key." On Friday, November 20, Kinney traveled to St. Louis to interview James E. Godlove, Dunn's father, "but the young man's father [so continues the

Globe], when seen yesterday, said he had not heard from his son in about four years, and that if he had gotten himself into trouble he must endure the consequences, as he does not feel it to be his duty to endeavor to protect him."

On April 6, 1892, E. Ellis Godlove pled guilty to the charge of forgery and was sentenced by Judge Ryland to two years in the penitentiary. Escorted to prison by Sheriff Smith, Godlove "feigned considerable grief just prior to his departure, and to a Bazoo reporter expressed himself as believing that the good people of Sedalia would eventually intercede in his behalf. On the train he wept, and tears flowed down his cheeks" (*Sedalia Bazoo,* April 6, 1892). He remarked to the same reporter, "I don't believe I will remain long in the penitentiary, and I trust that I am not mistaken. I have been many years tiding over my troubles, and today's sentence I hope is the end of it all. The verdict of to-day will, I believe, prove the best thing of my life for my future. I am going to write to the people of Sedalia and try and enlist their aid in my behalf."

John Joseph Kinney, also known as "Captain Jack."

Another view of Captain Jack.

Elizabeth Jeffers Kinney married John J. Kinney in 1877.

The Kinney family sometime in the middle or late 1880s. To Captain Jack's right is his eldest daughter Mamie. To his left are Dot and Nan. Nellie, the baby held by Elizabeth, died in infancy.

The Kinney house in Topeka around 1902. Captain Jack is on the far right in the shadows. The occasion for the photograph is probably the christening of his first grandchild.

*Captain Charles
La Flore*

*Charles La Flore
later in life.
Courtesy of the
Oklahoma
Historical Society.*

Captain Sam Sixkiller

Heck Thomas

*Chris Madsen and Bill Tilghman. Courtesy of the
Oklahoma Historical Society.*

Thomas Furlong

Detective Furlong (on the left) has just cleverly trapped this little girl into divulging the location of her Uncle Charlie, a fugitive from justice.

Al Jennings, dressed like the lawyer he once was.
Courtesy of the Oklahoma Historical Society.

Marshal E. D. Nix, Al Jennings, and Chris Madsen. Courtesy of Western History Collections, University of Oklahoma Library.

Judge Isaac Parker

George Maledon, the Prince of Hangmen. Courtesy of Western History Collections, University of Oklahoma Library.

J. Warren Reed, "The Lawyer Who Never Loses His Cases."

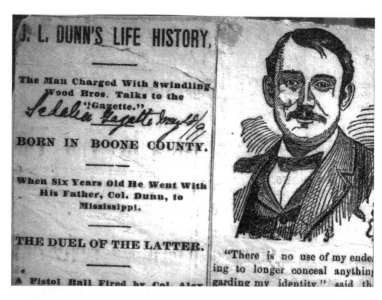

Newspaper clipping showing forger Jimmy Dunn (one of the newspaper clippings passed down by Captain Jack).

Lynching somewhere in east Texas. The black man posed in the center, behind the pile of logs, is about to be burned upon them.
Courtesy of Western History Collections, University of Oklahoma Library.

*United States Deputy
Marshal Frank
Dalton, killed in the
line of duty.*

*Bill Power, Bob Dalton, Grat Dalton, and Dick Broadwell (left to right).
Courtesy of Western History Collections, University of Oklahoma Library.*

Bob Dalton, Ransom Payne (?), and Grat Dalton. Somebody retouched the photograph to disguise the bullet hole through Grat's throat. Courtesy of Western History Collections, University of Oklahoma Library.

Mural in modern Coffeyville. Photograph by Judy Kinney.

Outline of Bob Dalton where he fell in "Death Alley."
Photograph by Judy Kinney.

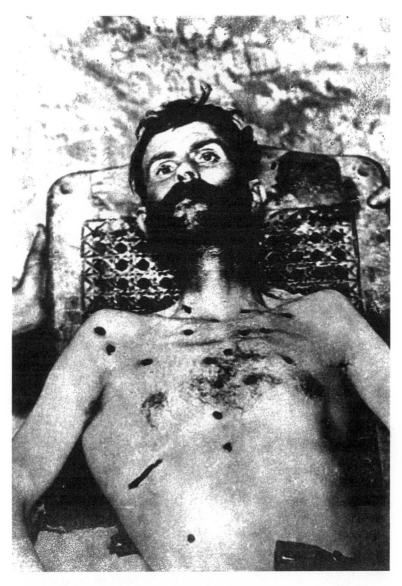

Bill Doolin, killed by Heck Thomas. Courtesy of Western History Collections, University of Oklahoma Library.

One of Captain Jack's railroad passes.

Captain Jack, late in life, dictating a letter to his secretary.

BRANCH LAW

Generations pass while some trees stand, and old families last not three oaks.
—*Sir Thomas Browne*

Do you know how long walnut trees live? The world's oldest trees, botanists estimate, have life spans of more than 5,000 years. On the North American continent, the longevity champions are likely the western red cedar, with some specimens celebrating over 2,000 birthdays, and the bristlecone pine. Pacific yews can live 1,800 years, and western hemlocks over 1,200. Walnuts, like most fruit-bearing trees (and the walnut in question here would bear sick fruit indeed), are comparatively short-lived, maybe 150 years or so, although some walnuts now living in France are estimated to be over 300 years old.

Thus it is very possible, although not probable, that a particular walnut tree still stands in Bedford County, Virginia, and has since well before the time of the Revolutionary War. That particular walnut had been planted in the front yard of a home belonging to the local justice of the peace and, by the time of the American Revolution, had fully matured into a stout, strong, and shady representative of its arboreal kind. The local justice was a staunch patriot, but many of his neighbors were not, and these "Tories," as those still supporting King George were called, when captured, were hauled before an entirely ad hoc court held on his walnut-shaded front porch. Although he had no authority to do so, the justice would mete out harsh punishments to those convicted, or simply accused, of lacking sufficiently patriotic sentiments. Some miscreants would be tied to the walnut's trunk and have their bare backs flogged. Others would be hung from a walnut branch by their thumbs until they cried "Liberty forever!" with a zeal indicative of a new political allegiance. More serious cases were tarred and feathered. The most grievous offenders would be strung up by a rope thrown over a walnut limb and hanged by the neck until they were dead. The name of the justice was Colonel Charles Lynch (1736–1796), from whose last name (or so goes one story) the term *lynching* was derived.

The practice of lynching is a cultural universal that probably predates civilization itself, and arguably, it has been a constant aspect of recorded history and before ever since people began living together in groups. Law itself may have evolved out of an effort to regularize and codify mob behavior, with some cave-dwelling Solon recognizing that a large enough mob could be defined as an abstract state, whose equally lethal actions would then become legal executions. Certainly, lynch mobs were a feature of American life from the earliest colonial times. One of the original Pilgrim founders who stepped ashore at Plymouth Rock was a querulous gentleman named John Billington, who had been punished on the journey over by Captain Miles Standish for his "blasphemous harangues." After the 1630 murder of John Newcomen, killed from ambush by a blunderbuss, Billington was strung up by a mob (or, depending on one's point of view, convicted and executed by a jury), thus becoming the first lynching, or legal hanging, victim in the new colony.[1] He would not be the last.

No individual or group was necessarily safe from the vigilante's rope, but as a general rule, the more foreign in appearance a suspected offender seemed, the more likely it was that he might face the dubious justice dispensed by an unruly mob. Chinese and other East Asians were often targets, as in Denver in November 1880, when a mob of 3,000 "illegal voters, Irishmen and some Negroes" set fire to Hop Alley, the thriving local Chinatown, lynched a young man named Look Young, and injured scores of other Chinese. In 1891 a group of eleven (by some accounts twelve) Italians, jailed in New Orleans over suspicions of their involvement in the murder of Police Chief David Hennessey, was murdered by a mob that stormed the jail and riddled them with bullets (lynch mobs did not necessarily always hang their victims). Mexicans and Indians were frequent targets, especially in the West, as were whites (see what became of "Yank" Kinney in Chapter 3). For some reason, San Francisco mobs seemed to specialize in lynching migrant Australians. Jews were not ignored. But it is fair to say that during the Reconstruction after the Civil War, when the number of lynchings dramatically increased, that the victims, particularly in the Old South and surrounding border states, were predominantly black.

We'd now like to think that, shameful as the lynchings were, most were instigated by radical fringe groups such as the Ku Klux Klan and represented only the sick hate and thirst for blood unfortunately characteristic of the lower orders common to any society. The original KKK, founded in Pulaski, Tennessee, in May 1866 by six former Confederate soldiers, was—at least in comparison to its later, more virulent appearance—a relatively benign group, if only because of its initially small size. The white robes and hoods were meant to simulate the ghosts of dead Confederate soldiers, useful in the then popular sport (as we have seen) of "affrighting negroes." In 1867 the group attracted attention by electing as its leader ("Grand Wizard") Nathan Bedford Forrest, the legendary Confederate cavalry general. But by 1869 General Forrest, perhaps retaining some sense of military honor and disturbed by the violent direction the group seemed to be heading in, resigned and ordered the group to disband. Some of the local chapters ("Klaverns") did; some didn't. A more cynical view is that Forrest's disbandment order, "General Order Number One," was in fact a ploy to create legal distance between the Klan's headquarters and the local operations.

In 1915 the Klan was revived, helped in part by the success of D. W. Griffith's film *The Birth of a Nation.* At its peak in the 1920s the Klan attracted nearly five million members and was responsible for electing numerous local and state officials. For example, at one point the Klan so dominated the city of Tulsa, Oklahoma, that the governor felt compelled to declare martial law, sending in the National Guard to restore order. One knowledgeable witness later recalled that "Klan membership [in Tulsa] permeated the entire population. I think it is safe to say that a large majority of the so-called middle- and upper-class men belonged to it; at least ninety percent of government officials and community leaders were Klansmen. The sheriff and his deputies, members of the police department, county commissioners, city councilmen, the county attorney, even most of the judges and court attendants belonged."[2] But by the 1930s, plagued by a series of internal scandals, Klan membership dropped to 30,000 and has been declining ever since.

This hopeful view, that the lynch mob and hate groups like the Klan were but aberrant and temporary stains upon our collective and continuing evolvement toward a higher ethical plane, simply cannot fit with a reading of the contemporaneous accounts, of which there are literally thousands. Here's just one (from the *Atlanta Constitution*, May 18, 1892, 1):

A TRIPLE LYNCHING

Takes Place Up In the Hills of Habersham,
And Three Negroes Dangle

At The End of Long Heavy Trace Chains
Locked Tightly About Their Necks

The Sheriff Overpowered, The Jail Broken Open and Three Negroes Journey Toward "The Beautiful Shore."

Clarksville, Ga., May 17.—Special—Padlocks and trace chains are rarely used in hanging. But this morning they played a leading part in a triple swinging a mile and a half from the Habersham county jail.

The three charms that hung from the three chains were Jim Redmond, Gus Robertson, and Bob Addison, the three negroes who were arrested last week charged with the murder of Marshal Carter, of Toccoa.

Before the negroes were brought here from Toccoa there were many threats of lynching and at one time it looked very much like the negroes would never reach the jail to tax the people for grub until the law could dispose of them. At first five negroes were arrested for the crime and had not one of them, Redmond, made a big talk there would have been five trace chains tested this morning instead of three.

Redmond, in his declaration, denied having any hand in the murder, but admitted that he had seen the bloody deed committed by Robertson and Addison.

That statement caused the release of the other two prisoners and on the evening it was made a mob was organized to lynch Redmond, Robertson, and Addison. Sheriff Gastly, however, managed to sneak the three prisoners out of town and to take them to the Clarksville jail.

Redmond's statement that he had seen his two fellow prisoners do the work was believed.

But his declaration that he had no hand in it was not believed.

For two or three days a systematic organization of a mob had been going on, and yesterday Sheriff Gastly received information that he would have a visit that night. The sheriff at once wired the governor, who ordered him to protect his prisoners, and a guard was organized and placed around the jail. Believing that he would have a determined crowd to deal with, Sheriff Gastly removed the other prisoners from the jail to the town calaboose. All night long a careful watch was kept up, and towards day the sheriff and his guards were growing easy.

They thought the crisis had passed.

But just before dawn a party, estimated all the way from one hundred to five hundred, came up and surrounded the jail, demanding the prisoners.

"You can't get them," answered the sheriff.

"See here, Gastly," said the leader, who was heavily masked, "we know it's your duty to protect these men. We know, too, that you have a lot of boys here to help you. We don't want to hurt you and those boys, but we are going to have the negroes. You better give them up."

The sheriff refused again, and instantly two or three men sprang upon him. Then the crowd advanced upon the jail and, brushing aside the guard like a cobweb, battered the door in. The keys to the cells were then taken from the sheriff and the door to the one occupied by the three negroes was unlocked. The negroes knew what was coming, and Redmond and Addison begged piteously for mercy but Robertson never opened his mouth. The negroes were carried about a mile and a half from the jail and the mob stopped. Three long trace chains and three padlocks were produced, and the chains were locked around the negroes necks. Then Redmond was made to stand upon a horse under a limb of a tree. A man who had climbed the tree made the chain fast and Redmond was questioned about the killing. He repeated the same story he first told.

"Let the horse go," said the leader of the mob.

Some one touched the horse with a whip and he sprang out from under Redmond. As the negro went down he exclaimed:

"Lord have mercy on my soul."

Addison came next, but he denied all knowledge of the crime. Just before the horse moved he dropped off as though dead and fell full length of the chain.

Robertson was put on the horse and asked the same questions which had been propounded to the others.

"All I know I'll die and go to hell knowing," he said, "before I'll tell."

The horse was touched and Robertson went down. His neck was broken, while the other two died of strangulation. Redmond's death was horrible. He could be heard breathing a hundred yards away.

The bodies were left hanging side by side until 3 o'clock this afternoon when the coroner took them down. The verdict was death from unknown hands.

Such accounts shock us not just because of what they report, but equally by the flip, jocular way the report is delivered, as if the lynching of three prisoners was best envisioned as decorating a Christmas tree with dangling, bloody ornaments. The mob is almost complimented on its novel and newsworthy substitution of chains and padlocks for ropes and nooses, and the saving to taxpayers, no longer responsible for the prisoners' care and feeding, is duly noted. Unless there is some sort of subtle sarcasm at play here (and I'd like to think there is, as the alternative is too depressing), the victims—not that they care any longer—are advised to feel not horror but almost gratitude at their treatment, charitably helped by new and deadly refinements on their spiritual journey toward "the beautiful shore" of a far better place.

Nor was the responsible mob here particularly large by the standards of the day, as lynchings would often attract crowds numbering in the thousands, reveling in a carnival atmosphere. Daguerre's beautiful process of "painting with sunbeams" would appear on the front of the new postcards, forever memorializing the awful spectacle of a packed crowd, including women and children, often dressed in their Sunday best, gawking at the swaying corpse—presuming, of course, that the corpse was allowed to dangle. Bonfires were often built, upon which the corpse was thrown, sometimes before it *was* a corpse. Then toasted human relics could be sold. Reportedly, a piece of dried bone went for a quarter. Portions of baked liver were even less expensive. A whole finger or a toe would command as much as a dollar.[3] Crowds of this large size would naturally attract the attention of political leaders, who, while vigorously or otherwise condemning mob violence, could not help but be impressed by the assembled number of potential voters. At least one such leader went further, the Honorable Ben Tillman, governor of South Carolina, who was quoted (*Atlanta Constitution*, August 17, 1892, 1) as saying "Governor as I am I would lead a mob to lynch a negro who would rape a white woman and before God I am not ashamed of it." One wonders if he gained or lost votes with that statement.

The NAACP, in statistics compiled in 1921, estimated that between 1889 and 1918, some 3,224 people were lynched, of whom 2,522 were black. The *Cleveland Gazette* published a study on January 1, 1903, calculating that from 1882 on, 3,233 lynchings occurred. A more recent study by the Tuskegee Institute, noting that there were three lynchings as late as 1964, and repeating the findings of an earlier study commissioned by the *Chicago Tribune*, broke down the number of lynchings on a yearly basis, concluding that the worst year for lynchings was 1892, when 230 people were summarily murdered by mobs, 69 white and 161 black.[4] A number of these studies classified the victims on the basis of their real or supposed offense, finding that, after murder, particularly that of a law enforcement official, a close second was rape, particularly the rape of a white woman by a black man. Of interest here is that on February 23, 1892, the very worst year for lynchings, Mrs. Charles L. Taylor, a white woman, was raped by a black man known, in the colorful language of the day, as the "Sedalia Fiend."

One must now wonder why Captain Jack chose to involve himself in such a matter. As a Sedalian, the crime would have outraged him as much as any other of the town's residents, and because the Taylors were both prominent and prosperous (they owned a local jewelry store[5]), there is a good chance Kinney was socially acquainted with the couple. But rape was hardly a matter for a railroad detective—unless, of course, the rapist used the railroads as a vehicle of escape. The Taylor assault was exactly the sort of crime most lawmen, personal feelings aside, would want to avoid. Rape was one of only four capital crimes in Missouri at that time (the others being first-degree murder, treason, and perjury leading to an innocent's execution), thereby producing the most desperate sort of criminal who would go to any lengths to avoid capture, because capture and conviction meant his certain death. Then, after catching the rapist—and especially if he was a black rapist—the lawman faced the daunting challenge of attempting to protect him from a mob that was likely to form, a lynch mob often consisting of his own friends and neighbors. All in all, it was a thankless and dangerous task.

Mr. Charles Taylor, accompanied by his "young and lovely" wife, attended a party the evening of February 23. They decided to walk home after it concluded. What happened next made national news. Taylor himself gave the following account, stung by "much criticism by the press and public" that he did not resist the attack with sufficient vigor:

> I noticed a man coming toward us. Nothing particularly suspicious could be seen at first. He wore a dark overcoat, thrown over his shoulders and buttoned at the neck. He was walking on the outer side of the walk, and when about a foot away stepped in front of us and abruptly commanded us to throw up our hands. In his right hand was a long knife, and in the other a large pistol. . . . My wife was about three feet east of me. She started to make an outcry, when the fellow said: "If you attempt to make any noise I will kill you." During all this time he kept me covered with the knife and pistol. . . . He secured my purse and then took my watch, breaking the chain while so doing. The robber said "Give me those ear-rings," and grabbed at them as if attempting to tear them from her ears. She said "I will give them to you" and took them out herself. . . . He then said: "I want you to walk around the corner a short distance." I thought he was going to the alley, by which he could escape more easily. . . . During all this time the streets were in total darkness, no lights save that on the court house could be seen. Not a single soul was seen or heard passing along the lonely street. At last we reached the Missouri, Kansas & Texas track, and walked west upon it about two blocks. Arriving at a secluded spot he compelled us to go down the embankment into a low, depressed lot of ground. . . . Even now I did not imagine that he intended to commit more than a robbery. . . . My wife thought the same thing, and had no idea what was to follow.[6]

One might note that in Taylor's own account that no mention is made of the assailant's color. Not so in the following journalistic frenzy, which strongly emphasized race, as if robbery and rape were somehow worse if committed by blacks against whites. As reported by the *Fresno Weekly Republican* (February 26, 1892, 1):

A Villainous Wretch

Sedalia, Feb. 24—A negro desperado last night burglarized a house and held up several people on the street at the point of a revolver. He met Charles Taylor and wife, stopped and robbed them, and then took them to a lonely spot where he tied Taylor hand and foot, and after a desperate struggle outraged Mrs. Taylor. The whole country is aroused and a reward of $1,500 is offered for the negro's capture. He will probably be burned alive if captured.

Similar predictions were offered by the Missouri *Chillicothe Constitution* (February 27, 1892, 1):

Sedalia's Sensation

Sedalia, Mo., Feb 26.—Everybody goes armed. The excitement is still at fever heat. If the fiend who ravished the young and lovely wife of Jeweler Taylor were to get into the clutches of the angry populace, in its present state of mind, he would meet the fiery fate of Coy, the Texarkana negro. There is no doubt, now, that Mrs. Taylor's assailant was a negro.

Governor Francis last night offered a reward of $300 for the apprehension and conviction of the perpetrator of the horrible outrage.

In Sedalia itself, the *Sedalia Bazoo* reported on March 3 that "many things are being said that should have been left unsaid." It was no secret: a lynch mob was forming.

Everybody had on their mind the sensational case of Ed Coy, "the Texarkana negro." As reported in the *Chillicothe Constitution* (February 22, 1892, 1):

A Terrible Scene—A Brutal Negro Burned at the Stake for Rape

The Poor Victim Herself Summoned to Use the Torch. Coal Oil Poured Over the Brute to Make Death Sure

Six Thousand Persons Witness the Scene

Texarkana, Ark, Feb. 20—Ed Coy, the negro who last Saturday evening outraged Mrs. Henry Jewell, a much respected white lady, at her house about four miles from this city, was captured this morning and this afternoon was burned at the stake in the presence of 6,000.

The wretch was captured last night, kept under a guard until this morning and then taken to the residence of Henry Jewell and was promptly and fully identified.

When taken into Mrs. Jewell's presence the negro said to her: "Are these the clothes the man had on?"

"No, but you are the rascal that assaulted me," came the instant rejoinder.

The wretch was taken back to town when a consultation was held and hanging was decided as the mode and Broad street as the place of death.

Coy was accordingly led out and marched to the place of execution. Arriving there some one threw a rope, but the 1,000 present set up a shout of "burn him."

"Burn him! Burn him!" went up again and again, and it was clearly to be seen that death by fire alone would appease the wrath of the surging multitude.

At this juncture Chas. M. Reeves, a leading citizen, mounted an elevation and besought the crowd that if they were determined to burn the wretch for the sake of their wives and children to take him outside the city. This appeal had the desired effect and the cry was turned to "out of town with him! Burn him! Burn him!"

The route to the suburbs was then taken and when just over the Iron Mountain railroad track, in front of a low, level opening a halt was made.

A large stake, to which had been fastened some guy wires, was what the crowd wanted and it was found here. A man who favored hanging tried to speak, but twenty leveled shot-guns silenced him. Up to the stake the avengers dragged the cringing negro and in a twinkling he was securely bound.

Some of the mob advanced with several cans of coal oil which had been secured from neighboring houses.

"Where's Mrs. Jewell," was the cry from many throats. "Let Mrs. Jewell set the fire," and she did it. The flames licked up around the negro's legs and he was soon enveloped, all the while yelling lustily. Death resulted in about fifteen minutes. . . .

When Jewell left home last Saturday after dinner to come to town, he left his young wife with her five months old babe in her arms in the best of health and spirits. Shortly after his departure, a negro appeared at the door and asked the whereabouts of Jewell. She informed him that he had gone to town. Then he said that he had some hogs to sell to Jewell. A considerable conversation was held between them and the woman thus had a good opportunity to note the general appearance of the negro.

After the negro had gone Mrs. Jewell concluded a visit to a neighbor half a mile distant, when the negro, who was hiding, sprang from his place of concealment, seized her by the throat, and after a desperate struggle outraged her. He then dragged his victim into the barn, where he kept her about an hour, assaulting her repeatedly.

A terrible logic of the time seemed to dictate that a lynch mob distinguished itself by escalating the savagery of earlier vigilantes. The likely fate of the "Sedalia Fiend," with so recent an example to inflame the mob, would not be pleasant. Suspicion first focused on a Mr. John Davis, brought to the attention of the authorities by his own brother-in-law, Tobe Ferrin, "who feels that his life is not safe as long as Davis is at large" (*St Louis Globe Democrat,* March 5, 1892). Davis was known to be in Sedalia at the time of the outrage and was also known to have left on the MKT railroad, bringing Captain Jack into the picture only hours after the crime occurred. It was observed after his arrival in Clinton that he had gone to some trouble to change his appearance, shaving off his beard and mustache. In addition, he was known to be armed with two pistols and a knife. "Several negro men are said to have met with him last week and talked with him," reported the *Globe-Democrat* (March 6, 1892), "but the negroes stand in great fear of him and offered no information when it could have been used to effect his capture. Davis is a bully and a gambler and boasts of many crimes almost as heinous as the one he is wanted for. Sheriff Smith received word from Detective Kinney today in regard to the case, but declines to give out anything for publication beyond the statement that Davis is not yet in custody." Perhaps sensing that the law was closing in on him, and certainly aware of the consequences should the public deem him guilty, Mr. Davis wisely disappeared.[7]

Meanwhile, another promising lead had developed, this time down in Denison where Captain Jack's assistant, Detective Ed Taylor, was based. On March 2, 1892, the *Globe-Democrat* ("Clew to the Sedalia Fiend") reported that

a negro who answers perfectly to the description of Mrs. Taylor's assailant entered a pawnbroker's shop in Denison yesterday and offered for sale a pair of diamond ear-rings identical with those taken from Mrs. Taylor. This morning at 4 o'clock the same negro assaulted and robbed two white ladies who had arrived on an early train. When the latter case was reported to Detective Taylor, and he learned of the offer to sell the ear-rings, he at once concluded that the Sedalia and Denison highwayman were identical, and immediately started in pursuit of the fugitive. Blood-hounds are being used on the trail, and Capt. Kinney feels confident the negro will be captured inside of a few hours.

Such confidence was premature, because somehow the suspect managed to elude his pursuers. Because the crime had generated nationwide publicity, reports came flooding in from all over, generating far more leads than could be thoroughly checked. Sedalia Chief of Police Prentice was dispatched to investigate a possible suspect in custody at Paris, Texas. The sheriff of California, Missouri, telegraphed Pettis County Sheriff Smith on March 3 that an "armed negro" had concealed himself in a car of shelled corn and, upon being discovered by the brakeman, fled the scene, but that a pursuit with bloodhounds was underway. "The California sheriff telegraphed that the man closely answered the description," announced the *Sedalia Bazoo,* "and his travel-stained clothing indicated that he had been hiding for days." Smith left to investigate further. A suspicious character was surrounded and trapped in the woods near Tipton, Missouri, by officer Charles Minter, one of "100 deputy sheriffs searching the country" (Omaha, Nebraska, *Morning World Herald,* February 28, 1892, 3). Other suspects were reported and investigated at Hannibal; Syracuse; Sedan, Kansas; and Lexington, Kentucky. One of the lessons Captain Jack had learned from the Dunn case was that the longer a fugitive remained at large, the more likely he would be discovered already in some jail. And just that again happened, although not until May.

An alert sheriff in Houston, Texas, arrested Mr. Charles McMillan for burglary and theft, and noticed his resemblance to the wanted description posted in the Sedalia matter. Captain Jack was sent to investigate. As reported by the *Sedalia Gazette* (in one of the undated clippings):

Detective Kinney Will Send a Photograph of the Houston Suspect
It begins to look like the negro suspect in custody at Houston, Texas, is the party who assaulted Mrs. Charles Taylor in this city the 23rd of last February.

Friday Sheriff Smith received a telegram from Detective Kinney, saying that the prisoner filled the bill in many particulars, but he (Kinney) would investigate further and wire later information on the subject.

Yesterday the sheriff received a second dispatch from Capt. Kinney, saying "Charles McMillan, under arrest here, fills the bill. Will get his picture today and send it to you."

The "shadow" will arrive tomorrow, when it will be submitted to Mr. and Mrs. Taylor, and if they are in any doubt as to the identity of the accused Mr. Taylor will make a trip to Houston.[8]

Taylor traveled to Houston and agreed that McMillan was the culprit. He then went to Chicago (where Mrs. Taylor was visiting to recuperate) and, without telling her about his identification of McMillan, escorted her to Houston to see if she would identify the same man. At that point, we have two significantly different descriptions of her conduct. The *Galveston Times,* later describing the incident (on May 19, 1892), observed that "she came, went down to the jail and picked out from among eight negroes who were brought into her presence the suspect and stated that he was the man to the best of her knowledge and belief." But the *Atlanta Constitution* (April 26, 1892) described the identification as follows: "A few days ago Mr. Taylor and Detective Kinney came to Houston and returned to Sedalia satisfied that McMillan was the man they wanted. Today they returned with Mrs. Taylor. On sight of the fiend who had outraged her, Mrs. Taylor fainted and had to be removed." If the latter account is correct, it would seem that Mrs. Taylor's identification—crucial for any trial—might remain suspect given the severe emotional trauma from which she had not yet fully recovered. Early on in the papers, it had already been reported (by the *Globe-Democrat,* March 6, 1892) that "Mrs. Taylor is beginning in a measure to recover her former spirits, and can discuss the affair without the intense suffering which for days almost caused dethronement of her reason. Mrs. Taylor was asked by a lady friend last night if she was positive she could identify the wretch, and with a thoughtful stare she responded that she was not absolutely certain that she could do so."

Sheriff Ellis of Houston, in whose custody the prisoner remained, sought to remove, were there any, all lingering doubts about McMillan's guilt. After ascertaining that McMillan "had some education and could read quite well," Ellis forged a telegram that was shown to the prisoner purporting to originate from Sedalia, demanding McMillan's extradition, both the sheriff and prisoner knowing quite well what was likely to happen should the citizens of Sedalia succeed in housing the "fiend" in any Missouri jail. After reading the telegram McMillan "showed evidence of much distress" (*Galveston Times,* May 19, 1892). Although the available record does not so indicate, it is reasonable to speculate that by then McMillan was willing, even eager, to confess to practically any charge Sheriff Ellis cared to make, just so long as he could avoid extradition to Sedalia. Ellis also had McMillan's outgoing correspondence, which he tried to smuggle past the guards, intercepted and opened. In one letter, after the visit of Captain Jack and the Taylors, he writes, "I think they have identified me." It was a potentially damning statement, but not quite the same thing as an admission or confession of guilt. In another letter, he notes, "I have enough crime over me at Sedalia, Mo., without anything else" (*Galveston Times,* May 19, 1892). With this, no one could doubt that McMillan was guilty of something, and at Sedalia, but again, the statement falls short of a confession to the particular crime for which he was most wanted.

Much has been written about the complicity between lawmen and lynch mobs, and it cannot be denied that upon many occasions officials were, to say the least, lax about their duties to protect prisoners in their charge, secretly or otherwise sympathetic to the goals, if not the methods, of vigilante justice. A common attitude then held that the courts were increasingly inclined to protect the rights of the accused, often self-confessedly guilty, at the expense of vengeance and retribution due the victim. Consider the intolerably difficult position of (the unfortunately named) Sheriff Gastly, facing an angry mob of 500 with their trace chains and padlocks. What, realistically, could he actually do? Like most sheriffs, Gastly was an elected official, and it was highly unlikely—which the mob knew full well—that he would order his deputies to open fire on some of the very voters who had elected him. One must suspect that, when seized by the mob, Gastly's resistance was only of a token nature. And why not? By then, the outcome was a foregone conclusion. Were the lives of three black prisoners, who were probably going to hang anyway, worth the bloodbath now required for their determined protection? Many sheriffs would find themselves in just such a predicament, and many would answer the question just posed negatively.

But such matters didn't always have to end so. By May, Captain Jack must have gotten to know the Taylors very well. On those long shared train rides, they had ample time for extensive discussion, which must have focused on an ethical dilemma they collectively faced. There was little doubt that McMillan was the "Sedalia Fiend," and it was completely in their power—indeed, it was their duty—to demand his extradition back to Missouri for trial. Even though Mrs. Taylor had publicly admitted that she could no longer be "absolutely certain" of her identification, and that for some time her very ability to reason had been "dethroned" by her ordeal (admissions defense attorneys were sure to pounce on), it seemed almost certain that, particularly given the evidence uncovered by Houston Sheriff Ellis, McMillan would be found guilty and executed. Did Mrs. Taylor really want to relive those sordid experiences, which would be gone over and over in salacious detail in a trial sure to generate huge publicity, particularly when (by the one account) she could not even bear to be in the presence of the accused without fainting?

The dilemma sharpens given the knowledge that the case was very unlikely ever to come before a court. Although tempers in Sedalia had cooled considerably, the general mood was still volatile, easily inflamed by headlines—and there were sure to be some—that the "Fiend" was imprisoned in a local jail. As prominent Sedalians, the three had to be concerned about the reputation of their town. Did they really want a repetition of the ugly scene in Texarkana, with neighbors canvassing door to door, seeking kerosene for a human bonfire? Would Mrs. Taylor, like Mrs. Jewell, be expected to light and apply the first match? The position of all those involved in the matter deserved careful consideration. Was it right to put Captain Jack's good friend Sheriff Smith in Gastly's impossible situation, sure to confront a mob of his fellow Sedalians, forced to choose between his duty as an officer of the law and the will of many of the citizens who elected him?

Then there was the prisoner. Perhaps he deserved death, but did he deserve the fiery death of Ed Coy? Did justice really require that diced bits of his baked liver be offered for sale to passersby?

Lynch mobs burning their victims was by no means unusual. For just one example, on December 30, 1897, Mrs. Mary Leard was with her children at her farm near Maud, in the Seminole Nation; her husband was off helping on another ranch. A lone Indian stopped by, asked to borrow a saddle, was refused, and later returned and with a rifle clubbed her to death in front of her eight-year-old son Frank. Almost immediately, a mob formed that began detaining and questioning, often by physical torture, Indian suspects. After a week, two Indians, Palmer Sampson and Lincoln McGeisey, despite the fact that the boy could not identify them, were somehow deemed guilty, and a fake confession was then read to the mob, who proceeded to chain them by their necks to a tree and burn them to death.[9]

Prominently figuring among the mob were members of the extended Lewis clan, many of whom had unsuccessfully applied for inclusion in the Choctaw Nation and later, after their expulsion, had settled primarily in the Creek Nation. It may be remembered that Alexander S. Lewis, whom we have met, farmed a plot in the Creek Nation, although there is no evidence, one way or another, that he or his close kin were involved in these events. United States Marshal Leo Bennett, whom we have also met, assisted by Heck Thomas and Bill Tilghman, led a successful effort to identify and arrest the mob's leaders, who were defended at trial, ably but unsuccessfully by—who else?—J. Warren Reed.

No matter what was decided, McMillan wasn't going anywhere for a long time. He'd already been convicted for other crimes and was now ready to confess to anything in order to avoid extradition. All in all, a powerful case could be made, and I believe was made, that the greater good lay in dropping the charges. And that seems to have happened. As reported by the *Galveston Times* (May 19, 1892), "despite these facts [the evidence in McMillan's intercepted letters], the parties seem indisposed to push the case and, in consequence, Sheriff Ellis said this evening that he intended to drop the matter and simply let McMillan be tried for burglary and theft, of which he has evidence that will send him to the penitentiary for twelve years."

This seems to me a remarkably wise decision, and makes the larger point that for every policeman at some level complicit in a mob's murderous action, for every official who sought to confront vigilante behavior only when it was too late to be stopped, at least some officers—and the evidence seems to indicate Captain Jack was one of them—had the intelligence to perceive that true justice was sometimes served by means other than its strict and rigorous application. A bedrock principle of law is that a crime against any citizen is a crime against every citizen. McMillan not only "outraged" Mrs. Taylor, but by so doing, equally "outraged" the entire people of the state of Missouri. And although it would be completely within the discretion of Mrs. Taylor to forgive her rapist, the people's mercy, were there to be any, must wait until adjudicated by a court in a trial that, given the circumstances, would in Sedalia likely be preempted by a mob. In effect, Captain Jack was a party to bending the laws he was sworn to uphold. For that, I'm proud of him.

Before we return to Adair on the night of July 14, 1892, it should be emphasized that the cases discussed thus far—the Tarver murder, the Dunn forgeries, the Taylor outrage—are atypical in the sense that most of Captain Jack's work was of a far more routine nature, on matters seldom noticed by the newspapers, or if they were, receiving only a brief mention. MKT locomotive engineer Beason's sixteen-year-old son, for example, was an arsonist who set a number of fires in the railroad town of Denison, Texas, burning first a Chinese laundry, then two warehouses, and finally a loaded Katy boxcar, thus coming to the attention of Captain Jack and his assistant Ed Taylor. Speaking of Denison (a city through which Kinney frequently traveled[10]), Captain Jack was clearly interested in a notorious multiple murder case that occurred there the night of May 18, but the available record does not indicate the nature, if any, of his involvement.[11] Somebody down in San Antonio was selling counterfeit MKT tickets. A "bold footpad" was stalking the rail yard at Parsons, Kansas, leaving one stunned victim (Mr. Monroe Wright, a Katy section foreman) lying unconscious across the tracks, whereupon his left arm was severed by a passing train. In Sedalia a party representing himself as a "conductor for the MKT" swindled the Van Wagner Brothers of "three pairs of shoes and two pairs of boots, all of excellent make." Forged money orders, petty thefts, vandalism, a case where a minor Katy official was suspected of making job offers contingent on bribes, suspicious derailments and collisions—such was the bulk of Captain Jack's caseload.

Such was the case until an event, which neatly sets the stage for Adair, occurred in Temple, Texas, on May 5, 1892. On that day, an MKT train driven by Engineer Pepple was signaled to stop by a group of men about a mile from the Temple station. The engineer, correctly suspecting a robbery attempt, pulled open the throttle and accelerated past the group at his best speed. At that, the frustrated robbers opened fire on the engine, forcing Engineer Pepple to crouch in the gangway. A week later, on May 12, the robbers again attempted to rob the same train at the same spot. "The train was flagged as before," reports the *Sedalia Gazette* (May 20, 1892),

> and again the engineer became suspicious and put on the steam. This time, however, the foiled robbers did not confine their attempt at killing the engineer. As the train pulled by them they fired indiscriminately into the coaches and sleeper, perforating the cars in several places, breaking windows and wounding Conductor Tom Hurley, a passenger who was in an upper berth of a sleeper. The shot struck him in the arm, but the wound was not serious. Other passengers had narrow escapes, although none were struck.

Certainly this could not be allowed to continue. And so Captain Jack, accompanied by Detective Ed Taylor, was off to Temple, where they met with City Marshal William Taylor (no relation, so far as I know, to Ed).

The case wasn't especially difficult to solve. Two attempted robberies in the same town only a week apart indicated the work of locals; a gang of strangers would surely have attracted attention. Because crooks and cops are usually well acquainted with each other, especially in so small a town, the investigation could begin simply by having Marshal Taylor recite his list of available local suspects, perhaps offering an opinion as to the likelihood of each. That accomplished, the lawmen, supported by a force of deputies, arrested the three Ward brothers, Bill Miller, Mr. O. L. Buchanan, and two gentlemen singularly named, respectively and colorfully, "Poker" and "Dead Eye Dick." "The Ward boys," noted the *Sedalia Gazette* (May 20, 1892), "are local toughs and are known as desperate characters. Miller is a telegraph lineman and jackleg gambler. Buchanan is well connected in Temple, but has been playing tough for some time. 'Poker' and 'Dead Eye Dick' have been in Temple for some time without visible means of support, and are noted as hard characters. Their real names are not known."

Following accepted procedures, the lawmen separated the suspects in two different jails, knowing that confessions were easier to obtain from isolated prisoners. The prospects for confessions were aided considerably by the discovery, during the arrest, of an arsenal of pistols and shotguns, plus cloth masks and other tools of the robber's trade. It so developed that the pistols had been stolen from the store of H. E. Ambold in Waco, providing another charge to bring against the group. Mr. Buchanan was the first of the gang to break, and he offered a full confession. Evidently the attempted train robberies in Temple had been preceded by a similarly abortive effort to hold up a Santa Fe train in the Indian Territory. At the time of their arrest, the bandits were planning to rob a Southern Pacific express at San Antonio. "The gang," concluded the *Gazette,* "is one of the toughest that ever operated in Texas, and the people of Temple and surrounding country are exceedingly grateful to Capt. Kinney and the local officers for having broken it up."[12] Captain Jack had just proven himself to be a first-rate detective against second-rate train robbers. But how would he fare against first-rate outlaws?

THE GIANT SPIDERS OF HERMOSILLO

*In vain do individuals hope for immortality or any patent from oblivion in
preservations below the moon.*
—*Sir Thomas Browne*

July 14, 1892. About 9:30 P.M. Captain Jack is seated in the smoker car
pulled by Engine No. 115 with Charles La Flore, Sid Johnson, Alf
McKay, Bud Kell, Mr. Ward, and two or three other heavily armed
guards.[1] The collective mood has considerably relaxed since the No. 2
northbound train passed through Pryor Creek without incident. Some
of the guards may have been discreetly drinking. Some of the guards
may also have been—to the silent disapproval of their superiors—
regaling other passengers with bloody and fanciful stories of what
would have happened had the Daltons dared to rob them. A long,
tense day was ending.

July 14, 1892, was not an otherwise particularly noteworthy day in
history. The train's newsboys had been selling various papers
throughout the day, the copies usually abandoned when read, free to
anybody who afterward wanted them. The lead story was that a "free
silver" bill had been defeated in the House of Representatives. As a
Republican, Captain Jack would have probably applauded the bill's
defeat. The free silver issue was a huge controversy of his time, culminating in William Jennings Bryan's famous Cross of Gold speech
during the 1896 election he lost to McKinley. It is difficult for us now
to understand the debate, particularly because most of us have lived
our lives in an inflationary economy, the currency we spend having
value only by governmental fiat, not because it is or could be exchanged (at least in theory) for an amount of metal, such as gold,
whose intrinsic worth equaled the denomination presented. But the

economy in Captain Jack's time was deflationary, meaning a limited and shrinking circulation of money whose value thus increased over time, a benefit to creditors but a disaster to debtors, who were forced to pay back loans in dollars the value of which, over time, greatly exceeded what they originally borrowed. One proposed solution to this situation was free silver, which was a call for a bimetallic standard fixing the value of silver to gold at sixteen to one, and requiring the government to buy and coin silver, thereby increasing the supply of money and creating an inflation beneficial to borrowers (who of course far outnumbered creditors).[2]

Other stories reported that federal troops had been sent to Wardner, Idaho, in an effort to intervene in a strike, but union miners were threatening to blow up the bridges over which the troop trains had yet to cross. Gladstone was elected prime minister in England by a narrow margin. In Peoria, Illinois, a night cyclone wrecked a river steamer, drowning at least nine people. Mount Etna threatened to erupt. Serious race riots continued in Paducah, Kentucky, where, in an unusual twist, a mob of black rioters attempted, in reprisal, to lynch a white man.[3] Russia suffered from an epidemic of cholera. Rival sectarian mobs fought pitched battles in Ireland. The Mississippi had flooded its banks, destroying thousands of acres of cotton. Featherweights Tommy Ward and Jack Dalley were due to fight in Atlanta. The day's most interesting story, widely reprinted from the *New Orleans Picayune*, featured

An Insect Terror

A strange spider, it is reported, has appeared in great numbers in the lowlands and valleys about Hermosillo, Mex., and is giving the natives great alarm. It is peculiarly ferocious and manifests no fear of anything, not hesitating to give chase to men who disturb it. It is considerably larger than the tarantula, common in those regions, and is terribly poisonous. Three deaths have been lately reported from its bite. It is a hairy insect and has legs as large as a pipe stem. It runs with remarkable agility, and climbs the stick or whip toward the hand of any one who strikes at it. It is a newcomer to the section, and, so far, no one has been found who has seen it before. One of the deaths was that of a Mexican who was riding along and saw one of the spiders. He struck at it with his whip, and before he could drop the whip the spider was at his hand and had bitten him. He died within three hours in great agony. The spiders hop along the ground in great leaps toward the object of their attack.[4]

As the men conversed in the smoker, discussing Daltons and spiders, idly flipping through the papers, they would have noticed the many advertisements, some for products still existing today. Hires' Root Beer aggressively promoted itself as "The Great Temperance Drink." The fast-growing temperance movement was also a huge issue of the day and would eventually result in the passage of the Eighteenth Amendment prohibiting alcohol in 1919 (until repealed by the Twenty-first in 1933). Probably the best-known crusader in the temperance cause was Mrs. Carry A. Nation (1846–1911), who, having suffered an alcoholic husband and then being inspired by God himself, smashed her first saloon on June 1, 1900. Although she favored hatchets as her instrument of God's wrath, she would also, in destructive sprees for which she was arrested thirty times, use rocks, bricks, iron rods, cue balls, and hammers—and not just any hammer, but what is known as a Crandall hammer, a particularly vicious-looking tool used by masons for dressing stone. It wasn't just the liquor that enraged her; just about everything a saloon contained inspired her, and God's, ire, from the slot machines to the pervasive tobacco smoking, from the card tables to the nude picture behind the bar. As to the latter, "it is very significant that the picture of naked women are [sic] in saloons. Women are stripped of everything by them. Her husband is torn from her, she is robbed of her sons, her home, her food, and her virtue, and then they strip her clothes off and hang her up bare in these dens of robbery and murder."[5] A large, formidable woman, nearly six feet in height and weighing 180 pounds, the very sight of her approach, Bible in one hand and blunt instrument in the other, would cause saloon keepers to tremble. Once she stormed into a saloon in New York owned by the great heavyweight prizefighter John L. Sullivan. He was reported to have meekly fled the premises and hid.

Other advertisements included Lea & Perrins's Sauce, which proudly featured a testimonial from a "Medical Gentleman" in Madras, India, reporting that the native population "highly esteemed" their product. One mysterious announcement, entitled "PERSONAL," briefly implored "MARRIED LADIES: send 10c for 'Infallible Safeguard' (no medicine, no deception) just what you want." "HARD DRINKERS," suffering in "mind, body, and purse from DRUNKENNESS," could be cured with CHLORIOGOLD, an advantage of which was that, "being tasteless, it can be given by a friend in tea, coffee, lemonade, beer, liquors, or food without the patient's knowledge." Even worse than drunkenness were

WHISKY AND OPIUM
An Awful Though Unintentional Error
is that of drinking whisky and using opium and morphine. Stop! Reflect! And apply to Dr. B. M. Woolley, Atlanta, Ga., and be cured as thousands of others have been who are now free with unclouded minds and happy families. A treatise sent free to all applicants.

One is further struck by the astonishing number of potions, elixirs, creams, salves, ointments, poultices, plasters, and electric and magnetic trusses, all promising to increase virility and restore manliness. Quite effective use was made of "before" and "after" sketches. The former would depict a feeble, bent figure, hair in patches, beard scraggly, cheeks sunken, eyes glazed, a perfect candidate for an invigorating dose of Professor Hood's "Infallible Notion," after which a muscular Adonis, beard full, erect in posture and presumably otherwise, appears before our very eyes.

It was just then, shortly after 9:30 that, perhaps meditating on the personal necessity of Dr. Hood's Notion, that the guards perceived the train slowing to a stop as it pulled into the Adair station, and what happened in the next forty-five minutes would generate accounts differing significantly, leading to opposite conclusions regarding the conduct of those involved. Perhaps the most neutral report, which can serve as an overview of what followed, appeared in the *Stillwater Gazette* (July 16, 1892):

The coolest and most desperate train robbery ever perpetrated on the Missouri, Kansas and Texas railroad took place at Adair station on the Cherokee Division of the road about 9:30 o'clock last night [wrong—the date of the robbery is the 14th], resulting in the killing of one man, the wounding of several others and the loss to the express company of a large sum.

The notorious Dalton gang, who had been camped in the Indian Territory between Adair and Pryor Creek for several days, made their way to Adair about 9 o'clock last night and at the muzzles of

Winchesters, pointed in the face of the station agent, ransacked the office of the station of all money and valuables. Having accomplished this, the robbers sat down at the station and coolly waited the arrival of passenger train No.2, due there at 9:42 o'clock.

When the train was slowing up at the station, the robbers covered Engineer Glen Ewing and his fireman with Winchesters and no sooner had Conductor George W. Scales and his porter stepped off the train than both of them were also forced to face Winchesters.

Three of the robbers then compelled the fireman to leave the engine and with his coal pick aid them in securing admission to the express car. Up to this time Messenger George P. Williams had persisted in his refusal to open the door. One of the bandits then shouted that he had placed dynamite under the car and would blow it to atoms if the door was not opened. He fired, by way of emphasis, several shots into the car, which passed uncomfortably near the head of the messenger and he gave in and opened the door.

The three men sprang into the car, and while one covered the terrified messenger with his gun, the other two turned their attention to the safe. The messenger was threatened with death if he did not open it. He finally succeeded and the robbers made short work of its contents, taking everything they could find, even things that were of no value to them. After relieving the messenger of his watch, the robbers bound him and dumped him in a corner of the car. While the three robbers were in the express car, another was seen to back a spring wagon up to the door and the contents of the safe were thrown into the wagon.

When the train stopped at Adair, Captain J. J. Kinney, chief of the detective force of the Missouri, Kansas and Texas, Captain LaFlore, chief of the Indian police, and seven other guards were in the smoking car of the train, expressly to protect the train from any attack from robbers. The robbers, the moment the train stopped, began firing their Winchesters and kept firing them up until they had accomplished their aims. Kinney and his men opened fire on the robbers and for a few minutes bullets were flying thick and fast. In the melee Kinney received a flesh wound on the right shoulder. LaFlore had one arm burned and a guard by the name of Ward suffered a slight flesh wound. None of the robbers were injured as far as known. Stray bullets entered a drug store up town and struck Drs. Youngblood and W. L. Goff, who were sitting in the building.

Goff has since died of his wounds and Youngblood is in a danger-ous condition.

After the robbers had loaded their plunder into a spring wagon, they headed for the woods, and after firing a parting shot at the train, were soon lost to view.

As the above article indicates, the shooting began almost from the "moment the train stopped," but there is considerable disagreement as to where the various combatants were located, or exactly who began firing first. Harry Sinclair Drago, a prolific and respected western historian, writes, "The night was warm. The car windows were open. One of the guards, a Cherokee half-blood named LaFlore,[6] thrust out his head to learn the meaning of the delay and the excited voices at the door of the express car. He hurriedly pulled it in as a splatter of rifle shots greeted him. It removed any doubt that this was a holdup. In-stead of rushing out and making a fight of it, Captain Kinney ordered his men to crouch down at the windows and shoot from there, which they were disgracefully content to do."[7] Elsewhere, Drago is not shy about using the word "cowardly" to describe the behavior of Captain Jack and his men.

Drago's source is probably an early account by the anonymous au-thor, known as "Eye Witness," of *The Dalton Brothers and Their As-tounding Career of Crime.* Upon first noticing the robbers,

> The guards looked at each other in silent dismay, but not a son of them budged an inch. Talk had died on their lips, and so had whatever measure of courage they might have ever possessed. Mice are not more discrete when they hear the steps of a housewife.
>
> The chiefs, Captain Kinney and Captain LaFlore, the latter a Cherokee [wrong!] half-breed and chief of the Cherokee Indians' special police force, stood up alone and began an animated but whispered conversation at the further end of the car.
>
> "How many are there, do you think?" said Kinney.
>
> LaFlore ventured his head out the window, but brought it back in a hurry, for a regular salvo from the enemy's Winchesters was fired as a threatening warning.
>
> "I saw seven of 'em," he whispered. "Might be a dozen or more for what I know."
>
> "Well, boys," called out Kinney, feeling that the situation was growing critical, "shall we go out and fight them—?"

This singular way of commanding his men to do their duty met with the expected answer—that is, no answer at all. They were not going to hazard their precious skins, not they, and the captain had better understand it right away.

Still it would never do to reach the next station and have to acknowledge themselves such arrant cowards; so, about the time the robbery was all over, these guards consented to become dimly aware of what was going on, and, rising cautiously from their seats, they opened a rapid fire at the freebooters through the car windows. The robbers replied with much promptness and vigor. Bullets whistled everywhere. (156–57)

This version, that the guards began to resist only when it was too late, plus the disturbing implication that it was the guards whose bullets killed one of the Adair doctors and injured another, is repeated by Eugene Block in *Great Train Robberies of the West:* "Word that a holdup was in progress had spread throughout the train but the guards remained in the smoker, reluctant to make any move—until it was known that the robbers were hurrying away. Then, in a sudden burst of activity, the guards started firing wildly through the windows and two of them jumped off the train, shooting in all directions. Bullets tore through the window of a nearby pharmacy, killing a physician, Dr. W. L. Goff. His companion, a Dr. Youngblood, suffered serious wounds" (99). Drago flat out states "that it was slugs from the high-powered rifles of the cowardly guards that felled the two doctors can hardly be disputed, since the bandits were firing in the opposite direction."[8]

Further making the case that Captain Jack and his guards were cowards, the anonymous "Eye Witness" included the following account purportedly given by one of the train's passengers:

Mr. J. T. Hearn, of St. Louis, arrived on July 16th at Coates Hotel, Kansas City, from the Southwest, where he had been on a business trip. He was one of the passengers on the Missouri, Kansas & Texas train that was held up at Adair, I.T., on that eventful Thursday night. He was awake and witnessed the entire fight and has some very strong opinions about the detectives and Indian police on board the train. He characterized their conduct as cowardly in the extreme and deserving of universal condemnation. In speaking of the very exciting episode Mr. Hearn said:

It was about 10 o'clock and every one in the sleeper had retired excepting myself. We were bowling along right merrily on the other side of Adair, and on stopping at that station I glanced out of the window, I saw some rather uncertain figures and a wagon standing near. Then came a few scattering shots, and then the batch of detectives piled out of the coaches.

Inside of ten minutes there were no less than 200 shots exchanged and, during that time, the passengers were secreting their valuables or crouching low to escape the rain of bullets from all sides. Then the firing let up a little and the valiant detectives came tumbling in pellmell, any way to reach shelter. Chief Detective Kinney had a slight wound in the fleshy part of the left arm. There seemed to be about fifteen of the detectives, and early in the evening I had noticed them and remarked what fearless looking fellows they were. Every one looked the typical 'bad man' and they were armed to the teeth.

A passenger asked the chief if the men were gone and he answered that they were in the express car. Then some one asked why the detectives were not outside trying to prevent the robbery, and they made scant reply. Several suggested that they could waylay the robbers as they emerged from the car, as by actual count there were only seven, or at most eight of them; but the detectives only replied by finding safe shelters behind the seats and on the rear platform. I had placed my watch and pocketbook under the edge of the carpet on the floor of the sleeper, but there were so many detectives on the floor that I thought the valuables would be safer in my pocket, so I returned them to their proper places.

After awhile, the robbers dumped all the stuff they wanted from the express car into the spring wagon, got up on the seats, and drove twice around the entire train, firing as they went. All the time the detectives were in their holes with the exception of one man about fifty-five years of age. He was fighting all the time until he received a wound in the shoulder from one bullet, while another plowed a furrow across his breast. Another man was shot through the left forearm, the bullet passing on and striking his watch. That stopped both the bullet and the timepiece. Afterward he laid the watch out on a piece of paper. It was in so many pieces that it could be gathered up and sifted through the fingers.

A stray bullet struck a physician in a drug store up town, cutting an artery in the thigh. They thought when we left that he would bleed to death.

That batch of detectives was on the train in the expectation of an attempt being made at robbery, and they were very brave until the time came for action. (160–61)

I would be the first to agree, were I convinced that the above accounts accurately described what happened that night in Adair, that Captain Jack and his men deserve "universal condemnation." But if I believed that, I would not have bothered to write this book. There is quite another version of the night's events—what I call the "coal shed" version—which presents the encounter in a considerably more favorable light. Harold Preece, generally supported by historians Robert Barr Smith (in *Daltons! The Raid on Coffeyville*) and Richard Patterson (in *Train Robbery*), writes as follows:

> Grat and Emmett climbed into the engine cab to cover Engineer Glen Ewing and the fireman. At that moment, four men dashed from the smoking car into a coal shed beside the track. The Daltons paid little attention to them. Scared passengers could be expected to run like rabbits into some convenient hole.
>
> A few men, later identified as special deputy marshals, then appeared on the smoker platform, yelling and flourishing weapons. Bob and two other bandits raised their guns threateningly. The bravos of the law scurried back inside the coach.
>
> Bob, Broadwell and Powers were meantime trying to gain entrance to the express car, but Messenger George P. Williams had locked himself inside at Pryor Creek and refused to open the door. Grat and Emmett forced the engineer and fireman from the cab to the side of the tracks opposite the depot. The engineer looked at his captors and said: "We expected you fellers at Pryor Creek."
>
> Grat gave him a prod with his gun barrel and growled, "We didn't wanta disappoint you—so here were are."
>
> Messenger Williams was still declining to open the express coach. Bob Dalton was threatening to blow up the car with dynamite.
>
> A volley of lead burst from the unlighted coal shed. Bullets spewed against the engine, around Grat, Emmett, and the two trainmen, standing in sharp silhouette from the glare of the en-

gine firebox. Three men who had dashed into the shed were no scared passengers but three of Oklahoma's top officers:

United States Deputy Marshal Sid Johnson, of the federal court in Wichita, Kansas; Captain J. J. Kinney, chief of detectives of the MK&T's special force for the Cherokee Division; and Captain Charles Le Flore, head of the Cherokee [!] National Police. A fourth man, too, had managed to reach the coal shed—a railroad guard named Ward.

In a brief but furious battle, the Dalton luck held. Their rifle fire seriously wounded Marshal Johnson. Kinney and Ward suffered minor flesh wounds and Le Flore had an arm "burned" by a bullet. The worst casualties were those from shots that went wild.

The town's two physicians—Doctors Youngblood and W. L. Goff—were sitting in a drugstore when the bullets sprayed through a window. Both were badly hit. Goff died a few hours afterward. Youngblood was many weeks recovering.

When the firing from the coal shed ceased, Grat and Emmett ordered the engineer and fireman to move to the other side of the track. There the bandits, holding guns on the trainmen, joined Bob, Broadwell and Powers, who were still trying to bully the messenger into opening the express car door. Newcomb kept riding herd on the loungers. Doolin and Pierce were standing track guard, the assorted lawmen inside the cars apparently hiding with passengers behind the seats and apparently forgetting all about the fight.[9]

Still another version of the event deserves consideration, as it was given by Captain Jack himself, shortly after the incident, in interviews with both the *Sedalia Gazette* (July 17, 1892) and the *Saint Louis Globe-Democrat* (July 16, 1892).[10] By then, Captain Jack was well aware that his actions, and those of his men, were under scrutiny: "I understand that our posse has been criticized for not having wiped the gang off the face of the earth. It is an easy matter to stand off 500 miles distant and tell how things should have been done. We did the best possible under the circumstances, and not a man in the party showed the white feather" (*Globe-Democrat*). As reported by the *Gazette,* the guards all "had the reputation of being brave men, and the smell of gun powder was no new thing to them. They were experienced fighters, knew how to handle border ruffians of all classes and did not know the meaning of the word 'cowardice'" The *Globe-Democrat* concludes its interview by stating

No one here doubts Capt. Kinney's bravery, and Capt. Laflore is conceded to be one of the bravest men in the Territory. He has been forced to kill several men, and in return he himself has been shot times without number. Kinney says the posse could have killed one or more of the robbers outright had they not been afraid of taking the life of the conductor, fireman, or engineer, who were always placed between the robbers and the railroad posse. There is one point that has been overlooked in all previous dispatches—the Indian police were all dismissed on June 30, as the appropriation was exhausted. Captain Kinney anticipated the attack, and two days before the robbery he appealed to Indian Agent Bennet at Muskogee for police assistance. Mr. Bennet wired Kinney's request to the Interior Department at Washington, and on the evening of the robbery received permission to retain in the employ of the Government all of the police who were on duty June 30, at which time the appropriation was exhausted. Had the telegram from Washington been received twenty-four hours earlier, the result of the battle might have been different, for instead of a posse of eight men Kinney would have had three times that number at his command.

It helps here to pause and visualize the scene. Adair, a small town founded in 1889, is bisected by the Katy tracks as they run straight in a north to northeasterly direction. The original depot (which no longer exists) and accompanying platform were on the west side of the tracks.[11] A short freight spur then switched off the tracks to the south and ran parallel with the main track further on the west side of the depot. The raised depot platform was perhaps 100 yards long, stretching primarily to the south with the depot located at its northern end. The town's major street (Mays Avenue) parallels the track on the west side. The station was originally located just to the south of the intersection of Mays and Main Street, the primary east-west road.

Something should also be said about the composition of the train and the order of its cars. Although I am not aware of any inviolable rule governing the placement of any particular car, as a general practice, the express car would be in the forward part of the train, usually right behind the coal tender, if only because the railroads liked to keep as much distance as possible between the passenger cars and the smoke- and cinder-belching engine. The smoker car in which Captain Jack arrived could have been located anywhere, although good train management would suggest separating it from the sleeper berths in order that noise from the former would not disturb those in the latter. Two other things to keep in mind are that by 9:30, it was completely dark, and as the train stopped, the engine would position itself just at or slightly beyond the north end of the platform, aligning the middle cars with the depot, taking care not to block any traffic on Main.

As Captain Jack relates the encounter (unattributed quotes here are from the *Sedalia Gazette*), shortly after the train stopped, he intended to visit the station agent (now bound and gagged in the small depot office) and inquire about "the Daltons, or any other suspicious characters in the neighborhood." After exiting the smoker and walking along its running platform toward the depot, he noticed that Conductor Scales, only a few feet away, is being held at the point of a Winchester by a robber. Unfortunately, Captain Jack had left his own Winchester behind in the smoker, "or he could have there and then have killed or disabled the man who was guarding the conductor." That is why I wrote, at the beginning of this book, that Captain Jack didn't carry a sidearm. Even if such was only his occasional practice, that night, of all nights, he would have so been armed, and because he wasn't (if he was, the lack of his Winchester could not have mattered at that close range), it's fair to conclude that, for reasons of his own, he didn't choose to wear pistols.

While running back into the smoker and grabbing his rifle, he called out, "They have got us, boys; get your guns and get out of here!" (The *Globe* reports his exclamation as "For God's sake, men, get a move on you. The robbers have got us, sure.") Such an announcement created something of a panic, resulting in shouting guards milling about and passengers frantically hiding their valuables.[12] Just here, as the confusion quickly sorted itself out, the posse—as best as I can reconstruct what happened—committed its first tactical, although perhaps understandable, error. The command ("get your guns and get out!") was promptly obeyed, with many of the guards running out of the smoker's rear door. Captain La Flore and most of the Indian police seem to have exited on the east side of the train while Kinney, by himself, dismounted on the west, or depot, side. It's not necessarily an error to split one's command given such a situation, as the Daltons were by then on both sides of the train, although most of them were at first to the east and between the engine, tender, and express car, but a split command should consist of roughly equal forces. My best guess is that some or all of the Indian police, accustomed to taking orders from La Flore, followed him out to the east side, while those who were supposed to support Kinney on the west mistakenly followed La Flore instead or simply remained behind.

To this point, by Kinney's account, not a shot had been fired. Although at some point he realized that he was entirely alone, Captain Jack circled behind the wooden depot office to a "position where he could have a good view of the express car. He saw one of the robbers standing between the engine and the mail car, and he blazed away at him." This prompted a furious return volley, shots being fired from (by Kinney's estimate) half a dozen Winchesters. Consider that an experienced Winchester marksman, and the Daltons were highly renowned for their ability in such matters, can fire two aimed shots in about a second. This would mean in only five seconds, some sixty accurate shots were fired back at him, many of them easily splintering through the thin walls of the depot behind which he crouched. La Flore and his command to the east, hearing the furious exchange, immediately opened fire, creating a diversion that enabled Captain Jack to roll off the depot platform into the high weeds, where, still clutching his Winchester and miraculously uninjured, he began to crawl east, first under the depot, then under the train, attempting to link up with La Flore. The Indian police were still firing, but, notes the *Gazette*, "they had to shoot with extreme care, for the robbers used the conductor, engineer and fireman as shields; they could not shoot into a group of men without running the risk of killing some of the train men. Their position was a peculiar one. When they rushed out of the car they were at first blinded by the darkness, but as their eyes became accustomed to the gloom they selected as targets the legs of the robbers who were on the other side of the train."

Captain Jack rejoined La Flore's group, who now had the undivided attention of the Daltons because they were no longer receiving any fire from the west. Captain Jack again opened fire and again received a strong volley in return: the "bullets fell around him like hailstones."[13] One of them struck his right shoulder: "'They have hit me, Captain,' he said to La Flore. That official put his hand to Kinney's shoulder and it was quickly covered with warm blood. Captain Kinney moved his arm up and down and was glad to find that no bones were broken and that he was not disabled."

Captain Jack and La Flore must have recognized the precarious position they were in. They and such guards who had followed La Flore were lying in exposed positions, fighting a well-armed force of unknown size. Kinney came to believe, from erroneous information later provided by the station agent, that the gang numbered fifteen outlaws who, in addition to the advantage of human shields, could fire from behind the bulletproof bulk of the massive locomotive itself. Already at least one of their leaders was wounded. At this point, there was nothing to prevent the Daltons from forcing Engineer Ewing to pull away from the station, which would enable them to loot the train at their leisure. Certainly the guards remaining on the train, however many there were, didn't seem to be putting up much of a fight. Accordingly (as the *Globe-Democrat* reported), they decided to reoccupy one of the Pullman coaches:

> The passengers had dropped out of their berths and were lying in heaps on the floor. The lights were extinguished so that the movements of those on the inside could not be seen from the depot platform. Then the guard passed out of the rear door and started across the tracks to take up a position where they could do more effective shooting.
>
> The robbers at this moment were busily engaged in robbing the express car, but they had an eye on the movements of the armed guard and when the police started across the track every one of the outlaws commenced to "pump" their Winchesters and the bullets flew fast and thick into the ranks of the guards. How any of them escaped alive is miraculous. Capt. La Flore was wounded in the arm. A bullet struck Sid Johnson's watch, glanced off and wounded his right arm below the elbow. Another chunk of lead knocked a piece out of the stock of Captain LeFlore's Winchester and three of the police received slight wounds. The police had to save their lives by seeking cover. The work of gutting the express car was quickly completed and the robbers fled with their booty. The hold up occupied only about forty minutes.

As the gang, numbering about fifteen men according to the estimate of the operator at Adair, rode through the village they saw

Drs. Goff and Youngblood sitting in front of a drug store, having just returned from a visit to a patient. Without provocation and with devilish spirit, they poured a volley of lead into the two doctors. Both were wounded, Dr. Goff dying in a few hours due to loss of blood.

So ends yet another account of the Battle of Adair. Captain Jack, himself injured and with various of the posse also having sustained wounds of varying degrees, thought the best thing to do was to gather up all the wounded and proceed north to Vinita, the next stop, where he could obtain medical treatment for those requiring it. The *Globe* reported that

"After the fight, which lasted forty minutes," continued Capt. Kinney, "we took aboard the three wounded in our party, and then made the discovery that the two doctors who were sitting in front of a store a block away had been wounded by the robbers, who fired deliberately while fleeing from the scene of their crime. The doctors were also taken aboard the train and it pulled out for Vinita, where Dr. Goff, of Fredericksburg, Mo., one of the victims, died a few hours later. After myself, La Flore and Ward had our wounds dressed, we took the first south-bound train and went to Muskogee, where I made an effort to organize a posse and go in pursuit of the fugitives. By hard work I got eleven men, only a portion of whom were mounted. I realized that it would be useless to go on the trail, however, with such an insignificant force, and after consultation the contemplated pursuit was abandoned."

When asked if he was certain it was the Dalton gang that committed the crime, Kinney said: "There can be no question about it. The Daltons are well known in that section, and a score of people have seen them in the vicinity of Pryor Creek inside of the past ten days. The people of that section are afraid of them though, and it is not going to be an easy matter to get a posse that will make an earnest effort to effect their capture."

Obviously, not all of these accounts can be right. The guards (or at least some of them) either left the train to fight or were "disgracefully content" to remain inside, firing a few potshots when it was too late to make any difference. Some of them either did, or did not, take ineffective refuge in a coal shed during the battle. None, some, or all of them were "arrant cowards." What killed Dr. Goff? Bullets fired "from the high-powered rifles of the cowardly guards"? Or bullets from the equally high-powered Dalton Winchesters as they galloped out of town?[14] It should come as no surprise that I tend to believe Captain Jack's account. After all, he actually was an eyewitness, and not an anonymous one, offering his version just days after the event, when the details would still be fresh in his mind. That said, some of what Captain Jack recalled does not now seem accurate. For example, he was under the impression, shortly after the battle, that "one of their [that is, the Daltons'] number had been mortally wounded during the engagement with the Indian police. And he died yesterday morning. A grave was dug and the body, wrapped in a blanket, was consigned to the earth. Such in brief was the report forwarded to MK&T officials last night and corroberated [sic] by Capt. J. J. Kinney, chief of the 'Katy's' secret service, who arrived home last night from Muskogee, I.T." (*Sedalia Gazette,* July 17, 1892).

This strikes me as wishful thinking, although Kinney was not alone in thinking so. The Decatur, Illinois, *Daily Review,* for example, reported (July 21, 1892, 7) that "the Dalton gang of outlaws, who committed the train robbery near this place [Adair] last Thursday night, are still in the vicinity. . . . It is supposed that the Daltons are delayed on account of some of their men being wounded, as they have made several trips into town for medicine." Then, too, Captain Jack's nice speech, about "how not a man" in his posse "showed the white feather," must be understood as a public gesture demonstrating loyalty to his subordinates. There is simply too much evidence to the contrary—some provided in other contexts by himself—that some (although not all) of the guards were, at best, confused during the fight, and at worst did indeed behave in a cowardly manner. Preece notes that "at Pryor Creek, so Kinney later told Chris Madsen, the sorry 'defenders' had become boastful, and prided themselves on driving the Daltons away without firing a shot. 'Not so when they reached Adair,' Madsen wrote in his journal. 'Here some of the posse threw their guns away.'"[15] The family story, speaking of "drunken, cowardly Indians," may indeed reflect Kinney's private feelings, although more probably it indicates embellishments later added by those who retold it.

Speaking of the family story, certain parts of it comport reasonably well with the account Captain Jack gives above (and certain parts don't—what became of the bloody door?). It might, on reflection, seem to him, as he leapt off the smoker on the west side of the train, but was not followed by any of the guards in what was probably a pre-planned pincers movement, that he had been abandoned by his own men, a common nightmare for any officer. One must wonder exactly when he discovered that he was by himself, charging most of the Dalton gang, and how he felt about it. In hindsight, the wiser course would have been to retreat back to the car and lead from behind by pushing his confused or recalcitrant supporting guards out first. Conceivably he did not discover his singular situation until he had already opened fire, when it was too late, forcing his ignominious roll through the high weeds beneath the depot platform.

But if elements of Captain Jack's account remain open to reasonable question, so do the competing versions of the incident at Adair. Passenger Hearn's unfavorable report, although admitting that a "batch of deputies piled out of the coaches" after the first shots, condemns them for returning too quickly to the dubious safety of the sleeping coach during a lull in a battle that, despite his assertion to the contrary, could only have seemed in the distant sleeper as a series of confused flashes and explosions in the fully dark night. It never seemed to occur to Mr. Hearn that, in response to his querulous questions, the deputies' reported silence might not have been an admission of cowardly shame but instead an indication that they had other, more important matters before their attention than answering his many questions, like being right in the middle of a furious gunfight. Confidence in the acuity of Mr. Hearn's observations is not increased when he reports, contrary to every other source which discusses the matter, that Captain Jack was wounded in the "fleshy part of the left arm."

Some aspects of Drago's highly critical account, and the primary source on which he usually depends ("Eye Witness"), continue to puzzle me.[16] After asserting that Captain Jack initially ordered his men to shoot from the smoker's windows, "which they were disgracefully content to do," Drago then remarks that "their cowardly behavior explains, perhaps, why they were not riding in the express car, close to the money they were hired to protect, instead of drinking and lolling in the smoker."[17] But aside from the tempting allure of strong drink, the smoker was in many ways, for a force like Captain Jack's, a location markedly superior to confinement in the fortresslike express car. The railroads, realizing that the express car was the primary focus of robbery, designed them to partially resemble the safes they contained. We now have no way to know what type of express car (there were numerous models) Engine 115 pulled that night, but in 1892, many of them were still constructed of wood and thus vulnerable to rifle fire. Some models, for added security, did not even have end doors, limiting access to a ramped freight opening and a narrow, heavily barred side door. Windows, if there were any, were small and placed so that it would not be easy to threaten at gunpoint the messenger locked inside. To any force similarly confined, that meant limited portals of observation and correspondingly restricted fields of fire. Given the widespread use of dynamite, the express car was a potential death trap. The best way to protect the express car was to protect the entire train, which meant having a force capable of dispersing throughout it as the situation required. Such a force would also offer far better protection from robbers disguised as passengers. The express car would be the very last place to headquarter such a posse.

Similarly, the accusation of "disgracefully" firing from the smoker's windows instead of "rushing out and making a fight of it," as if the choice of a firing location necessarily determined the mettle of a combatant, simply doesn't make much sense. If that's all that happened (by these reports), such firing would involve, for any aimed shot, not just firing through but leaning completely out of the window, because the targets were all near the front of the train, and doing so in a car initially backlighting the shooter's position, the near equivalent—facing expert marksmen like the Daltons—of committing suicide.[18] If Kinney really gave such an order, and that was the only order he gave, then he deserves to be condemned not for cowardice, but for stupidity. Although Drago and "Eye Witness" concede that eventually some of the guards left the smoker, when the robbery was almost over, one is struck by the breezy confidence of assertions that seem to be just that, divorced from the reported experience of any of the actual participants. Here's the "Eye Witness" account, which Drago follows: "somewhat emboldened now, and the two captains not being after all such absolutely despicable funks, a few of the guards followed their lead out of the smoking car down on the side of the track where the robbers were not and began shooting between the cars at the retreating forms of the bandits. Undaunted, though and briskly firing back, the robbers, none of whom seem to have been hit by the wild firing of their pusillanimous adversaries, loaded their wagon and drove merrily off towards the woods, firing as they went."

At least so merry a drive did not include, as described by passenger Hearn, whose report "Eye Witness" appends to bolster his own account, a double circuit "around the entire train," sort of a contemptuous victory lap, indicative of their jaunty spirit. Absent a detailed log of the robber's exact positions, there is no way "Eye Witness" could plausibly assert that the guards only advanced "on the side of the track where the robbers were not." I'm not saying he's necessarily wrong; I am saying he cannot know he is right. He has here claimed to know that the bandana was red. To further assert the obvious, that in a fight of this size "wild firing" occurred, but to attribute such to only one side, seems again to stray into clairvoyance, and reveals more about the agenda of the writer than the events he is describing.

I am certainly not alone in my distrust of "Eye Witness" whom Robert Barr Smith suspects was a correspondent for the *Kansas City Times*. Smith refers to the "egregious" "Eye Witness" (*Daltons!*, 66) and elsewhere describes him as "an inventive sort" (59). Similarly, Nancy B. Samuelson suspects "Eye Witness" was, or was a ghostwriter for, U.S. Deputy Marshal Ransom Payne, and produces a letter from Payne's superior, William Grimes, in which Grimes fires Payne for, among other things, "mis-statement of facts in every particular."[19] In *Shoot from the Lip,* Samuelson describes the "Eye Witness" book as "mostly fictitious" (48). Emmett Dalton (*Beyond the Law*) has a similarly low opinion of Payne: "United States Marshal Ransom Payne, the joke of the United States Marshal's office, who never attempted to use his gun and later on was fired by United States Marshal Grimes for allowing the usage of his name as a hero in a 'fake book' purporting to give lives of the Dalton boys" (64). Interestingly, Deputy Marshal Payne was among the passengers on the train robbed by the Daltons at Wharton in May 1891. He sensibly, if not heroically, offered no resistance.[20]

This brings us to Drago's most damning assertion, which "can hardly be disputed," that the guards' wild firing killed and wounded the doctors, "since the bandits were firing in the opposite direction."[21] Let us ignore for now that (as Robert Barr Smith writes in *Daltons!*) "according to the local press, as the robbers clattered past the Skinner store, they fired eighteen or twenty rounds at two inoffensive men on the porch of the store. Both men went down with leg wounds" (65). One such account, presented above (*Sedalia Gazette*) notes that "without provocation and with devilish spirit, they [the Daltons] poured a volley of lead into the two doctors." Most of the contemporary reports presume the doctors were shot as the battle concluded, with the Daltons escaping west down Main Street. If these reports are correct, the doctors must have been in or in front of the pharmacy located at 138 Main. And it is further true that unless the Daltons deliberately fired at the pair (which the contemporary accounts assert), they most likely would have been hit by the guard's fire, because at the conclusion of the battle, it was then aimed in a westerly direction at the fleeing outlaws. But such reports by themselves do not conclusively disprove Drago's claim. The death of Dr. Goff had to be explained somehow, and even if the journalists privately suspected that friendly fire caused his death, in the absence of definitive proof, their inclination would be to blame the Daltons—blame they deserved, because their actions were at least indirectly responsible for all the firing that night, wild or otherwise.

But Drago's claim will stand or fall upon examination of the details, as best we can now know them, of exactly where the doctors were and the likely patterns and directions of the shots exchanged. Although Smith identifies the "Skinner store" as the doctor's location, most accounts refer to a "drug store" or a "pharmacy" and are divided as to whether the doctors were hit inside the store or as they sat on its front porch. Interestingly, the most specific location is given by Drago himself, who says they were in a drugstore, "one of the several stores facing the back of the depot across an open space of a hundred yards or more."[22] If Drago's description is accurate, then the drugstore must have been located not (as has always been supposed) on Main Street but instead on Mays Avenue, because that is the only location where stores could be said to face the depot's back. A Sanborn-Perris plat map of Adair, dated June 1896, does indeed show a drugstore located at 410 Mays Avenue, right next to "Drs. offices" at 412 Mays.

As the train stopped the engine, tender, and mail express cars would have been positioned slightly to the north of the depot and its siding, themselves located on the west side of the train. The Daltons, variously clustered around on both sides of the engine and express car, would have been firing generally due south, southwest, but primarily southeast during the different phases of the battle, depending on the placement of La Flore's posse as they fired back to the north and northwest. Yet by Drago's information, the doctors were in a drugstore facing the back of the depot, or west of the train. If I am right in identifying the location as 410 Mays Avenue, then the pharmacy was also approximately one block south of the depot. On only one occasion would there have been any reason for fire to be directed, inadvertently or otherwise, in their direction, and that was as the battle began.

As he left the smoker, alone, on the west side of the train, Captain Jack then "passed around the rear of the depot," which would put him behind its northwest corner, and began firing northeast (at a distance of only some twenty yards) at a robber standing between the tender and the express car. This provoked a vicious return volley, perhaps as many as sixty shots, heading southwest. I think it is logical to assume that these were the bullets that killed Dr. Goff and wounded Dr. Youngblood. The 1896 plat of Adair supports this thesis. If one places a straightedge from where the Daltons were shooting to the northwest corner of the depot where Kinney first opened fire, the line of the Dalton's return fire directly hits the pharmacy at 410 Mays, 125 yards distant. If that is what actually happened, it would further explain the reports that the doctors were hit (if they were) while sitting on the porch. Presumably intelligent men, they would have certainly realized that a nearby gunfight is not a spectator sport and would have immediately sought shelter. If indeed they were on the front porch, it must be because the battle had not yet begun. And it didn't, according to Captain Jack, until the exchange described above.

Yet even this seemingly obvious assertion, that intelligent men would seek shelter during a furious gunfight, is subject to dispute. Nearly fifty years after the robbery, Mrs. Louise Rider, wife of Indian policeman Charlie Rider, told an interviewer,

> Through my husband's work, I have had a wide knowledge of the different outlaws and bad men of those days. Our home at the Hills was eight miles northwest of Pryor. We were living here when the Daltons held up a train at Adair. There were only two trains a day each way on the Missouri, Kansas and Texas Railroad then. The marshals and police got word of the intended holdup which was to be staged that night as the train neared Adair.
>
> Dr. Goff had just come to that place from St. Louis and he and another doctor had been out in the country that day but had returned and were sitting on the porch of the little hotel when they were told by the officers of the intended holdup. Dr. Goff said that

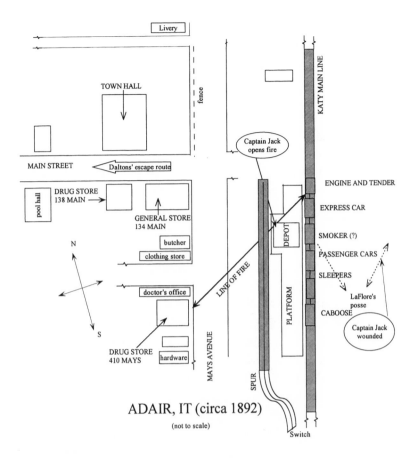

ADAIR, IT (circa 1892)

(not to scale)

he had always wanted to see a holdup, so he and his friend continued to sit. . . .

The officers killed one of the gang and drove the others off and
as they left they spied the white shirts of the two doctors on the
porch and as the Daltons passed they fired. . . . Dr. Goff was shot in
the legs and the other doctor was shot in the heel. Realizing that
they would have to come out in the open for help, Dr. Goff said "We
will have to crawl to the train. I've got forty dollars in my pocket and
I'll put it under the porch." They put the wounded doctors on the
train and brought them to Vinita where they cut off one of Doctor
Goff's legs and he died.[23]

One must emphasize that the doctor's precise location is not
known. Another version has the doctors, wherever they were, running toward the gunfire as the robbery began, thinking their services

might be required, and they were shot as they approached. The *Fort Smith Elevator* (July 22, 1892) recounts these events as follows: "When the robbery was completed three or four men started down the street west of the depot and 200 feet west of there, sitting on a porch, they passed Dr. W. L. Goff of Fredericksburg, Mo., and Dr. T. S. Youngblood, of Adair. They fired on them, and Goff fell forward, exclaiming 'I am killed'" (3). The 1896 plat does indeed show a drugstore (138 Main) near the reported location. By this account, Youngblood was shot twice, once on the porch and once as he ran to the depot to get help, sustaining a wound that eventually resulted in the amputation of his instep. Goff, whose left leg was amputated at the knee by Drs. Fortner and Bagby in Vinita, died the next morning at 6 A.M., apparently from loss of blood and not, as Emmett Dalton later claimed, from blood poisoning. In Emmett Dalton's account of the robbery, he notes that the doctors "were in a drugstore across the way from the depot" (*Beyond the Law,* 121), which would again seem to support the thesis that the pharmacy was located not on Main but on Mays Avenue.[24]

What about the coal shed? Captain Jack says nothing whatsoever about seeking shelter in such a shed, where various later historians contend he, along with La Flore, Johnson, and Ward, was wounded. But unless one suspects that Captain Jack is lying (and he did in my opinion tell a "white lie" about the "white feather"), there is no good reason not to believe his own account of what happened to him, particularly on so inconsequential a detail. He alone is the best authority on his own actions until proven to the contrary. Very probably this "coal shed" business is one of those cases, more common than I had once thought, where some spurious detail of history somehow surfaces, from where nobody really knows, and because it erroneously figures in one account, it tends to appear similarly in many of the later accounts, gaining an undeserved authority through sheer repetition. I can think of no other way to explain its presence.[25]

How much did the Daltons get? The simple answer is that nobody knows how much, or whether they got anything at all. The Ogden, Utah, *Standard* reported on July 16 that "the amount taken from the express car is unknown and conjectures run all the way from an insignificant sum to $75,000" (1). Similarly, the Trenton, New Jersey, *Times* asserted "the robbers secured the contents of the safe of the Pacific Express, amounting it is said to $75,000, and made good their escape" (July 16, 1892, 1). On July 21, 1892, the Hagerstown, Maryland, *Herald and Torch Light* announced that the Daltons' take, "it is asserted by an official who knows, [was] certainly between $50,000 and $75,000." The *Saint Louis Globe-Democrat* later reported "about $4,000" (October 6, 1892). The MK&T policy in such situations, cited by much of the press, was to refuse to disclose any specifics. Al Jennings, as has been earlier described, says they got $27,000, but he cannot be said to be a credible source.

Seeing Mr. Al Jennings mentioned here, I am reminded that back in Chapter 2, I awarded him the honor of writing the most inaccurate account ever written of the Adair robbery. Upon due reflection, I must retract that award and present it instead to the Hagerston *Herald and Torch Light*, whose report (mentioned above) is a truly astonishing compendium of error masquerading as fact. Although they correctly report that the No. 2 train was robbed, they have it traveling the exact opposite direction it did and leaving from Vinita, which they believe is located forty miles east of Adair. Captain Jack's name is spelled right, but Captain La Flore is "L. A. Flora." The two doctors, neither of whom "is likely to die from the injuries received," are described as fellow passengers on the train. They assert the safe was blown up. After the train is stopped "a few miles from Adair," Captain Jack and "Mr. Flora," accompanied by the two doctors, all open fire on the robbers with pistols and are forced to retreat back to the car when their guns run out of bullets. The robbery over, the train continues on to Adair, where a posse is supposedly gathered. At least the story concludes in a generous fashion: "Captain Kinney, the chief of the detectives, is a man noted for his bravery and the odds must have been greatly against him to force a retreat on his part."

Most historians, figuring that the Daltons must have gotten something, repeat the $17,000 amount claimed by Emmett Dalton many years later. In one intriguing description of the robbery's aftermath, Glen Shirley (although few other historians repeat his claim), writes that

> hardly had news of the Adair robbery hit the papers when the robbers [that is, the Daltons] appeared in El Reno, on the Choctaw Coal and Railway Company's lines, one morning when the streets were crowded with people, and entered the leading bank of the city. The only person in the bank at that time was the wife of the president, who fainted at the sight of their guns. The bandits leisurely helped themselves to all the money in sight, remounted their

horses, and rode away. The raid netted them $10,000, which was such a severe loss to the bank it was forced into liquidation.[26]

This can be interpreted in two completely different ways. That the Daltons would risk, if they did, another robbery so soon after Adair might be explained by the fact that they needed money, not having gotten any at Adair. Or then again, precisely because the Adair robbery was successful, if it was, they may have felt their good luck would continue. Another way to examine the question is from the perspective of the railroad and express company, particularly because many accounts say they were forewarned the robbery would occur. Drago notes that "several explanations are offered for the presence of an armed guard of that strength on Number 2 this particular night. One commentator says that the Missouri, Kansas and Texas had got word that it was to be attacked. It is easier to believe that it was because the $17,000 in the express car was an unusually valuable shipment for the financially impoverished Katy to be carrying that Captain Kinney and his men had been hired to see it through from Muskogee to Vinita."[27] But if the shipment was really all that valuable, why risk it at all? The wisest policy would have been to let it seem the shipment was going through under guard as planned, hope the guards would exterminate the robbers, and then actually ship the money when it was safer to do so. Nobody can now know.[28]

Still another way to analyze the question is from the standpoint of the seven (by my best estimate) robbers: Bob, Emmett, and Grat Dalton, "Bitter Creek" Newcomb, Dick Broadwell, Charlie Pierce, and Bill Doolin (and if eight, probably Bill Power). Assume they got $17,000 from Adair and $10,000 from the El Reno bank. Add to that another, let us estimate, $10,000 from their recent train robberies at Red Rock and Leliaetta. That totals $37,000, or $730,360 in today's dollars. From July 15 to October 5, when Emmett claimed they were broke and stated such as the motive for Coffeyville, they would *each* have had to spend, in the eighty-two-day interval, over $1,300 a day. Although that might be possible in New York City, the bleak Indian Territory offered consumers far fewer venues for spending on that scale. The logical conclusion is that, if Emmett can be believed, their combined take wasn't anywhere near what was reported. Unless, of course, somewhere "in the rolling hills near Grayhorse," there indeed lies buried a fabulous treasure.

News of the robbery spread quickly and angered much of the country. Shirley writes that the Daltons'

> bold attack on such an armed force, which they must have known to be on the train, spread great alarm throughout the territories and the Border States. It shook political circles all the way to Washington, and territory officials were ordered to resort to every means at their disposal to wipe out the bandits. The Katy, the Santa Fe, and Pacific railroads and Wells Fargo and Company pooled their resources to raise to $5,000 [other sources say $6,000] the reward for the apprehension and conviction of each member of the gang, making a grand total of $40,000—the most money ever offered for an outlaw band in America.[29]

Even if their take had been far less than what was reported, it cannot be denied, as Robert Barr Smith writes, that "the bandits had gotten the best of this brief skirmish."[30] But not for long. Almost immediately, determined posses led by Heck Thomas and Wells Fargo Chief Detective Fred Dodge began to scour the Indian Territory. Emmett Dalton later admitted that the gang was thereby "hard pressed." Other experienced lawmen soon joined the hunt, but above all, the gang feared Heck Thomas (whom they called "Nemesis"). Smith notes that

> Deputy Marshal Chris Madsen and dozens of other lawmen were also out on the hunt. Indian trackers headed some of the posses, and the combination of five thousand dollars a head in blood money and the killing of Dr. Goff meant that no place was safe any longer. It was hard to know whom to trust now. . . .
> Nemesis was even closer behind them now, the worst possible bunch of manhunters to have on your backtrail. Fred Dodge was very close to them, and with him were veteran posseman Burrell Cox, and Sac and Fox tracker Talbot White, and that most dangerous of pursuers, the implacable Deputy U.S. Marshal Heck Thomas, whom Fred Dodge called "a man that was known to always get his man—sometimes dead but he got him."[31]

Although the Daltons had won the skirmish at Adair, in doing so, they sustained great damage to their reputation. Until Harry Sinclair Drago later claimed otherwise, nobody then doubted that the Daltons were

MISSOURI, KANSAS & TEXAS RAILWAY COMPANY

Parsons Kas   July 15th 1892

$ 5000 Reward!

The Express car on the north bound

train of the M K & T Ry was

robbed by masked men at Adair

Indian Territory Thursday night July 14th A Reward of Five
Thousand Dollars will
be paid by the undersigned for the Arrest
and conviction of each of the men engaged in
this Robbery to an amount not exceeding
Forty Thousand Dollars

Signed M K & T RR
by Chas Grady
Senior Vice President
Pacific Express
by L. A. Fuller
Vice President

responsible for the attack on the two doctors, and this was a clear violation of the unwritten code that although it was almost acceptable for robbers to target the generally hated banks, railroads, and express companies,[32] one did not, in the process, kill or injure innocent bystanders, particularly women, preachers, or doctors. Although the Daltons were greatly feared by the populace, by more than a few, they were secretly admired, and it was this tacit admiration mingled with fear that allowed them to successfully remain so long at large. Killing Dr. Goff changed that, deflating the then-prevailing myth of the train robber as a latter-day Robin Hood, plundering only those whose wealth derived from exploiting the common man, stealing only from those who became rich by robbing the poor.[33]

"For the first time," Smith writes, "virtually every man's hand was against the Daltons." He continues:

The robbery of the Katy train at Adair, and especially the death of Dr. Goff, had generated massive public indignation and official energy. The public and the press saw Daltons behind every bush. They were accused of robbing a bank in Southwest City, Missouri, just after the Adair raid. And when robbers took ten thousand dollars from a bank in El Reno, Oklahoma, shortly after the Adair raid, the crime was instantly blamed on the Daltons. Some experienced lawmen doubted the Daltons had had a hand in the El Reno job, but the public leaped to a conclusion and clung to it staunchly.

The reward for the gang was now the biggest bounty yet offered for a single bunch of outlaws. It was plain that even the dugouts down in the Nations were no longer safe havens. The whole countryside was becoming too hot to hold the gang for many days more. It was time to go.[34]

And that they did, perhaps only hours ahead of the man they called "Nemesis." The *Saint Louis Globe-Democrat* (October 7, 1892) reported that "Fred Dodge, chief of the Wells-Fargo detectives, and Deputy United States Marshal Heck Thomas arrived here [Guthrie, Indian Territory] to-day from the Osage Reservation, where they have been for six weeks hunting the Daltons. They had located their headquarters, gotten full information about their movements, and were about ready to lead a posse to take them when the gang suddenly pulled out for Coffeyville, and Dodge and Thomas lost track of them." But the Daltons were mistaken about nemesis—that lay not just behind but just ahead at Coffeyville, a town near which many of them had grown up, a town that even today features the painted red silhouettes of their bullet-riddled corpses strewn about Death Alley.

Captain Jack's reaction to the robbery at Adair, of the train that it was largely his responsibility to guard, is not well documented. From the clippings he saved reporting the aftermath, the only one—aside from general articles on the Daltons, including a false report of their burying one of their members, and a lengthy account of the Coffeyville raid—that specifically discussed the events that immediately followed was a short piece, probably from the *Sedalia Gazette*, observing that "word was also sent to Adair to the effect that their [that is, the Daltons] band now numbers twenty-six members, sixteen having joined the gang recently. They are very bold and almost daily send some one to a trading post to purchase provisions, always paying for them without any trouble. With all their boldness and daring deviltry, no one appears to possess bravery enough to tackle them."

Recalling that the reason Kinney gave for abandoning pursuit the night of the robbery with his own posse was that it would have been "suicidal" to engage what he then believed was a far larger force than it actually was, it may be that the above clipping interested him by its (almost certainly equally erroneous) estimate of the size to which the gang quickly grew. This gives the appearance of a man seeking justification for his own actions.

He cannot have been, to say the least, pleased with the outcome at Adair. The railroad guards were under his (at least joint) command, and he and they had failed in their duty to protect the train and its contents. Because by many accounts the Daltons knew the train was guarded and they attacked anyway, the robbery almost amounted to a personal insult, as if no collection of guards could match the gang's daring, skill, and courage. What must have been particularly irritating was the appearance (bound in lurid yellow covers) of the anonymous "Eye Witness" tract—wherein Captain Jack is soundly excoriated as a "coward"—which was aggressively marketed to the passengers on the very trains he was still sworn to protect. Burton Rascoe writes, "it [the book] was what nowadays, in the publishing business, is called a 'quickie,' and no doubt it was hawked by the newsbutchers in the coaches of all the railroad trains of the mid-West, as was the custom in those days, by mid-November, 1892, or thereabouts."[35]

It's very possible that his superiors were equally displeased, both at the robbery and what they may have felt was on his part an insufficient zeal in either preventing it or immediately tracking down those responsible for it. Curiously, Captain Jack does not seem to have taken any active role (or if he did, no record remains) in the intensive manhunt that followed the robbery. Perhaps his wound was more serious than first reported. One contemporary account, which inaccurately presents many other details of the robbery, did note that "the wounds are not fatal, but Kennedy [sic] and Ward will be laid up for many days—one with a ball through his shoulder and the other with a broken leg."[36]

Something needs to be said here about Sid Johnson, the other wounded officer. His experience at Adair would be repeated two years later, in a fierce battle at Blackstone switch, when (on November 13, 1894) a Katy train was stopped by Tom Root, Buz Luckey, Will Smith, and Nathaniel "Texas Jack" Reed. Guarding the train with Johnson were Paden Tolbert and Bud Ledbetter ("The Fourth Guardsman"). During the attempted robbery, in which hundreds of shots were fired, Ledbetter managed to shoot Texas Jack in the hip, the bullet piercing his intestines and bowels. The gang was eventually captured, but at the cost of the life of Deputy Marshal Newton LeForce. Texas Jack voluntarily surrendered and was given a light sentence in exchange for testimony against the alleged mastermind, Jim Dyer. Dyer's conviction was later reversed by the Supreme Court, and at a new trial, now represented by Attorney J. Warren Reed (see Chapter 4), he was acquitted. As for "Texas Jack," he

> became an evangelist, traveling the West preaching the consequences of outlawry and sin. He often exhibited himself with carnival companies and Wild West shows as "Texas Jack, Famous Bandit and Train Robber."—replete in a battered Stetson, high-topped boots, fringed buckskin jacket literally covered with badges and souvenirs acquired in his travels, and selling a yellow-backed pamphlet purporting to be his true life story—until his death in Tulsa in 1950.
>
> Ledbetter frequently heard of his peregrinations. When occasionally asked about Texas Jack, he would remark: "I saw him 'hunkering' for them crossties with the sack of loot, and let him have it. That shot made a preacher out of him."[37]

In any event, by 1893 Captain Jack had left the Katy and accepted a position as a "Special Agent" for the Atchison, Topeka & Sante Fe railroad, a position he would occupy until at least 1898 (by the evidence of his railroad passes). Exactly when or why he left the Katy I have been unable to discover. Kinney's wife Elizabeth may have influenced his decision, particularly as some evidence suggests she was at the time pregnant with George, their second son. (Their first son, John, my grandfather, had been born in 1888.) She cannot have been pleased with her husband, father of a large and growing family, trading shots with train robbers. Although railroad detecting would never be considered an entirely safe occupation, it was possible to seek employment on relatively safer lines of track. Still, his leaving so soon after the robbery at Adair strongly suggests mutual dissatisfaction.

One probable source of such dissatisfaction, an irritant just waiting openly to erupt (but for all I know, he simply got a better job offer[38]), is that the ideal railroad detective would necessarily have a Dr. Jekyll/Mr. Hyde personality, combining skills and behaviors unlikely for any individual to possess equally. Preece notes that at Pryor Creek, when Captain Jack announced that they would continue on to Adair, Kinney "guessed that the Daltons had pulled a ruse. The intuition of a born lawman had forced the bandits, cocky after three unchallenged train boardings, into a fight that so injured their prestige."[39] This was all fine to a point—but what the railroad wanted was a man who would win the fight not by damaging the bandits' "prestige," but instead by shooting them dead, leaving "their corpses strewn along the track."[40]

In other words, at the penultimate moment of his career, Captain Jack found himself in a situation requiring just the sort of skills and experience he most lacked. The word most often used to describe him was "genial." Naturally gregarious, he generally liked people, inspiring them in turn to like and trust him, invaluable assets for eliciting confessions (as from Holloman). He was a hard worker, clever, and excelled at detailed investigations, as in the Lewis case, which he worked up "fine as silk," according to one of his saved clippings. He made a good impression, important when dealing with prominent clients like the Wood Brothers in the Dunn forgery. He had constructed an effective and extensive network of law enforcement friends and colleagues, and he could depend on their unstinting help as his investigations required. He was an asset both to his employer and his community, recognizing (as in the case of the Sedalia Fiend) that occasionally the well-being of the latter trumped the narrow interests of the former. He presented a good appearance in court and was just the man to count on for unraveling a complicated financial fraud, apprehending a confidence man, tracing a counterfeiter, outwitting a swindler, or negotiating a financial settlement with an irate customer. One of his professional mentors and social friends was Detective Pat Lawler, a man he obviously emulated and admired, whose obituary (which he saved) noted that "he treated everybody, including the criminals with whom he came into contact, in a gentlemanly manner, and never used the rough, boisterous methods of some thief-takers. He was in himself a refutation of that long exploded belief that a detective cannot be a gentleman."[41]

Again, this is all well and good to a point. But Captain Jack was not the sort of man who would at night happily dream about busting union skulls. He was not, at heart, much of a killer. And for all his other abilities, that was what the situation at Adair required. The Daltons couldn't be reasoned with. They couldn't be charmed. They were not fellow gentlemen willing to discuss their differences in a civilized fashion. They had no respect for the law. Out-fighting them was more important than out-thinking them. The situation demanded the sort of man who, rifle at his hip and standing beside Bob Dalton, could plug the thrown tin can four times to Bob's three. Captain Jack was not that man. Captain La Flore might have been, which may explain why the guards would instinctively follow his lead, and not Captain Jack's, as the battle began.

He would have been less than human had he not, while convalescing in his South Prospect Street home, speculated on what might have been. To have captured or killed the Daltons, a chance afforded few, would have elevated him from the footnotes to the main text in the annals of law enforcement, capping an already successful career, creating a future largely of his choosing. If only the Daltons had attacked at Pryor Creek, where he was fully prepared to meet them. If only some of the guards had followed him, as they were supposed to do, off the west side of the smoker. If only his first shots had been more accurate.[42] If only he had been able, weakened as he was by shock and loss of blood, to assemble a larger posse for pursuit. If only. Captain Jack couldn't know it then, but his law enforcement career—with one spectacular and perhaps redeeming exception—had just peaked, and not on a pleasant note. His fate was to be remembered, to the very slight extent he is remembered at all, within obscure parentheses, by brief asides. He was the man who failed to stop the Daltons that night of July 14, 1892.[43]

DALTONS AND DESTINY

*Who knows whether the best of men be known, or whether there be not
more remarkable persons forgot than any that stand remembered in
the known account of time?*
—Sir Thomas Browne

Benjamin Franklin is *not* responsible for the Dalton's death. Quite the
contrary. If only city planners and road designers had followed his
quite sensible advice on a particular point of street construction, the
Daltons, or at least some of them, arguably would have survived their
ill-fated attempt to rob two banks simultaneously in Coffeyville,
Kansas, on the morning of October 5, 1892. From an early age,
Franklin, who would later invent such useful items as fire insurance,
an electrical apparatus for humanely slaughtering turkeys, swim fins,
bifocals, and the stove bearing his name, had an interest in paving and
quarry stones. The young Ben, when the approaches to his favorite
fishing hole turned into a quagmire, organized an effort by his peers
to pilfer paving stones from a nearby construction site, using such to
construct a wharf shoring up the muddy banks. He was caught and
punished, learning that "nothing was useful which was not honest."[1]
Much later, Franklin was (as he says) "instrumental" in convincing
the city of Philadelphia to pave its streets, as he "saw with pain the in-
habitants wading in mud while purchasing their provisions."[2] He further realized that even paved streets had to be maintained, which focused his attention on how best to design a street in order that its
periodic cleaning would require a minimum of labor.

Most paved streets then typically featured a slightly convex design,
allowing water and debris to flush to curbs and gutters lining both
sides. Franklin had a better idea:

And let me here remark the convenience of having but one gutter in such a narrow street, running down its middle, instead of two, one on each side, near the footway; for where all the rain that falls on a street runs from the sides and meets in the middle, it forms there a current strong enough to wash away all the mud it meets with; but when divided into two channels, it is often too weak to cleanse either, and only makes the mud it finds more fluid, so that the wheels of carriages and feet of horses throw and dash it upon the foot-pavement, which is thereby rendered foul and slippery, and sometimes splash it upon those who are walking.[3]

The installation of curbs and gutters was an occasion of considerable civic pride, particularly in the west, signaling that a given town had reached new levels of prosperity and sophistication, and that its passageways were no longer the near exclusive domain of driven cattle. So the citizens of Coffeyville, on October 5, probably didn't mind the annoying disruptions caused by fitting out Eighth Street with curbs and gutters. But because Franklin's wise advice was not heeded, the new gutters were positioned along the street's sides, requiring the temporary removal of certain appurtenances—like horse hitching rails—also there located. That absent hitching rail, at the corner of Eighth and Walnut just in front of McCoy's Hardware store, about a half a block behind the C. M. Condon & Company Bank, which itself faced the First National Bank, was just where the Daltons had planned to tether their horses.

One might here ask why, planning to rob two banks, the Daltons simply didn't (as one account reports[4]) hitch their horses instead immediately outside on Union Street, on either side of which the banks stood? One reason is that horses are easily spooked by gunfire, something that must be anticipated in such an enterprise. Horses also make good targets, so it was best to locate them far away enough from the scene to be reasonably safe, yet near enough to enable a speedy exit. Why didn't the Daltons, unable to hitch their horses where they had planned, delegate one of their members to hold the horses in a similarly convenient spot? The answer to that is that the five (or six[5]) robbers—Bob, Grat, and Emmett Dalton, Bill Power, and Dick Broadwell—had set an ambitious task for themselves, one that required all their available manpower. After some indecision, the gang rode down an adjacent narrow alley, near the end of which they found a suitable hitching rail at the back of a lot owned by the local judge. "Their choice of tethering places," writes Robert Barr Smith "is astonishing. For the fence by which their horses were tied was a long 350 feet away from Walnut street to the east, and across Walnut lay the gang's targets, the Condon and First National banks. The banks and the horses were a very long way apart, a long way for an armed stranger to walk to his target. It was an even longer way for a desperate, hard-pressed man to run, especially with a whole town shooting at him."[6]

Because the Daltons were well known in Coffeyville, as they rode in from the south (by other accounts from the west, right down Eighth Street), some reports indicate that they disguised themselves with false beards and moustaches, but evidently, as they searched about for a new hitching spot, they were recognized anyway. Even before they entered the banks, word quickly began to spread throughout the town that a robbery was about to happen, an event confirmed when Aleck McKenna, the owner of a dry goods store, saw through the windows of the Condon bank a robber pull out a rifle. Citizens began to gather and erect barricades and firing positions in the streets. In two local hardware stores, clerks began passing out firearms and ammunition to those determined to protect both their town and their money.

Broadwell, Power, and Grat Dalton targeted the Condon bank, confronting three employees and two customers, demanding cash at the point of Winchesters. In the front of the vault, Grat found bags of silver dollars, but most of the cash was in a safe equipped with a time lock that cashier Charley Ball claimed couldn't be opened for another ten minutes. This was a courageous bluff, but it worked: the robbers were dutifully content to wait until the safe could be opened. Across the street at the First National, Bob and Emmett Dalton forced cashier Tom Ayers to open his safe, which yielded large stacks of currency plus gold coins. Neither party of raiders then seemed to have any idea that by then the streets outside were teeming with armed men awaiting their exit.

As the Daltons left the two banks, Emmett and Bob pushing employees of the First National ahead of them, general and heavy gunfire began. Bert Ayres, son of First National Cashier Tom Ayres, gave the following account to the *St. Louis Globe Dispatch* (October 6, 1892):

> They then put us in front of them and marched us out through the front door. Father was the first to go out. Just then the shooting

began on the street, and the robbers closed the door and conducted Mr. Shepard and myself out of the back door in the alley and turned us loose. They left father on the outside, in front of the bank. Just as we got into the alley Lucius Baldwin came out of Isham's store with a pistol in his hand, when one of the Daltons, whom I recognized as Emmett, pulled his Winchester and shot Baldwin. The robbers then ran out of the alley on to Eighth Street, and we put ourselves out of their range. About this time I heard that father had been shot, and I ran into the hardware store and found him dying on the floor. When the robber put him out of the front door he ran to Isham's and secured a Winchester, and, kneeling down in the doorway, was looking in the direction of the bank. Just then a shot from one of the Winchesters struck him in the face.

During all this, the Condon bank was under heavy fire directed at Power, Broadwell, and Grat Dalton. Over eighty shots were fired by the citizens outside, wounding at least one of the bandits in his arm. The three decided to make a run for it. Smith explains,

They ran the gantlet of a murderous swarm of bullets, an interlocking cross fire from Boswell's and Isham's, tearing at them as they ran diagonally across the coverless expanse of Walnut. They turned to fire at their tormentors, snapping bullets back at the phalanx of flaming rifles concentrated in front of Isham's. Behind his iron range, Henry Isham "was throwing bullets up that alley as fast as he could pull the trigger" and everybody else was banging away furiously at the men running for their lives down Death Alley.[7]

They didn't make it. The *Globe-Democrat* (October 6, 1892) reported that "five of them fell within a space of 20 feet of the point where their horses stood in the alley. One of the party [Broadwell], however, managed to get on his horse and rode a half a mile west of town, where he fell from the animal and died by the roadside. His horse was also wounded and died within a short distance of his rider. The citizens acted coolly and deliberately. Four of the gang fell pierced with from five to fifteen shots, whereas another [Emmett Dalton], who was shot through and through, is still alive."

The cost of this victory was four dead, including City Marshal Connelly, shot in the back by Grat Dalton. The dead outlaws were then collected and laid out on the plank floor of the city jail, conveniently located just off what would become known as "Death Alley." At one point—I don't know by whom or when—somebody outlined the corpses's positions where they fell. Then crowds of relic seekers and at least two photograpers went to work. Emmett's pistols were snatched up by the editor of a local newspaper. The live and dead horses had hairs plucked from their tails. During all this, Deputy Marshal Ransom Payne, who may have been "Eye Witness," arrived on the scene. Wishing to include himself in the photographic record, but fastidiously deciding that it would be unseemly (and also dirty) to lie between the corpses, Payne instructed that Bob and Grat be hoisted from the planks, and he posed for pictures between them.[8] Payne also evidently hoped to confiscate their bodies and ship them to California for rewards still offered by that state.[9] But that didn't happen, and shortly afterward, Payne was fired by U.S. Marshal Grimes.

The raid's bloody end did not bring immediate closure and relief to Coffeyville. On October 10, 1892, one of the citizen heroes of Coffeyville, Mr. John Kloehr, received the following anonymous and ominous note:

> I take the time to tell . . . the citizens of Coffeyville that all of the gang ain't dead yet by a damn sight . . . and we shall come and see you. I would have given all I ever made to have been there the 5th. You people had no cause to take arms against the gang. The bankers will not help the widows of the men that got killed there and you thought you were playing hell fire when you killed three of us but your time will come soon when you will go into the grave and pass in your checks. . . . So take warning.
>
> Yours truly,
> DALTON GANG[10]

Many believed, as did Captain Jack, that the gang numbered considerably more than the five who attacked, and there were persistent and panicked rumors that the town could expect quick retaliation in the form of an attempted rescue of Emmett. So reported the *Globe-Democrat* (October 6, 1892):

> Business is practically suspended, while a feeling of sadness pervades the entire community over the death of four esteemed citizens at the hands of the red-handed murderers, and the probable loss of another.

It is reported that the gang consisted of fifteen men, and that ten of them are camped out by Rock Creek, about fifteen miles south of this city, in the Indian Territory. The city is carefully guarded, and any attempt at a rescue will result in great bloodshed.

A large part of that guard was supplied by the Katy railroad at the direction of their general superintendent at Parsons, Mr. J. J. Frey, whose signature authorized Captain Jack's railroad pass, because he had been telegraphed that a robbery was in progress. Fifty armed men were immediately rounded up and sent south to Coffeyville on a special train. (If Captain Jack was still with the Katy, he would have certainly been on that train.) A similar rumor—that remnants of the gang planned to attack the town—spread a week later, so again, a special Katy train was organized, this one reportedly carrying two hundred guards, but before it left, word was received that the expected number of raiders was less than what was first feared, and that the Coffeyville police by themselves could probably defend the town.[11]

Nor was the situation calmed when, hardly had the gun smoke cleared, brother Bill Dalton showed up in town and claimed, outrageously, that the citizens of Coffeyville had stolen $900 from one of his brother's bodies, a sum he demanded the town repay to the estate. Given that there was already widespread talk about lynching Emmett, one can only be amazed by his brother's foolishness, a foolishness that came due in June 1894 when, after a series of robberies, Bill Dalton was killed near his house in Elk, Oklahoma, by Marshal Loss Hart.[12]

Whether or not Bill Dalton actually participated in any of the robberies he was popularly credited with, in particular a bank in Longview, Texas, is still very much a disputed point. As for Bill's death, some accounts describe Deputy Marshal Selden (or Seldon) Lindsey as the man who killed him.[13] Still other accounts say that both Hart and Lindsey were responsible, a version that once seemed to be supported by an autopsy that supposedly found two different slugs in Dalton's body matching the firearms the two deputies were known to carry. Other versions insist Bill Dalton was killed by a single bullet. In the aftermath of Bill's death, members of the posse who killed him were charged with murder, although no records of their trials (if indeed they ever stood trial) have yet been discovered.

That sums up the fate of most of the Adair robbers, with two exceptions: "Bitter Creek" Newcomb and Charlie Pierce. After joining up with the Doolin gang, Newcomb was present in Ingalls, Oklahoma, on September 1, 1893, when eight members of the gang—after visiting Arkansas Tom, who was laid up sick in a nearby attic—decided to play poker in George Ransom's saloon. A pair of covered wagons hiding a posse of thirteen men under the command of Deputy Marshal John Hixon pulled up near the saloon. The deputies quickly took up firing positions. While leaving the saloon to check on his horse, Newcomb recognized and was recognized by one of the posse, leading to an exchange of gunfire. Newcomb, wounded either by a cartridge exploding on his belt or by a piece of his bullet-shattered Winchester, which lodged itself in his thigh, eventually managed to mount his horse and escape, but not before figuring in one of the enduring but entirely fictional myths of the West, a scene depicted in Tilghman's *Passing of the Oklahoma Outlaws*.

Supposedly, as Newcomb lay wounded in the street, his rifle smashed, a lady (who may have been his wife or girlfriend) known only as the "Rose of Cimarron" fashioned a rope of bed sheets and rappelled down from the attic, where she was tending Arkansas Tom. She carried a rifle and ammunition secured in her dress, and ran through a hailstorm of bullets to Newcomb's side. Rearmed, Newcomb effected his escape, the distracted posse in collective awe over the woman's bravery. It's a nice story, and an even better myth, for it probably never happened. By the time the battle ended, nine men were killed or wounded, and the gang escaped, with the exception of Arkansas Tom, who surrendered, but only when he ran out of ammunition defending his attic fortress. After serving time in the penitentiary, Arkansas Tom reprised his role at Ingalls in Tilghman's film, which gave credence to the mythic Rose. But film actors were not paid as much then as they are now. And so Arkansas Tom, whose real name was Roy Daugherty, resumed his profession as a bank robber, which lasted until he was killed in a shootout with lawmen on August 16, 1924, near Joplin, Missouri.

Ironically, if there was a "Rose of Cimarron," even one with less bravery than her myth extolls, she was probably Rose (or "Rosa") Dunn, and her association with Bitter Creek would not help his escape but, years later, indirectly cause his death. Or so goes one story that, until recently, was widely believed. Supposedly, her three brothers in Payne County were notorious cattle thieves and were arrested for that crime by Deputy Marshal Frank Canton. In order to avoid charges, the Dunn brothers came to an agreement with Marshal E. D. Nix, promising to alert him if they saw any of the remaining Doolin gang members, notably Charley Pierce and Newcomb, who (because of Rose's romantic relationship with Bitter Creek) they knew well. They also learned that Newcomb and Pierce had rewards of $5,000 each for their capture, dead or alive. In May 1895 the Dunns lured the pair to their ranch, where they were murdered as they slept. The bodies were loaded into the back of a wagon and covered with a tarp during a trip to town to claim the bounty. During the journey, Bee Dunn (himself later killed by Frank Canton) noticed that the tarp was moving and threw it back to discover that Bitter Creek, although his brains were exposed, was not quite dead but only unconscious. So he shot him again through the head.[14]

Sometime in 1893 Captain Jack joined the Atchison, Topeka & Santa Fe (ATSF) railroad, and in 1894 was described as their "Chief Detective."[15] Also by 1894—perhaps indicating a middle-level management shakeup at the Katy—his former boss and friend, J. J. Frey, had similarly secured employment at the ATSF as a general manager, as had (in 1893) his assistant at the Katy, Mr. E. F. Taylor, who would retire or be replaced by 1894. Although the corporate headquarters were in Boston, the ATSF's operational headquarters were in Topeka, Kansas, the town where it had been founded in 1859 by Cyrus K. Holliday, a town to which, at some unknown date late in 1893, Captain Jack moved with his family into a three-story house he had built at 1435 Topeka Avenue. His duties were probably much the same as they had been for the Katy, the difference being where he performed them. Although the Katy was primarily a north-south railroad, the ATSF stretched from Chicago in the east to a complicated crisscross of lines in Kansas, one branch going south through Oklahoma City down eventually, by way of Dallas–Ft. Worth, to Galveston (with a spur up to Houston), and another heading west through Santa Fe and Albuquerque, continuing on to both Los Angeles and San Francisco.

Among his first duties at the ATSF was attending to the enormous amount of work generated by the opening of the Cherokee Strip (or Outlet) on September 16, 1893. The Strip, which consisted of over six million acres, was the location for the largest of Oklahoma's land runs. It had attracted a crowd of over one hundred thousand prospective settlers, boomers and sooners, land speculators, and adventurers, plus pickpockets and crooks of every stripe, most of whom traveled to the borders by train, creating considerable railroad logistical difficulties. Once they arrived, the huge masses impatiently waited for the starting gun (except for those who tried to sneak across sooner—hence "sooners"), precipitating a mad rush whereby the homesteaders, riding everything from ancient Conestoga ox-drawn wagons to bicycles, would stake their claims.[16] Above all, this presented an immense crowd control problem, requiring all available police personnel in addition to military troops. On September 13, 1893, Captain Jack, writing on his new ATSF stationery, describes the scene to his wife Elizabeth:

> I leave this a.m. for the opening of the Cherokee strip. I have to place men at several points in the strip. There never was known such a rush of people to any place as there is to the opening of the strip. . . . I am feeling well but working hard. Love and kisses to yourself and the children.
> From your husband,
> Jno J. Kinney.

Captain Jack must have soon discovered that, in at least one respect, his new position was a disappointment. On June 30, 1891, he had proudly recorded in his diary that the MKT was finally able to emerge from bankruptcy. But the ATSF, along with many other railroads and businesses, was in 1893 just about to be forced into bankruptcy. Financial panic had

> broadened into a major depression. In the following year [1894] railroad traffic for the second time in history suffered an absolute decline. Railroad construction fell off drastically, reaching its lowest point since 1851. . . . By the end of June, 1894, more than 40,818 miles and one-fourth of the capitalization of American railroads were in the hands of receivers. Three-fifths of railroad stocks paid no dividends. . . . During the worst months of 1894 it is safe to conclude that as much as 20 per cent of the labor force was unemployed. In New York the police at one time estimated that 67,280 were out of work and 20,000 more were not only out of work but

homeless and vagrant. In Chicago, more than 100,000 were jobless during the winter of 1893–94.[17]

Still, unemployment breeds crime, providing people like Captain Jack with job security, and railroads were, as they had been for some time, leading targets of opportunity for robbers. One such attempted robbery—of the Colorado and Utah westbound passenger express on the Santa Fe tracks near Gorin, Missouri, early in the morning of September 18, 1894—became (with the exception of the Collins murder in 1898) Captain Jack's last major case.

The Gorin robbery generated national news coverage, every bit as much as that at Adair, resulting in headlines from Bangor, Maine, to Fresno, California, which is astonishing considering that the robbers weren't famous outlaws like the Daltons, but young Missouri farmers who were probably, like much of the rest of the population, down on their luck. However, any sympathy for their impoverished condition would have quickly vanished, given their behavior as the robbery began. This was almost certainly their first train robbery, but despite their inexperience, they had obviously given some thought to planning the details of their crime. One matter that never occurred to them to consider was that one of their members, W. E. McDaniel (also spelled "McDaniels" and "MacDonald"), was, in fact, a spy.

As best as I can now reconstruct from the many conflicting accounts, some three weeks before the robbery, Mr. McDaniel appeared in one of the local Missouri offices of the Santa Fe railroad, asked to speak to a detective, and, upon being introduced to Mr. J. A. Matthews, announced that he wished to confess.[18] He had fallen in with bad companions who were plotting to rob a train as it carried the weekly Santa Fe payroll, an amount they estimated to be nearly $50,000. He was basically a good man (obviously I'm guessing at the details here), and didn't want his conscience burdened by such a deed. Nor could he bear the thought that people might be hurt, even killed, if the robbery took place. As expiation for his sins, for even being tempted to participate in such a foul plot, he wanted to maintain the pretense of cooperating with his evil companions, but he would secretly provide the railroad with all the particulars necessary to anticipate and prevent the crime. Perhaps the railroad might, in return, reward his modest services with a cash sum?[19] Agent Matthews, whether he believed McDaniel or not, would have immediately wired this information to Captain Jack in Topeka, who in turn would have, accompanied by his new assistant Mr. G. C. Montgomery, left east on the next train.

Clearly, McDaniel was a spy, but it is by no means clear exactly for whom he was spying. Possibly his confession was sincere—but a grand jury later didn't think so. More likely, he had conceived a remarkably clever and devious scheme, a way (so he thought) he would profit, regardless of how the robbery turned out. Perhaps the robbery would succeed, despite—or because of—the information, or misinformation, he supplied to the railroad. In that case, he would be due a share in $50,000, then a fabulous sum (roughly a million dollars in today's money). If the robbery failed, he could take credit for its failure, earning the reward a grateful railroad would surely offer. The most ingenious part of his plan was that by securing the trust of both sides—and he already had the trust of his fellow outlaws—he would then put himself in a position where, within reason, he could decide the outcome. The only downside of this scheme is that he would actually have to participate in the robbery, a dangerous business. But even that angle he was able to cover: "Orders were given that no matter if every one of the robbers got away, there was to be no shooting to endanger the life of the spy, who had in fact taken his life in his hands in order to frustrate the robbery."[20]

The criminals chose the spot for their robbery with cunning intelligence. The nearest night telegraph station was ten miles away in La Plata. The rail line at that point was but a single track, requiring eastbound trains to switch out at Hurdeland to allow the western express to pass. This further meant that the railroad personnel were used to being flag stopped anywhere along the section, as they would be if there was any question as to the positions of trains heading their way. The terrain was also favorable for such an enterprise:

> It is also evident they made a careful study of the topography of the country. For nearly a thousand feet before the spot at which the red light was swung across the rails the road winds on a reverse course through a cut, with embankments from ten to forty feet high. Then comes a little fill, followed by a stretch of track almost on a level with the surrounding country. On either side of the right-of-way are dense clumps of oak and hickory, not to mention an undergrowth as bad as that of the northern Michigan pine woods. But the

timber, though apparently thick and impenetrable, is only so for less than a quarter mile from the track. Beyond that the country stretches practically clear and is easily traversed almost to the Iowa line.[21]

The law enforcement officials quickly devised a plan. McDaniel was ordered to assume responsibility for flagging the train, which he was to do by waving a red lantern in a certain way and also by placing a torpedo (a pressure-activated firecracker used to signal danger) at a certain spot on the track. By these measures, the officials could determine whether the stop was for criminal purposes. The railroad guards would, singly or in small groups, unobtrusively board the train at various stops up the line, in order to avoid attracting the notice of any accomplices the robbers might have aboard the train. Such men were to be dispersed in the engine and tender, the mail car, and the smoker, with most of them in the smoker. The engineer, fireman, conductor, and other employees were advised of the situation and ordered to make no resistance. Stockton, the Wells Fargo superintendent, had converted the express car into a deadly fortress. The express messenger was told, in the event of a holdup, to let the robbers in the car—and then, as fast as he could, to get out of the way. In the rear of the car, behind a barricade of cotton bales, heavy merchandise, and piles of stout trunks, lay concealed seven guards, all armed with "specially modified" Winchesters (more about that later) and Colt revolvers. The robbers were to be given one chance to surrender and shot down if they didn't.

The Colorado and Utah express left the Polk Street station in Chicago on a rainy Sunday afternoon, September 2, 1894. Early Monday morning, the train passed the section where the robbery was expected, but nothing happened. Detective Matthews, who was the link to the spy McDaniel, reported that the gang (who all lived on nearby farms) had indeed assembled and started for the track, but became discouraged by the heavy rain, which they argued would make them easier to follow after the robbery was over. Again, this may have been the truth. But it could also be that McDaniel, whose profit would be far greater if the robbery actually succeeded, knew they had no chance that night given the forces arrayed against them. Conceivably, McDaniel may have even told his associates that he was pretending to be a spy for the railroad, convincing them that his knowledge of the railroad's precautions would increase their own chances of success. This may have been the plan from the outset, providing the railroad with what would prove to be a false alarm, after which, when everybody relaxed and procedures returned to normal, an actual robbery would come as a complete surprise.

But if that was the plan, it didn't work, and so the next Sunday, September 9, when the express again left the Polk Street station, the guards were all on alert. But as before, it passed through without incident. Captain Jack was later reported, in reaction to this, to be "badly chagrined."[22] McDaniel again claimed that the robbers had turned back, discouraged by the still-muddy ground, but this time, Captain Jack checked out his story and sent two men to examine the trail the robbers supposedly had followed. His men reported that indeed, a party estimated to number eight riders had passed that way. If he wasn't suspicious from the outset, Captain Jack would have certainly by then been wary of McDaniel's claims, and it is likely that he gave the spy a lecture on the legal consequences of providing false information. Captain Jack resolved to repeat the run one more time, and McDaniel, reasoning that a small actual reward was better than a large potential return, and likely further aware of the increasing suspicion directed at himself, silently vowed this next time to let the robbery proceed.

So yet a third time, the Colorado and Utah No. 5 express left Chicago at 5:00 P.M. on September 16. The train, as it approached Gorin, was driven by "Dad" Prescott, "the white-bearded engineer." F. M. Wilson was the Pullman conductor. George Blue was the general conductor. J. P. Mooney attended the rear brakes. Fred McGraw, the regular fireman, was relaxing somewhere in the train, having been replaced at Joliet by a gentleman—Captain Jack himself—clad in blue jumpers, "looking for all the world like an apprentice to the art of firing an engine."[23] In addition to his shovel, Captain Jack had a double-barreled shotgun nearby.

Kinney may have been armed with one of Wells Fargo's specially designed double-barreled shotguns, originally developed to protect stagecoaches but still in widespread use during the 1890s. Each barrel contained a charge of twenty-one pellets, prompting one expert in its use—Wyatt Earp, who at one point rode shotgun for Wells Fargo—to explain that firing both barrels "means a shower of forty-two leaden messengers . . . each fit to take a man's life or break a bone if it should reach the right spot." Earp further extolls the virtues of this weapon: "the Wells-Fargo shot gun is not a scientific weapon. It is not a sportsmanlike weapon. It is not a weapon wherewith to settle an affair of honor between gentlemen. But, oh! in the hands of a honest man hemmed in by skulking outlaws it is a sweet and a thrice-blessed thing. The express company made me a present of the gun with which they armed me when I entered their service, and I have it still."[24] Anyone doubting the power of such a weapon is invited to view the death picture of Bill Doolin, included in this book.

Kinney's new chief assistant, G. C. Montgomery, was similarly armed and concealed in the coal tender behind. Other guards had boarded at Streator, Galesburg, and Fort Madison and dispersed themselves throughout the train. Sheriff H. H. Saling of Scott County and City Marshal L. E. Bryne, in whose jurisdictions Gorin was located, were aboard with deputies. Superintendent Stockton and four guards were barricaded in the express car. The express messenger, whose name I have been unable to discover, was nervously sitting in the front of the car, listening to Stockton brag about his rifle, wondering whether he could get out of the way safely when the firing started.

Stockton, it seems, was a firearms collector, and he fancied himself a gunsmith and ammunition technician. His Winchester rifle, which he had sawed off for the occasion, was a Winchester with a history: "It belonged to Bill Dalton, and it was but poetic justice to turn it loose upon followers in the footsteps of the Kansas desperado."[25] Now, there may be good reasons for sawing off a Winchester, although doing so will greatly decrease its accuracy. So shortened, the gun will be more maneuverable, an advantage in the close confines of the express car, where the fight was expected to take place. The rifle is also more easily concealed, which cannot have mattered to Stockton's force, already hidden in the car, but may have been a factor in convincing many of the other guards, instructed to board unobtrusively, to adopt similar hardware. Stockton further decided to modify the Winchester's factory cartridge loads, which would have a significant bearing on the following fight. As reported by the *Fort Wayne Weekly Sentinel:* "But it was in the forward end of the smoking car that the forces were massed. A partition and door incloses [sic] half a dozen seats and shuts off the rest of the car from it. There the men, a dozen of them, were planted. Each had one of the 'sawed-offs,' every cartridge loaded especially for the event with two dozen buckshot by Superintendent Stockton" (September 18, 1894, 1). This assertion is repeated in many of the accounts, although the Ogden, Utah, *Standard* sensibly lowers the number of "buckshot" packed in each cartridge to a single dozen (still too many).

Again, this tampering may have made sense for the guards in the express car—but only there. In effect, they had converted their Winchesters into quick-firing shotguns, which could be expected to be quite lethal at short ranges. But the crucial point that seems to have been overlooked is that the Winchester's firing chamber and extractor mechanism can only fire and eject a cartridge, however it is packed, of a fixed dimension. The more buckshot you load up front, the less gunpowder you can load behind. The trade-off is between the weight and dispersal of the projectiles and their velocity. The result is that many of the train's guards, who must have thought that these new rounds looked especially deadly, were going into a fight with short-loaded weapons.

The *Fort Wayne Weekly Sentinel* describes how the engagement began:

In the little compartment filled with armed men the lights were out [the time was approximately 3:30 in the morning] and the windows were up. In each seat were two men sitting sideways, the muzzles of their guns protruding just a trifle over the sills. Behind them stood others, seemingly statues, with Winchesters at the half-cock, resting on their arms. They were waiting for the torpedo.

Out from between two high embankments, just one mile from Gorin, sped the train. One minute more and the anxious watchers would know whether they again had their labor in vain. Then came the crack [of the railway torpedo]. There was but one. A moment and a shrill, sharp whistle gave token that the engineer had heard, and almost before his hand had left the valve, across the tracks, not fifty yards away, swung a red light. A grinding of the wheels along the rails told that the air had been applied, and within twenty seconds from the explosion of the torpedo the train was at a standstill. (September 18, 1894, 1)

After two false starts, McDaniel had finally fulfilled his pledge to appease his conscience (and perhaps fatten his wallet) by betraying his comrades, who began slipping out of the underbrush, surrounding the train. At the caboose, brakeman Mooney dismounted and saw two men holding five horses a short distance away. One of them left the horses, ran toward Mooney, shoved a pistol in his face, robbed him of $19, and ordered him back aboard. But it was at the engine where the real action began, when the gang's leader, Charles Abrams, approached the cab as his four or five (accounts vary) accomplices rushed the express car. "We have got you!" he shouted, ten feet away from white-whiskered "Dad" Prescott. "Hold up your hands!"

By 1894, train robbing was something of a well-established profession, and like many professions, it was conducted by a set of unwritten rules, one of which was that if the trainmen complied with the outlaw's orders, they would usually not be shot. Instead, betraying his inexperience, or brutality, or both, Abrams decided that the aged "Dad" was not moving fast enough and shot him in the chest. "The bullet," reported the *Atlanta Constitution*, "struck him in the breast, glanced from his collar bone, and fell on his shirt front, beneath his blouse" (September 19, 1894, 1). This shot also shattered all of the guards' carefully laid plans, for it signaled the frenzied and unpredictable behavior of a dangerous madman who had to be stopped immediately. So Captain Jack, in his coal-smudged blue overalls, jumped on top of the tender and, with a resolute action that perhaps exorcised some of Adair's lingering ghosts, leveled his shotgun at the robber's face, and fired off both barrels.[26] As reported by the *Fort Wayne Weekly Sentinel:* "His [Abrams'] aim was true, and 'Dad' fell to the floor of his cab with a bullet in his right breast. With one bound Kinney gained the top of the tender, and bringing his gun to his shoulder, sent a load of shot almost into the face of the masked individual. How on earth the fellow ever managed to move six inches is a mystery; but he did, and made for the woods" (September 18, 1894, 1). The *Fort Wayne Gazette* described the event almost identically: "Chief Detective Keney [*sic*] jumped from the cab to the coal on the tender and thrusting his gun in the face of the man who had shot Prescott, pulled the trigger. How it was that the robber escaped having his head blown off no one seems to know" (September 19, 1894, 1).

Did Captain Jack flinch at this crucial moment? How could anybody survive being shot in the face at "point blank range" (as reported by the Oshkosh *Daily Northwestern*) by a double-barreled shotgun? Many of the accounts (*Atlanta Constitution, Fresno Weekly Republican*) describe the blast as being "full in the face." Others (*Ogden Standard, Fort Wayne Weekly Sentinel*) qualify this by saying "almost" full in the face. The *Colorado Springs Gazette* provides the most detailed description of the wounds the robber suffered: "Abrams wound was made with a load of buckshot fired from close range and from above, striking him in the right shoulder and ranging downward. There is slight chance of his recovery" (September 19, 1894, 1). I'm inclined to believe this latter account, which would seem to indicate that, wherever Captain Jack was aiming, the charge actually hit the robber's shoulder. Unless the shotgun contained defective cartridges or cartridges that had been tampered with (and there was a lot of that going on), there is little chance a person could survive a blast to the face, let alone, as Abrams did, later walk sixteen miles back to his farm. If his intent was to blow the man's head off, Captain Jack missed, but I don't think he flinched. An important point here is that he fired the shotgun after leaping atop the loose and shifting coal piled in the tender, which is far from a stable firing platform.

The fight—a rather one-sided fight, between some five outlaws and maybe as many as twenty guards—was on. The detectives in the smoker immediately began blasting away with their sawed-offs, pumping out rounds at the quickly retreating bandits. Superintendent Stockton and his men charged out from behind their barricade, jumped from the express car, and began firing their modified Winchesters as fast as they could lever the actions. G. C. Montgomery with his shotgun would have rushed from his hiding place to Captain Jack's side, defending him while Kinney reloaded his own shotgun. Sheriff Saling and his deputies were similarly blazing away. The *Fort Wayne Weekly Sentinel* describes the action:

> The shot which laid Engineer Prescott low was the signal for a fusillade, and was echoed and re-echoed from bank to bank and through the woods. It was also a signal for a hasty retreat to the shelter of the timber on the part of the greatly surprised individuals whose features were hidden by masks. Not until they reached the timber did they answer; then they only fired two shots. But their aim was not good, and although men were leaning from the car windows and pulling the triggers as fast as possible, while others had jumped to the earth and were after them on foot, they failed to hit a man. (September 18, 1894, 1)

However furious this protective barrage was, it was not accurate, and one would be forced to agree with the Stevens Point, Wisconsin, *Gazette,* as they subheadlined their account, that the guards "Did Some Mighty Poor Shooting." "The peculiarity of this affair," so the

Gazette continues, "is that any of the gang got away alive." Kinney "up and shot the robber with a double-barreled shotgun, while the men in cars poured a volley of bullets into the gang, or over it—for it seems that nobody was hurt" (September 26, 1894, 1). Indeed, the only casualty besides "Dad" Prescott and Abrams was Abrams' gray horse, which was killed as it galloped north: "A well directed shot brought it low, but there was no rider on its back." Almost certainly, the poor marksmanship was not the result of high firing but from the short-loaded rounds, exactly the wrong type of ammunition to use in a fight over any distance. The lesson here is that too much planning can be as dangerous as too little, in that the more complex the plan, the greater the number of assumptions—like the range at which the fight will occur—that may or may not prove true.

Inside the train, many of the passengers panicked, adding to the general confusion. The Sandusky, Ohio, *Register* provides one such account:

> It is not likely the passengers in the rear and those who were dozing in the chair car and a half a dozen or so sleepless ones in the sleepers will ever forget the experience. With the first shot every man near a window opened it and looked out. With the second he drew his head in and when the volleying commenced he hadn't time to close the window, but just dropped flat down on the floor of the car. Then [the shout of] "train robbers" went through the train and women went down on their knees, lifted their hands and screamed vigorously and persistently as if a mouse was in sight. It was absolutely impossible to walk through the cars without climbing over the seats. When the excitement was at its height, the brakeman put his head in the door and shouted: "Keep your heads down, ladies and gentlemen. Train robbers are outside" (September 19, 1894, 1).

Two women ran shrieking from their sleeper berths and attempted to jump off the train in their nightgowns, but they were captured and restrained by Conductor Blue who "forcibly prevailed on them to go back to bed."

F. M. Wilson, the Pullman conductor, described a similar scene in an interview he provided to the *Colorado Springs Gazette:*

> Such a scramble for safe places . . . I never witnessed. The women were frantic in their endeavors to get out the way and the

men no less eager, showing as much fright as they could possibly display. Some lay flat on the floor, others concealed themselves in their berths or clambered underneath, while others ran frantically up and down the aisles, apparently bewildered.

One man, probably about 50 years of age, when the shooting began to be fierce, knelt down in the aisle and prayed long and loud for deliverance. (September 19, 1894, 1)

Conductor George Blue notes what happened to the outlaws, led by Lincoln Overfield, who split off from Abrams and charged the express car:

I was in the rear part of the train when I heard the engineer answer the flagman's signal. The train soon came to a standstill, and in a few minutes I heard gun shots. I hurried back and sent out my flagman to protect the rear end of the train. By the time this was done, the firing began. When I reached the ground I saw three men by the side of the express car. One man fell to the ground and I suppose he was shot. Whether or not he was able to get up or was carried away by his pals, I do not know. The other two men went in under the car and escaped to the south. They did not get away immediately, however, for they were surrounded by the guards who began shooting rapidly. On either side of the track there is a dense timber and the robbers had only to run a few feet to get under cover. (*Colorado Springs Gazette,* September 19, 1894, 1)

With that the fight ended, the robbers fleeing for their lives through the thick woods, the deputies quickly organizing themselves into search parties, assisted by bloodhounds, in close pursuit.[27] But it was too dark. Sheriff Saling examined the dead horse and recognized the saddle. He knew the horse's owner. He knew where its owner lived. "Dad" Prescott was unloaded from the train and taken to a house nearby, where he was attended by Dr. Cruickshank, a railroad doctor who happened to be aboard.[28] Fireman McGraw assumed the controls for the remainder of the trip west, leaving one to wonder who shoveled coal for the rest of this journey.

The next morning, Sheriff Saling gathered a posse and, as described by the *Fresno Weekly Republican,* captured four men:

Memphis, Mo., September 18—Chas. Abrams and Lincoln Overfield, two of the farmer bandits arrested for their part in the attempted Santa Fe robbery, were only captured after a stubborn fight. Both had made their way directly to their homes, situated sixteen miles south east from here in a lonely part of the country.

Abrams, who had received a full load of buckshot in the face, was compelled to walk the entire distance, it being his horse that was killed by the detectives. Arrived at home, Abrams was secreted behind a dresser, and when Sheriff Saling and his posse came to the house soon after his arrival, he was in a faint. When he knew that escape was impossible he made a bold attempt to stand off his captors with a revolver. The officers had the drop on him and he finally gave in. Search for the other bandits was resumed.

At the farm of Mrs. Tull nearby the officers found Overfield, who had crawled under a bed. The house was first surrounded. Mrs. Tull and her two daughters stoutly denied that Overfield was in the house. Overfield showed fight when he was discovered. A fierce struggle ensued with the bandit, but he was finally overpowered. Then both men, with two brothers of Overfield, upon whom suspicion also rests, were handcuffed and taken to Memphis. (September 21, 1894, 1)

The following day, while in jail "awaiting the action of the Grand Jury," reported the *Reno Weekly Gazette and Stockman,* "Overfield, beyond admitting that he was present at the scene of the attempted robbery, refuses to talk. He lies in bed with his head covered, crying most of the time. Charles Abrams, the dying robber, says that the informer, McDaniel, planned the robbery and coaxed the others into it" (September 20, 1894). He was believed. The *Fresno Weekly Republican* records the aftermath:

W. E. McDaniel, informer of the Gorin, Mo., train robbery fame, was held to appear before the grand jury on $1500 bail upon the charge of conspiring to rob a train. He pleaded not guilty to the information filed against him before Justice C. F. Sanders, and so far has failed to secure bondsmen, his own father refusing to go on his bond. He persists in his story that he had nothing to do with planning the robbery, simply followed Overfield's instructions and also keeping the railroad company informed. (October 5, 1894, 1)

At their trials—there could be little doubt as to their guilt—the robbers continued to accuse each other of masterminding the plot, with

McDaniel (as reported by the *Atlanta Constitution*, October 12, 1894)
asserting that Overfield "had planned the robbery over three years
ago." Almost certainly, they were convicted and sentenced to the penitentiary.[29] That is, all except one of them, who the railroad and authorities declined to prosecute under the charming legal theory that
he was a "simple minded and harmless sort of fellow."[30]

CONCLUSION

To be nameless in worthy deeds exceeds an infamous history.
    —*Sir Thomas Browne*

Here Captain Jack's trail largely disappears, at least insofar as I can now follow it, with only a few dim markers of how his life continued. He maintained his interest in Republican politics, and as a reward for his services to the party (of which he was once the Pettis County chairman) was appointed as assistant sergeant of arms at the 1896 convention that nominated McKinley for president. On April 30, 1896, eight representatives of seven western railroads gathered in the lobby of the Savoy Hotel in Kansas City, Missouri, for the purpose of forming the Railway Special Agents' Association of the United States and Canada. Captain Jack was elected the first president of this body, which, under different names, existed until the 1980s. He resigned from the Atchison, Topeka & Santa Fe railroad sometime in 1900, involving himself in various short-lived mining and retail ventures, and for a while he bought a partial ownership interest in the Coughlin Hardware Company in Topeka. At some point he became active in the Knights of Columbus and was elected the Grand Knight of Topeka Lodge No. 534 from 1902 to 1904.

He was certainly living in Topeka during the great flood. In late May 1903, the Kaw River began flooding, resulting in one of the worst natural disasters in Topeka's history. Before it was over, all of north Topeka was under water, at some places to a depth of ten feet. In addition, the flood caused a major fire, and first reports (greatly exaggerated) were that as many as 350 people had died and that some 8,000 were homeless. This was well before the days of federal disaster relief, although President Roosevelt did send the following telegram to Governor Bailey:

Cheyenne, Wy. May 31—Hon. W. T. Bailey, Topeka, Kan.—Am shocked at the calamity that has befallen Topeka. If there is anything the federal authorities can do, of course, let me know.

(Signed) Theodore Roosevelt

Because most of the railroad bridges were under water, there was little anybody could do, and for days, hundreds of people were stranded in trees and on rooftops. "The work of relief is being carried on nobly," reported the *Fort Wayne Weekly Sentinel* (June 3, 1903, 1); "fraternal aid societies, banks, and commercial societies are bending every energy to the stricken. A city of tents will be erected on the high ground. A thousand have been secured and the chances are that they will be inhabited for at least a month." The actual number of drownings in Topeka was twenty-nine, with some 4,000 having to abandon their homes. Captain Jack was prominent among those helping in the aftermath. The record indicates that he organized and chaired a committee to raise relief funds for the victims. In 1905 he served as a trustee for the Knights' executive council. But one of the great enemies of history is fire, and just as many of the Katy records were similarly destroyed, any further information about those years was lost when, on May 15, 1962, a Knights of Columbus records repository burned.

Selling hardware could not interest such a man for long. Because law enforcement seemed to be in his very blood, he accepted a position with the Metropolitan Police Department of Kansas City.[1] As late as 1908 there is a mention of a "Detective Kinney" escorting by rail a prisoner (something he would often do) wanted for theft of an automobile[2] to Chicago, a brief story that was newsworthy in that the prisoner—taking a "desperate chance to regain liberty"—jumped from the window of a speeding Pullman car and escaped. Kinney kept active to the end of his life. In early 1918, the year he died, he was appointed a member of an auxiliary committee of the Knights of Columbus "War Fund," a national effort to raise $3 million to provide "recreation centers" for the troops both at home and abroad. This subscription was endorsed by such spiritual and secular notables as Woodrow Wilson, Teddy Roosevelt, William Taft, William Jennings Bryant, and Pope Benedict himself.[3] He died in Kansas City at the age of sixty-six, and is there buried in St. Mary's Cemetery.

He had been born into a time of horses and carriages, currycombs and candles, sailing ships, surreys, saddles, and steam engines. He had arrived in an uncertain country about to tear itself apart with civil war. He saw Winchesters evolve into tommy guns, telegraphs become telephones, and women verge on the vote. He died amidst electric streetcars and airplanes, movies and automobiles, radios and radium, traffic lights and temperance, leaving behind a country just establishing itself as a major player on the world's stage. One of the few constants in his life were the railroads—and he was, to his core, a railroad man.

So as well ends the family story. Time for the diary and the fading, tattered clippings, wrapped in their plastic shrouds, to be reinterred in the file cabinet's dark crypt, allowed finally to regain their perpetual sleep in the black infinity of past information. I'd be surprised if there are not other stories, similarly told by other families, about how their ancestors figured in the minor incident of July 14, 1892, the night when Daltons and destiny, chance and necessity, briefly conspired to include them in an event by which they would be rescued, if only temporarily, from the complete historical anonymity to which most of us are doomed. Although I'm not at all sure I have been able to preserve from decay "the remembrance of what men have done," I can hope, more modestly, to have revisited some of one man's experiences, at least those parts of them he thought to preserve and thereby share. I'll never know whether my account accurately mirrors what happened that night, for history is not a smooth mirror but a rough and partial mosaic created by the fractured tiles of stories most of which we will never hear, stories equally supported by facts as solid as the painted red silhouettes on Coffeyville's streets and as fanciful as the giant spiders of Hermosillo. Time past is a potter's field where lie buried, shallow and deep, the urns of lives and deeds that shatter as they are exhumed, the brittle shards and recumbent dust only remaining to suggest the flesh of moments long dead.

Let me conclude by making it clear that the point of this account is not to bemoan Captain Jack's fate as a human footnote, an historical afterthought. That's more than most of us will achieve. I'm not nominating him as the Fourth or Fifth Guardsman. Most of his work was routine (but so was theirs). I'm not saying he deserves to be better remembered. It's quite something that he is remembered at all. Life afforded him certain challenges, and he met them to the best of his abilities, not always successfully. It's hard to imagine Heck Thomas complaining—as Captain Jack wrote in his diary on August 7, 1891—that his hotel bed in Rhome, Texas, was "too rocky to sleep in."

Bill Tilghman or Chris Madsen would have simply unfurled their bedrolls. He was a mostly ordinary man who on one night was compelled by history to occupy a small stage in a brief role whose script thereafter threatened forever to define him. Above all, I'm not saying that history has treated him unfairly, that there is something fundamentally wrong with a culture that lavishly memorializes the Daltons but largely ignores those who fought them. Well, I suppose I really am saying something like all that, knowing my saying so can make no difference. History's harsh verdict, like that of Judge Parker, can seldom be successfully appealed. For reasons I cannot understand, reasons I'm not sure I want to understand, some historical figures, the Daltons among them, flash through time like a furious comet through space, blazing with a powerful light we can still see, their quick, bright passage briefly illuminating adjacent dark bodies we would otherwise never notice, bodies far more solid than the frenzied, fiery gas by which they attain their momentary visibility. The cosmos of history is filled with just such dark matter, men and women like Captain Jack.

Still, he made a difference in his time, and what times they were. One of his cases reached the Supreme Court, but he also gave his daughter a pair of diamond earrings on her birthday. He relentlessly pursued and captured the forger Dunn, but he also found time to take his family to the Sells Brothers Circus. He tracked down the "Sedalia Fiend" and had enough sense to let him go, but he also enjoyed baseball games and worried about suitable colleges for his children. Seldom home, riding the long western rails, greeting friends at every stop, investigating matters large but mostly small, recording the day's events and the price of meals in his Excelsior diary—he must have been a familiar figure as he repeatedly passed through the stations and depots, many of which have by now been replaced, destroyed, or similarly forgotten. And all that is but a small part of a life briefly touched by history on the night of July 14, 1892.

NOTES

INTRODUCTION

1. Other sources claim the amount stolen in this robbery was as much as $26,000. See Dale Walker, *Legends and Lies: Great Mysteries of the American West* (New York: Tom Doherty, 1997), 93.

2. Thomas J. Schlereth, *Victorian America: Transformations in Everyday Life* (New York: Harper Collins, 1991), xi.

3. Nell Irvin Painter, *Standing at Armageddon: The United States, 1877–1919* (New York: W. W. Norton, 1987), xvii.

4. Sir Thomas Browne, *Hydriotaphia (Urn Burial) and The Garden of Cyrus,* ed. F. L. Huntley (Northbrook, Ill.: AHM Publishing, 1966), 42.

CHAPTER 1

1. The Winchester Model 1873 ("The Gun that Won the West"), and its subsequent variants, was then the weapon of choice for both outlaws and lawmen. "The major advance represented by the Model 1873," writes Dean K. Boorman, "besides its stronger and lighter steel frame, was its use of the more powerful centerfire [WCF] cartridge. The nomenclature of the .44–40, the size which came out first and was the primary caliber used for the Model 1873, refers to its .44 caliber [slug] and charge of 40 grains of black powder. This compared with only 28 grains of powder used in the rimfire cartridge for the Henry and Model 1866. A larger load cannot be used in a rimfire cartridge because the metal must be thin enough to be indented by the firing pin, making the case too weak for heavy loads" (*The History of Winchester Firearms* [New York: Lyons Press, 2001], 36). Over 720,000 Model 1873s were produced from 1873 to 1924. The most common configuration allowed for a capacity of fifteen rounds in the magazine, plus one in the chamber. Another advantage is that the .44 cartridge was the same used by the popular Colt .44 revolver, eliminating the need for different types of ammunition.

2. The sources variously refer to Captain Jack's title as "chief of detectives," "special agent," or even "head" of the MKT "Secret Service." The Norfolk Southern Railroad Police Department's Web site explains that "the title 'detective' was commonly used in the East. Because the responsibility of the

railroad policeman was to protect the agency and the agent, the western railroads entitled their policemen "Special Agents" (http://www.nspolice.com/historyo.htm).

3. The express messenger, or agent, had a hard job. Carolyn Lake explains, "on trains, the Messenger rode the express car, acting as the entire express business in that car—porter, receiving and way-bill clerk, money clerk, freight deliveryman, transfer agent, route agent, cashier and auditor for the contents of his car, not to mention defending the company's safe from train robbers who always outnumbered him. He was necessarily a good man. Actually, there wasn't room in the express business for any other kind" (Fred Dodge, *Under Cover for Wells Fargo*, ed. Carolyn Lake [Norman: University of Oklahoma Press, 1969], 22).

4. Leflore County, Oklahoma, is reportedly named after him (or his family), which is a strong indication for spelling the name with an "e." Art Burton, a leading authority on the history of the Indian Police, assures me that is the correct spelling. In the newspaper clippings Captain Jack saved, the spelling is variously "Leflore," "Laflore," and "La Flore." A biographical sketch published in 1891 lists him as "Capt. Charles La Flore" (see note 15). A contemporary photograph (included in this book) identifies him similarly. In Kinney's diary, which mentions the Captain more than a dozen times, the name is always spelled "La Flore." This is the spelling I elect to use, because I have a hard time understanding how Captain Jack could so often and consistently misspell the name of a man with whom he was so closely associated.

5. See Nancy B. Samuelson, *Shoot from the Lip: The Lives, Legends, and Lies of the Three Guardsmen of Oklahoma and U.S. Marshal Nix* (Eastford, Conn.: Shooting Star Press, 1998), 12. Samuelson also claims that Madsen's service in the U.S. army was occasionally less than meritorious, in that he was court-martialed at least twice, once for stealing grain in his capacity as a quartermaster and again for shooting cattle.

6. Pryor or Pryor Creek? The original name of the town, although it was not yet then a town, was "Coo-y-Yah," which is Cherokee for "huckleberry." "Pryor" refers to Captain Nathaniel Pryor, a member of the Lewis and Clark expedition, who settled in the area around 1816. The town's Web site explains that "the white man's difficulty in both spelling and pronouncing the Cherokee name of the town soon forced postal officials to formally change the name to Pryor Creek on April 23, 1887. In 1909 the post office, for the sake of brevity, dropped the 'Creek' from the name and shortly afterward both the Katy and the map publishers followed suit. So today the city is known as Pryor, although officially it is still Pryor Creek and is so written on all legal documents." The town of Wagoner, where this account opens, is named after Henry Samuel "Bigfoot" Wagoner, who built (evi-

dently at his own expense) a switch and siding at the site, the better to load his cattle and lumber. Although the original depot no longer exists, a replacement built in 1896 featuring a passenger car and a Katy caboose now houses a roadside (Route 69) diner. The chicken-fried steak is excellent.

7. Harold Preece, *The Dalton Gang: End of an Outlaw Era* (New York: Hasting House, 1963), 200.

8. One cannot say with any certainty which members of the gang were present at any given robbery. In addition to those listed, the gang also (according to Emmett Dalton) upon occasion included Charley Bryant, Bill Power(s), and William McElhanie (also known as the "Narrow Gauge Kid").

9. Messenger F. C. (or E. C.) Whittlessy was also in charge of the express car during a later train robbery by the Doolin gang on May 30, 1893, at Cimarron, Kansas. Upon this latter occasion, Mr. Whittlessy, having by then obtained some valuable experience in such matters, succeeded in hiding $10,000 in cash and jewelry from the robbers.

10. For the record, Emmett Dalton claimed the take at Red Rock was $7,800. Whether or not the Daltons routinely (or ever) robbed passengers is a disputed point. Nancy B. Samuelson asserts that "they were, in fact, rather gentlemenly train robbers, for they never molested nor stole from a passenger, unlike many other practitioners of this profession" (*The Dalton Gang Story* [Eastford, Conn.: Shooting Star Press, 1992], 3). The *Fort Smith Elevator* (July 22, 1892), discussing the robbery at Adair, went on to state, "In all of these robberies no passenger has ever lost a dollar, and in the majority of them the express company has escaped with slight losses" (3). Evidently, the class hierarchy among train robbers dictated a higher status should one refrain from robbing passengers. A similar claim is made for the Wild Bunch by Brown Waller in *Last of the Great Western Train Robbers* (New York: A. S. Barnes, 1968), 156.

11. I'm not sure that anybody has any accurate count as to how many such robberies occurred. One source claims, with suspicious exactitude, that "between 1890 and 1900 there were 250 Western train robberies, and in that same period sixty-five lawmen were killed. No count had been kept of saloons held up, of cattle rustled, of horses stolen, but the number was great" (Floyd Miller, *Bill Tilghman: Marshal of the Last Frontier* [New York: Doubleday, 1968], 101). Miller presents no documentation for the number he cites. Another similarly undocumented source (cited by Philip L. Fradkin) asserts that "from 1890 to 1903, however, there were 341 attempted or actual train robberies, resulting in 99 deaths, mostly in the Southwest" (*Stagecoach: Wells Fargo and the American West* [New York: Simon and Schuster, 2002], 121).

12. Samuelson also supports this view (*Dalton Gang Story*, 5, 87 ff.). James Hume, then the chief detective of Wells Fargo, gives his version of

these events in Richard Dillon, *Wells, Fargo Detective: The Biography of James B. Hume* (New York: Coward-McCann, 1969), 248 ff. I might add that aside from the Alila robbery, other sources claim that the Dalton Gang had killed at least two people by 1891. After the Wharton robbery, pursuing posseman W. T. Starmer was supposedly killed by the gang, as was a telegraph operator at Red Rock (by Blackface Charley) as he called for help. See Paul Wellman, *A Dynasty of Western Outlaws* (New York: Bonanza Books, 1961), 166–67. Other accounts insist Starmer was killed shortly before the Wharton robbery in a battle with horse rustlers who may, or may not, have been the Daltons.

13. This situation cannot have pleased Mary Angelina, La Flore's beautiful wife ("Hi! We're here to see the skeleton!"). Skeletons are also notoriously difficult to dust, they attract ants, and they do not integrate well with most tasteful schemes of interior decoration.

14. The "Christie" mentioned here should not be confused with the infamous Ned Christie, whose exploits are briefly discussed in Chapter 4.

15. H. F. O'Beirne, *Leaders and Leading Men of the Indian Territory: Choctaws and Chickasaws* (Chicago: American Publishers' Association, 1891), 1:88.

16. Ibid.

17. Ibid., 1:89.

18. Although the Rangers would continue to exist under various organizational guises well beyond the date discussed here, their heroic reputation would suffer considerable eclipse. During the middle 1930s, the Texas state government offered "special commissions" in the Rangers seemingly to practically anybody who wanted one, including "liquor dealers, nightclub bouncers, gambling-house operators, barbers, dentists, and wrestling referees" (Wayne Gard, *Frontier Justice* [Norman: University of Oklahoma Press, 1949], 233).

19. The actual legal authority of railroad detectives varied widely on a state-by-state basis, a situation complicated in that Oklahoma would not become a state until 1907. The best account to date of the origins of the railroad police, including a discussion of their legal status, is in Dorothy Moses Schulz, "On the Track of—and with—Railroad Police: Separating the Real Cops and Special Agents from the Fictional Bulls and Cinder Dicks," *Proceedings*, St. Louis Mercantile Library, 2002, 19–23.

20. Pryor Creek would have been a logical place to expect a robbery. One old-timer reports that Pryor Creek was "a rather notorious spot on the line . . . which often occupied the headlines of public print as a favorite place for the boys to hold up the Missouri, Kansas & Texas trains. The spot was isolated, the natives friendly, and the escape route always open" (Joseph Bristow, *Tales of Old Fort Gibson* [New York: Exposition Press, 1961],

153). Bristow tells the story of one such robbery, during which the outlaws discovered that a passenger was a locksmith by trade. They immediately invited him, at gunpoint, to ply his skills on the express car safe. This he did so successfully that the appreciative robbers awarded him a valuable gold watch, which they had just stolen from another passenger.

21. There is some dispute as to whether Adair was a regular stop on the No. 2 route. In an almost illegible account of the incident written by the Fireman (on Form 705—Revised, Missouri, Kansas, & Texas Railroad Company, Cherokee Division, Special and Accident Report), Mr. Brandenburg seems to indicate that the train was flagged to a stop. In any event, it stopped. A photographic reproduction of this report, the entire text of which is quoted in Chapter 7, can be found in V. V. Masterson, *The Katy Railroad and the last Frontier* (Norman: University of Oklahoma Press, 1952), 256.

22. Of the vaunted Three Guardsmen, "Heck Thomas," writes Samuelson (who debunks the myths surrounding these gentlemen) "came the closest to actually living the legend" (*Shoot from the Lip,* 8). Henry Andrew Thomas, born in 1850, served in the Confederate Army as a young man. After later moving to Texas, Heck worked for the Texas Express Company and was rewarded by his employer when his quick thinking saved the company $22,000 during a train robbery by the Bass Gang in Hutchins, Texas, on March 18, 1878. In 1885 Heck was appointed as a deputy for Judge Parker's court, where by all accounts he excelled in capturing fugitives. Heck finished his career as the chief of police of Lawton, Oklahoma, and died in 1912.

23. Glen Shirley, *The Fourth Guardsman* (Austin: Eakin Press, 1977), 58–59.

24. The historical and popular accounts of the railroad police are largely negative, a situation resulting from the fact that "most of what has been written about the railroad police has been by their adversaries" (Schulz, "On the Track of—and with—Railroad Police," 19). Railroad detective Thomas Furlong, who was Captain Jack's boss at the Missouri Pacific during the 1880s, wrote that "the pettifogging lawyers and irresponsible penny liners of the press have educated [the general public into] believing that all detectives are thieves, thugs, and black guards" (*Fifty Years a Detective* [St. Louis: C. E. Barnett, 1912], 5).

25. Furlong, *Fifty Years a Detective,* 3. The title of Furlong's book was certainly intended as an insult to the far better known Pinkerton Detective Agency, whose founder, Alan Pinkerton, published in 1889 a similar autobiographical book entitled *Thirty Years a Detective.*

26. Robert C. McMath, *American Populism: A Social History 1877–1898* (New York: Hill and Wang, 1993), 75–76.

27. Cockfighting was illegal in all but three states—Louisiana, New Mexico, and Oklahoma. Cockfighting remains legal in Louisiana and New Mexico, but Oklahoma passed a law in 2002 banning it, although the law is widely ignored. Zoe Tilghman reports that Kinney's interest in game chickens was shared by both Bill Tilghman and Heck Thomas (see *Marshal of the Last Frontier* [Glendale, Calif.: Arthur H. Clark, 1949, 1964)], 191).

28. *New Yorker,* March 24, 2003, 80.

29. Ben Townsend, "Buried Loot in Oklahoma," *Lost Treasure Magazine,* May 1977, 13.

30. Readers with metal detectors may be interested in Townsend's conclusion that the Daltons buried their loot "in the rolling hills near Grayhorse." Kinney saved a clipping from the *Saint Louis Globe-Democrat,* October 6, 1892, which quotes Emmett Dalton (who survived the Coffeyville raid the day before but was thought to be on his deathbed) as follows:

> The story of a hidden treasure, he said, was nonsense. "If there had been a treasure," he said, "we would all have been alive today. It was because we were all broke that we planned the Coffeyville raid. We were being hard pressed by the officers down in the Territory, and Bob decided that we would have to get out of the country. He planned the robbery about two weeks ago, while we were in the Osage country. He said he would out-do the James boys' exploits and raid both banks at the same time." It was with great difficulty that the bandit told his story, as he was suffering terrible agony from the wound in his side. The physician attending him says he can not possibly recover.

Despite having been shot (by some accounts) more than thirty times, primarily with buckshot, Emmett would live until 1937, having been employed (after his pardon in 1907) as a special police officer in Tulsa, Oklahoma, and later as an "authenticity consultant" by the movie industry. He died—where else?—in Hollywood, California.

31. Emmett Dalton, *Beyond the Law* (Coffeyville, Kans.: Coffeyville Historical Society, [1918]), 121.

CHAPTER 2

1. In another version of these events, Temple's friend, ex-sheriff Jack Love, also actively participated in the fight. See Glen Shirley, *Temple Houston: Lawyer with a Gun* (Norman: University of Oklahoma Press, 1980), 212 ff. For the information about Houston inspiring Yancey Cravet, see Nancy Samuelson, *Shoot from the Lip: The Lives, Legends, and Lies of the Three Guardsmen of Oklahoma and U.S. Marshal Nix* (Eastford, Conn.: Shooting Star Press, 1998), 137. The story about Houston shooting up the courtroom

is in Jay Robert Nash, *Encyclopedia of Western Lawmen and Outlaws* (New York: Da Capo Press, 1994), 168. Also see Shirley, *Temple Houston,* 3–7. The structure in which the Cabinet saloon was located still stands in historic downtown Woodward, and it still presides over mayhem of a more modern sort, housing as it does the local offices of a nationally syndicated tax preparation firm.

2. See Zoe Tilghman, *Marshal of the Last Frontier* (Glendale, Calif.: Arthur H. Clark, 1949), 241. I should note that the available historical record is confused as to exactly when and what Al robbed. Although most criminals are on some level ashamed of their acts, Jennings instead took delight in his notoriety, to the point where he would later imply his involvement in crimes unlikely to have been committed by his gang. For another account of Jennings's criminal history, which differs significantly in some of the details I have presented, see Michael Tower, *Dialing "911" Was Not an Option! Tales of Lawlessness Along the Middle Washita River* (privately published, 2004), 98–99.

3. Reproduced in Glen Shirley, *The Fourth Guardsman* (Austin, Tex.: Eakin Press, 1997), 72–73.

4. Ibid., 162–63.

5. Zoe Tilghman's remarks are from *Marshal,* 311.

6. Thomas Schlereth, *Victorian America: Transformations in Everyday Life* (New York: Harper Collins, 1991), 202–3. Film historian David Cook has some minor quibbles with Schlereth's account, asserting that the movie was filmed in Paterson, New Jersey, and lasted more than twelve minutes. Both agree that the film was a great success: "So spectacular was the commercial success of *The Great Train Robbery* that the film was studied and imitated by film-makers all over the world. It is frequently credited with establishing the realistic narrative, as opposed to the fantastic narrative of Melies, as the dominant cinematic form from Porter's day to our own" (David Cook, *A History of Narrative Film* [New York: W. W. Norton, 1981], 27). Nor was such success momentary. Frank Beaver writes in *On Film: A History of the Motion Picture* (New York: McGraw-Hill, 1983), "The sensational nature of *The Great Train Robbery* caused this motion picture to remain the most popular film in the United States for at least a half-dozen years after its release" (50).

7. Zoe Tilghman, *Marshal,* 310–11.

8. Shirley, *Fourth Guardsman,* 164.

9. Dale Walker, *Legends and Lies: Great Mysteries of the American West* (New York: Tom Doherty, 1997), 104.

10. See Nancy B. Samuelson, *The Dalton Gang Story* (Eastford, Conn.: Shooting Star Press, 1992), 164.

11. Samuelson claims Roosevelt witnessed the demonstration "in the spring of 1905," and that it occurred in the Oklahoma Territory. See *Shoot from the Lip*, 88. Another version of this story can be found in Colonel Charles W. Mooney, *Doctor Jesse* (Oklahoma City: Pro-Graphics, 1978), 172 ff.

12. See Samuelson, *Shoot from the Lip*, 90–91.

13. Further details of this remarkable story can be found in Zoe Tilghman, *Marshal*, 312–15. I should add that other sources (see Samuelson, *Shoot from the Lip*, 109) indicate that the wolf-wrestling clips were released as a separate short titled "The Wolf Hunt."

14. Bill Neeley, *The Last Comanche Chief* (New York: Wiley, 1995), 223. Parker died on February 23, 1911. Also of some interest is that one of his earliest biographers was the prolific Zoe Tilghman, who published *Quanah, the Eagle of the Comanches* in 1938.

15. Who contributed what to this account is not known, but it is reasonable to suppose that Jennings wrote most of the rough draft that Porter polished for publication. On receiving the draft from Jennings, Porter cautioned his friend that "we have to respect the conventions and delusions of the public to a certain extent" (letter from Porter to Jennings quoted in *The Complete Works of O. Henry*, vol. 2 [New York: Doubleday, 1953], 1091).

16. Ibid., 890.

17. Ibid., 838.

18. I'm not aware of any way to verify Brady's claim that "two-thirds" of train passengers were likely to be armed. But guns were cheap. Schlereth notes during the 1890s that one could buy "a Harrington & Richardson pistol for $2.98" (*Victorian America*, 144). Anecdotal evidence from another source indicates that as late as 1908, Sears Roebuck offered in their catalog .32 caliber revolvers for $2.95. One gentleman later remembered that "everybody carried a pistol and a Winchester in those days, not only for protection, but from habit. I always wore two pistols, and would have felt lost without them" (Oklahoma *Indian Pioneer Papers*, interview with Claude Timmons).

19. O. Henry, *Complete Works*, 837–38.

20. Ibid., 838.

21. See Glen Shirley, *Shotgun for Hire: The Story of "Deacon" Jim Miller, Killer of Pat Garrett* (Norman: University of Oklahoma Press, 1970), 32–33.

22. All the quotations in this paragraph are from Richard Dillon, *Wells, Fargo Detective: A Biography of James B. Hume* (New York: Coward-McCann, 1969), 250–51. My information about the possibility of poisoned whiskey from the reminiscences of E. C. Ott, a former express car agent, who claims that during a robbery of his car by outlaws he thought were the Dal-

ton Gang, he was forced to drink some whiskey because the bandits suspected it might have been poisoned. See "Railroad Tales on the Air," *Kansas City Times,* January 2, 1938, 6.

23. Harold Preece, *The Dalton Gang: End of an Outlaw Era* (New York: Hastings House, 1963), 201.

24. Ben Townsend, "Buried Loot in Oklahoma," *Lost Treasure Magazine,* May 1977, 14.

25. Harry Sinclair Drago, *Outlaws on Horseback* (New York: Dodd, Mead, 1964), 217.

26. "Eye Witness" writes that the railroad guards "proceeded 'to imbibe' and to exchange jocose and boasting remarks . . . but when Pryor Creek was passed without unpleasantness, and also the next station, Perry, the drooping spirits of the 'brave' police revived marvelously, and a festive drink was absorbed in honor of this narrow escape, which the men boisterously qualified of '—— bad luck.'" ("Eye Witness," *The Dalton Brothers and Their Astounding Career of Crime,* introduction by Burton Rascoe [1892; reprint, New York: Frederick Fell, 1954], 155).

27. In point of fact, Houston did get at least one movie—*Oklahoma Territory* (1960), starring Bill Williams as Temple—but of course it counts for more when the title includes one's name.

28. This is a must-see movie for those interested in the period's history. In one scene, Bill Tilghman, dutiful and loving father of two young boys, is entertaining them with slides on the family stereoscope (a viewing device as common then as televisions are today). "But Daddy, why is that man full of holes?" The picture is the famous death pose of Bill Doolin, his corpse riddled with buckshot fired by none other than Heck Thomas. "All in a day's work, son" (I can't resist making up the dialog). Then there's Marshal Bill, charged with cleaning up the town, barging into the local saloon/whorehouse. Everybody expects violent confrontation. Instead, he pulls out a sheaf of handbills advertising his movie *The Passing of the Oklahoma Outlaws* (purported scenes from which often appear, intercut into the narrative) and implores the gamblers and prostitutes to attend. (This I'm not making up.) Finally, shortly after Bill is murdered by the dastardly revenue agent Wiley Lynn, we cut to his teary-eyed wife Zoe, clattering away on a primitive typewriter, no doubt writing his biography, *Marshal of the Last Frontier.* So Death is defied.

It must be said that the young Bill Tilghman was no stranger to saloons and whorehouses because he had owned and operated both. Nancy Samuelson reports that "William Tilghman was arrested [in Gutherie, Indian Territory] for operating a bawdy house on June 2, 1889 and again on June 14. He was arrested for gambling on October 7 and November 5, 1889, and on June 1, November 25, and December 26, 1890. . . . During July 1892 several women and William Tilghman were all arrested and charged with prostitution" (*Shoot from the Lip,* 44).

Sadly, two of Tilghman's sons (Woodie and Richard) came to bad ends. In October 1929, the pair (accompanied by their uncle, Zoe's brother) attempted to rob a poker (or craps) game near Minco, Oklahoma, during which Richard was shot through the liver. He later died of his wounds.

29. The 1909 film featured Emmett playing both himself and his brothers. The camera work for this short film was shot at the actual location by John Tackett, one of the photographers credited with taking the Dalton's famous death picture (of which there are at least three versions) of the four gang members laid out on the plank floor of the Coffeyville city jail. Other photographs of this scene were taken by local Coffeyville photographer C. G. Glass.

30. This movie appears to be the entire output of the Dalton Film Company, whose president, Russell W. Kurtz, had married Jennie Perrier, one of Emmett's granddaughters, to whom he assigned all his literary copyrights. On the basis of this assignment, Kurtz sued the National Broadcasting Company and a number of sponsors over their production of an early TV show, *The Daltons Must Die*. See Samuelson, *Dalton Gang Story,* 160.

31. Samuelson (*Dalton Gang Story,* 60) reports the Meade "Hideout Museum" is probably a hoax, and that some local Kansas residents remember the tunnel being dug by the Works Progress Administration during the Depression.

32. Perhaps something needs to be said here about the then-widespread practice of photographing in bloody detail the criminal dead, a custom that to modern sensibilities may seem barbaric. And no doubt such pictures pandered to morbid sensationalism and also served as cautionary icons depicting sin's gory wages. But what may be now overlooked was the difficulty of definitively identifying criminals at that time. Outlaws frequently used aliases, and they routinely operated in locations where they were not known. Death photography was thus important simply as a means of visually preserving their appearance for evidentiary purposes. In any event, it was certainly a less gruesome practice than pickling severed heads in jars, a method occasionally used by some early lawmen and bounty hunters who needed proof to claim rewards.

33. The awesome Coffeyville hailstone must now apparently settle for second place, eclipsed by a stone measuring 18.75 inches in circumference that fell on Aurora, Nebraska, on June 22, 2003.

34. Robert Barr Smith, *Daltons! The Raid on Coffeyville* (Norman: University of Oklahoma Press, 1996), xiii.

35. Whether or not the local Coffeyville physicians aided Emmett Dalton is a disputed point. The Dalton Defenders Museum has on display the surgical case of Dr. Wells, and notes that he used these instruments to dig assorted buckshot and slugs (also on display) out of Emmett.

36. The best Dalton genealogy is by Samuelson (a Dalton relative) in *Dalton Gang Story*.

37. General Santa Anna's contributions to North American history and culture have not been sufficiently appreciated. The state of Texas, of course, in large measure owes its existence to the atrocities committed by Santa Anna's army against American rebels at both the Alamo and Goliad, atrocities repaid with ample interest some weeks later in 1836 when General Sam Houston's army defeated and captured Santa Anna at San Jacinto. (The resulting treaty between the two may have been the only time in history that such an important negotiation was conducted by leaders both intoxicated on opium.) Surely even more importantly, in 1869, during one of his periodic exiles from Mexico, Santa Anna happened to share a room on Staten Island with inventor Thomas Adams, who was trying to formulate a substitute for rubber. Santa Anna helpfully suggested that "chicle," a saplike substance native to trees in southern Mexico, might aid in this quest, and even had a ton of the stuff imported for Adams to experiment on. Although this didn't make a good rubber, it did make a superior chewing gum, eventually evolving into a multibillion-dollar industry and providing the basis for many personal fortunes, including that of William F. Wrigley Jr. Wreaking a terrible vengeance on America, Santa Anna, the Butcher of the Alamo, is thus indirectly responsible for the existence of the Chicago Cubs. So butchery begets botchery. See Jeff Long, *Duel of Eagles: The Mexican and U.S. Fight for the Alamo* (New York: William Morrow, 1990).

38. This document is reproduced in James D. Horan, *The Outlaws: Accounts by Eyewitnesses and the Outlaws Themselves* (New York: Gramercy Books, 1977), 148.

39. A similar, more modern exploration of this thesis of familial ties is presented by Paul Wellman in *A Dynasty of Western Outlaws* (New York: Bonanza Books, 1961).

40. As reported in the *Ft. Smith Elevator,* September 4, 1891, 2.

41. Oklahoma *Indian Pioneer Papers,* interview dated April 21, 1937.

42. Oklahoma *Indian Pioneer Papers,* interview dated April 22, 1938.

43. Nancy Samuelson disputes that Bob Dalton ever served as chief of police for the Osage Nation. The records she has examined state only that he served as a detective for that organization.

44. Samuelson argues that "Power is the correct spelling of the name though it generally appears as Powers in most of the literature" (*Dalton Gang Story,* 100). Emmett Dalton (*Beyond the Law* [Coffeyville, Kans.:

Coffeyville Historical Society, (1918)], 68) spells the name "Powers," but on a tombstone he had commissioned many years after Coffeyville and set above the grave containing Bob, Grat, and the gentleman here under discussion, the name is shown as "Power." A descendant of the outlaw has advised me that "Power" is indeed the preferred spelling.

45. Within six months of Captain Jack's inquiry, Deputy Marshal Jim Yates would be ambushed and killed by Robert Hall after a dispute over a card game. Hall's trial is of some interest in that his guilty verdict was overturned by the Supreme Court (150 U.S. 76 [1893]). During the original trial, the prosecutor, Clayton, attempting to show that Hall was a dangerous man, introduced into evidence the fact that he had been arrested and tried in Mississippi for murdering a "negro." The defense objected that Hall was acquitted of that charge. Then Clayton (see Chapter 4, note 31) said something like, "Well, everybody knows a Mississippi court will not convict a white man for killing a negro." Although many people, then and now, may have perhaps agreed that this statement contained some measure of objective truth, the Supreme Court ruled this was improper argument and remanded the case back to Ft. Smith for a second trial. At this second trial, Hall was acquitted.

46. See Robert K. DeArment, *Alias Frank Canton* (Norman: University of Oklahoma Press, 1996). Also, Canton was part of, and arguably one of the leaders of, a large mob or posse that murdered Nate Champion during an incident early in the Lincoln County War.

47. Fred Dodge, *Under Cover for Wells Fargo*, ed. Carolyn Lake (Norman: University of Oklahoma Press, 1969), 132.

48. O. Henry, *Complete Works*, 839.

49. Harry Sinclair Drago, in *Road Agents and Train Robbers* (New York: Dodd, Mead, 1973), claims that during the Wharton robbery, the station agent was killed as he telegraphed for help (211). No other source (except Wellman, who claims the agent was killed at Red Rock—see Chapter 1, note 12) I've found mentions this. One source does mention that "young Smith," a telegraph operator, was killed at Wharton by "Six Shooter Jack," then suspected to be a member of the Dalton Gang, but it makes it clear that this crime occurred "months" before the Wharton robbery (see the *Chillicothe Constitution*, May 11, 1891, 1). Drago further claims that William Starmer, a member of the posse pursuing the gang, was also killed (212). The Ft. Smith National Historic Site, which maintains a list of deputies killed in action, lists W. T. Starmer as "unconfirmed."

50. A fame perhaps undeserved. Nix was fired as U.S. marshal in 1896 for extensive financial irregularities. This did not prevent him from later making highly exaggerated claims about his effectiveness in office. Nix, a shameless self-promoter, even secured (along with Al Jennings) a job as

radio commentator in 1941, touting himself as the "Fighting Marshal," which very much amused his granddaughter and niece. Samuelson writes, "they both say that E. D. Nix never owned a gun and probably did not know how to shoot one" (*Shoot from the Lip*, 137). In fairness to Nix, a photograph included in this book (which may be a ceremonial posing) shows him wearing a pistol, though whether he actually owned it, or knew how to use it, is not known.

Al Jennings, as has been discussed, took vast pride in his ability as a marksman. But Joseph Rosa quotes a contemporary of his, General Roy Hoffman, "a Rough Rider and veteran of World War I," that he "knew Al Jennings personally, and his marksmanship was notoriously poor. He was one of the kind of fellows who could have qualified as the traditional bad shot who couldn't hit the side of a barn" (*The Gunfighter: Man or Myth?* [Norman: University of Oklahoma Press, 1969], 186).

51. E. D. Nix, *Oklahombres: Particularly the Wilder Ones* (1929; reprint, Lincoln: University of Nebraska Press, 1993), 43.

52. Dalton, *Beyond the Law,* 91.

53. Also see Samuelson, *Dalton Gang Story,* 64–65.

54. See the *Kansas City Times,* January 2, 1938, 6.

CHAPTER 3

1. Thomas Schlereth, *Victorian America: Transformations in Everyday Life* (New York: Harper Collins, 1991), 46.

2. Mark Svenvold, *Elmer McCurdy: The Misadventures in Life and Afterlife of an American Outlaw* (New York: Basic Books, 2002), 29.

3. Maury Klein, *The Life and Legend of Jay Gould* (Baltimore: Johns Hopkins University Press, 1986), 30.

4. By some accounts, the phrase "watered stock" derives from the practices of Daniel Drew, an associate of Gould, who, while employed as a cattle driver, would compel his herd to eat salt before their being weighed for slaughter, the resulting thirst swelling both their bulk and his profit. See Klein, *Life and Legend,* 77.

5. Ibid., 66. To this list one might add outright bribery, although it was usually disguised as loans, special stock issues, paid seats on a board, or campaign contributions. At the high levels where moguls like Gould and Vanderbilt operated, justice occasionally seemed a commodity for sale like any other. During their battle for the Erie Railroad, Vanderbilt found a New York state supreme court judge who issued orders forbidding a crucial board of directors meeting from taking place. The Gould faction then promptly turned up a compliant judge of equal authority who compelled that meeting to occur. Charles Francis Adams Jr. noted, "One magistrate had forbidden them to move, and another magistrate had ordered them not

to stand still. . . . If the Erie board held meetings and transacted business, it violated one injunction; if it abstained from doing so, it violated another" (Klein, *Life and Legend,* 82).

6. On another matter perhaps of interest, if the Second Missouri participated in the Battle of Pea Ridge (and there is still controversy as to whether they did), then Private George may well have noticed the presence of the Confederate Cherokee Mounted Rifle Regiment, commanded by then Colonel Stand Watie under General Albert Pike. The conduct of these Cherokee soldiers at Pea Ridge created quite a controversy because there were reports that some of the Indians scalped their Union adversaries, and not always after they were dead. (See Colonel Charles W. Mooney, *Doctor in Belle Starr Country* [Oklahoma City: Century Press, 1975], 8.) Watie would later be promoted to general of the Confederate Army, and his command was the last organized force to surrender in the Civil War, on June 23, 1865. Acting as the chief staff surgeon for General Watie was Dr. Walter Thompson Adair (1838–1899), for whom Adair, Oklahoma, is named. In the ranks was Sam Sixkiller.

7. Klein, *Life and Legend,* 96–97.

8. Gould's control over the overseas cable earned him the implacable hatred of James Gordon Bennett Jr. (1841–1918), one of the period's most flamboyant figures. He inherited the *New York Herald* from his father, an even more famous newspaperman, but Jamie is now best remembered for sending correspondent Henry M. Stanley to find Dr. Livingstone, then presumed to be lost in Africa. Similar publicity stunts did not always fare as well. Jamie, who was interested in arctic exploration, sponsored what was to be a three-year-long survey of the Bering Straits, but the party of thirty-five or so sailors and scientists, led by G. W. De Long, was trapped by ice flows for two years, and their ship (the *Jeanette*) eventually crushed. Only two of the party survived to tell the story to the *Herald*'s readers.

Bennett's contemporaries probably remembered him best because of an unfortunate lapse on January 1, 1877. While attending an elegant party in the posh estate owned by his fiancée's high-society family, Jamie, perhaps due to overindulgence in spiritous liquors, or perhaps due to shockingly poor eyesight, mistook, in full view of the assembled guests, and with predictably unsanitary results, the parlor grand piano for a urinal. (Some versions of this story identify a fireplace as the inappropriate vessel of his micturate requirements.) That behavior immediately ended the engagement, a point emphasized the next day when his ex-fiancée's brother publicly horsewhipped him in the street. This in turn led to a duel in which neither man was wounded. After his self-exile to Europe, Jamie was compelled to run his paper at a distance by means of Gould's cable pool, which he "condemned as 'the most gigantic system of organized robbery in existence in any civilized country'" (Klein, *Life and Legend*, 313). So great was Jamie's disdain that he spent much effort and money organizing a cable system of his own.

Bennett, who is credited with introducing the sport of polo to the United States, was a huge sports enthusiast, organizing and sponsoring many races of yachts, balloons, automobiles, and even airplanes. But scandal plagued his life, so much so that the explicatory phrase "Gordon Bennett!" became a feature of British slang, indicating unpleasant surprise and dismay.

9. Gould's methods and tactics attracted strong opposition, to say the least. During the Southwestern strike of 1886, the Knights of Labor published and posted the following "Revenge Circular" (April 1886): "Mad with the frenzy of pride, and self-adulation, begotted as it is of the success of outrage and infamy there stands before us a giant of aggregated and incorporated wealth, every dollar of which is built on blood, injustice, and outrage. That giant of corporate wealth has centralized its power in and is impersonated in the eager fiend who gloats as he grinds the life out of his fellowman, and grimaces and dances as they writhe upon his instrument of torture. . . . Gould, the giant fiend, Gould, the money monarch, is dancing, as he claims, over the grave of your order, over the ruin of our homes, and the blight of our lives" (http://www.umkc.edu/labor-ed/kclh/2.htm). This same website is the source of Gould's quotation about the working class

Although such enmity from the laboring classes is understandable, what remains puzzling is the hatred of Gould by nearly all elements of society, which seems to need villains as much as heroes, Gould perfectly filling the role of the former. One contemporary writer (Robert Bruce in 1877) likened him to a "furtive and deadly" spider, "fattened on the ruins of stockholders." Another early historian (Gustavus Myers in 1909) declared Gould to be a "freebooter who, if he could not appropriate millions, would filch thousands; a pitiless human carnivore, glutting himself on the blood of his numberless victims . . . an incarnate fiend of a Machiavelli in his calculations, his schemes and ambushes, his plots and counterplots" (both quotes are from Klein, *Life and Legend*, 1–2). Klein's excellent book serves as a necessary counterweight to such hysterical rhetoric, and his conclusion—that Gould's ethics and business practices were no worse than many of his time and often better than some—seems quite fair.

10. I've found no evidence indicating that Gould and Fisk bribed, or attempted to bribe, Grant directly. But shortly after Grant assumed office, Gould "loaned" Corbin $10,000. Gould also offered $1.5 million in gold purchases to Corbin, who at first refused but then agreed so long as the purchases were listed in his wife's name (his wife being Grant's sister). Gould also approached Grant's private secretary, General Horace Porter, offering to buy gold for him. Porter refused. But then, as Klein notes, Porter "received from New York a sheet of note paper, addressed and

signed by Gould, noting that $500,000 in gold had been purchased in his name. Annoyed, Porter wrote Gould at once to repudiate this and any other transaction in gold on his behalf" (*Life and Legend*, 106).

11. I am told that most of the early Katy employment records were destroyed by fire. However, Captain Jack's Excelsior diary came equipped with a pocket flap containing some of the railroad passes he was issued. The earliest, 1888, is from the Katy, where he is listed as "Special Agent." In 1889, the Chicago, Burlington, and Quincy railroad listed him as an MKT "Special Agent." In 1893 he seems to have changed employment and was issued an Atlantic and Pacific (Western Division) pass as a "Special Agent" for the Atchison, Topeka & Santa Fe railroad. He is listed that way in 1898 by the International and Great Northern Railroad. Another 1898 pass, from the Terminal Railroad Association of St. Louis, notes that he is a "Supervisor of Special Services" for the AT&SF.

12. This description can be found at http://www.plantpath.wisc.edu/pp300/docs/pathogen.html.

13. Letter from Jonathan Swift to Alexander Pope, August 11, 1729, in *Eighteenth Century Literature,* ed. Geoffrey Tillotson with Paul Fussell Jr. and Marshal Waingrow (New York: Harcourt Brace and World, 1969), 447.

14. Jonathan Swift, "A Modest Proposal," in *Eighteenth Century Literature,* 447.

15. Swift, "Modest Proposal," 448.

16. Nancy Samuelson claims that Grat was named for a Kentucky neighbor of the family (who might have himself been named after the Irish statesman) and goes on to assert, "but so far no proof of any Irish ancestry has been located for this Dalton family" (*The Dalton Gang Story* [Eastford, Conn.: Shooting Star Press, 1992], 68). Nevertheless, she writes that "by the thirteenth century the name [Dalton] was well established in the British Isles" (6). She does concede that Emmett was named after Irish patriot Robert Emmet. Emmett Dalton himself, in *Beyond the Law* (Coffeyville, Kans.: Coffeyville Historical Society, [1918]), writes that "Dalton" was a "good old Irish name" but gives no further particulars.

17. Peter Fry and Fiona Somerset Fry, *A History of Ireland* (New York: Barnes and Noble, 1988), 183.

18. Ibid., 188.

19. Ibid.

20. Ibid., 215.

21. Ibid.

22. Ibid., 228.

23. Ibid., 230–31.

24. From the Web site http://www.botany.hawaii.edu/faculty/wong/BOT135/LECT06.HTM.

25. Fry and Fry, *History of Ireland,* 231.

26. See Chapter 5 for further information on one of the "Young Ire-landers" leaders.

27. The treaty offered by Lloyd George (ably assisted by the wily Winston Churchill) proposed the creation of the "Irish Free State," but many con-temporary Irishmen noticed that the "Free State" was not quite that, and instead offered dominion status similar to that enjoyed by Canada, as Irish parliamentarians were still required to take an oath of allegiance to the crown. Although this new state was significantly more independent than what it replaced, it was not quite the republic that many of the more radi-cal Irishmen desired, and so a civil war was fought essentially over the question of whether the proposed "Irish Free State" was free enough to sat-isfy a majority of Irishmen.

A leading figure in this war was one Mr. Emmet (one "t") Dalton (1898–1978), whose career curiously paralleled that of his American coun-terpart. Variously outlaw and lawman, the Irish Emmet was also an expert with firearms and resembled (noted one contemporary writer) "a Wild West cinema star, the butt of a service [pistol] peeping from his hip pocket" (Tim Pat Coogan, *The Man Who Made Ireland: The Life and Death of Michael Collins* [Niwot, Colo.: Roberts Rinehart, 1992], 234–35). After the war, the Irish Emmet, in common with his American namesake, went on to a career in cinema, and produced and directed a number of films in both London and Hollywood. Perhaps his best-remembered work is *This Other Eden* (1959), a movie adapted from a play by Louis D'Alton, whose surname is arguably the basis of both the American and Irish Dalton clans.

28. Fry and Fry, *History of Ireland,* 236–37.

29. An article in the *Sedalia Gazette,* May 28, 1891, quotes Mr. J. L. Dunn (who will later be discussed in greater detail) as having visited St. Louis sometime in the mid-1880s, where he was for some months a guest at the Southern Hotel, "during which time I heard of and afterwards knew Mr. Kinney, who was a prominent ward politician." The *St. Louis Globe Demo-crat,* on May 7, 1891, notes that "Detective Kinney is an old St. Louisian." In another clipping (source and date unknown), Mr. Dunn says Kinney "is an ex-politician and gained considerable notoriety in St. Louis (his former home) several years ago as being a connoisseur on chicken fights and box-ing matches."

30. One might speculate that the Missouri Pacific sought to increase se-curity that year by hiring more detectives after an abortive attempt to as-sassinate their president, Jay Gould, on January 9, 1882. The *Atchison Globe* (January 21, 1882, 1) reported that "on January 9, when the special train containing Jay Gould and party ran from Sedalia to Denison, Tex., a most dastardly attempt was made near Rockville, Bates county, Mo., to wreck the

train." Someone had loosened one of the rails, and the sabotage was only discovered when a handcar, scouting just ahead of the special, was thereby thrown into a ditch. The article went on to note that "for several days the chief detective of the Missouri Pacific, Tom Furlong, was working up the case." August Joanmeyer, a local farmer, was soon arrested and charged with the crime.

31. See the *Atchison Globe*, October 21, 1882. It's hard to say how much Captain Jack might have earned in his new job. One source (William T. Hagan, *Indian Police and Judges* [Lincoln: University of Nebraska Press, 1966]) notes that in 1880 Captain Sam Sixkiller had been hired as a special agent for the Missouri Pacific at about "$1,200 a year" (60). But Sixkiller was by then a highly experienced law enforcement officer, surely commanding a greater salary than a novice like Kinney. On the other hand, Sixkiller's job was understood to be only part time.

32. Harry Sinclair Drago, *Road Agents and Train Robbers* (New York: Dodd, Mead, 1973), 97.

33. Ibid., 99.

34. Ibid.

35. "Captain" Kinney served with the Union army during the Civil War, but the records indicate he did not arise above the rank of private.

36. Even preachers with unsavory backgrounds were then in great demand, given the Ozarkian ubiquity of Beelzebub and his minions. The Bristol, Pennsylvania, *Bucks County Gazette* (February 7, 1889, 4) reported that "if there is any place in the country where a living spirit of evil, the personal devil, is believed in unquestioningly, it is here. Satan travels up and down the gulches and ravines and peers in at the open doorways at the firesides or, finding an open door, 'just melts his way in.'" This same source reports the belief that, after his death, Captain Kinney's ghost "stalks forth by night clad in mask as of old, but now with a blood stained shroud around him instead of the marshal's coat of blue that was his pride."

37. *Atchison Daily Globe*, August 22, 1888, 1.

38. Such masks were the signature primarily of the (by comparison more vicious) Christian County Bald Knobbers, many of the original Taney group, at least at first, not even bothering to wear disguises, because they felt they were doing nothing wrong. It should also be noted that the group's large claimed membership was achieved, so many later said, by coercion and intimidation. Indeed, the Knobbers' slogan was "Join the Band or Leave the Land."

39. Mary Hartman and Elmo Ingenthron, *Bald Knobbers: Vigilantes on the Ozarks Frontier* (Gretna, La.: Pelican, 1988), 49–50.

40. The quote, and many of the details about W. Kinney's life, are from the Web site http://www.angelfire.com/mi2/billythekid/kinney.html.

41. Another account of this skirmish reports that the Kid shot Kinney's mustache clean off, surely adding insult to injury at a time when men took great pride in their facial hair. But by 1898, in a picture of Kinney taken in Santiago, Cuba, one notices that his facial bristles had either completely regrown or else been replaced by a realistic-looking fake. See Frederick Nolan, *The West of Billy the Kid* (Norman: University of Oklahoma Press, 1998), 164.

42. Reciprocity was then a code word figuring prominently in one of the major political issues of the day, the always-contentious issue of tariffs and import duties, pitting free trade factions against various shades of protectionists. Advocates of reciprocity desired not free but fair trade—in other words, a selective protectionist stance. Those with free trade sympathies therefore viewed the fast-growing movement with alarm. An editorial writer for the *Atlanta Constitution* (June 6, 1891, 4) scathingly observed that "the Knights of Reciprocity will be to the republican party what the Danites [a sect of religious assassins] were to the Mormons, with the murder business left out. Like the Danites, they will be used for secret and dishonorable work that their employers cannot afford to do openly and accept the responsibility."

43. Baseball's origins remain obscure and controversial. In 1748, Lady Hervey, writing a letter describing the family activities of Frederick, Prince of Wales, observes them "diverting themselves in baseball," but whether that game has any resemblance to the modern activity cannot be known. The first recorded mention of the sport in the United States seems to be in the July 13, 1825, Delhi, New York, *Gazette*, which posts a challenge for any nine men in Delaware County to meet and play a New Jersey team at baseball at the home of Mr. Edward B. Chance, the winners to receive $1. Although Abner Doubleday, a Civil War general, has been popularly identified as modern baseball's founder, most historians agree that honor should go to Mr. Thomas Cartwright, who in 1845 first codified the rules. The first recorded game, in which Cartwright participated, was in 1846 at Elysian Fields, Hoboken, New Jersey, where the Knickerbockers lost to the New York Nine 23–1. The first openly professional (that is, paid) team, the Cincinnati Red Stockings, formed in 1869, the same year in which the record was set for the largest score of a nine-inning game, with the Niagaras beating the Columbians 209 to 10.

44. This quote, and more information on the Sells Brothers Circus, is from the Web site http://www.shortnorth.com/CircusTown.html. Eventually, the Sells sold their interest to Barnum and Bailey, who were in turn acquired by the Ringling Brothers in 1906. One hopes the circus roustabouts were better behaved at Sedalia than on a later stop in Trinidad, Colorado, where thirty-four of them were arrested and jailed on charges of disorderly

conduct (as reported by the Decatur, Illinois, *Herald Dispatch*, July 30, 1892, 1).

45. These animals wintered with the Circus in Columbus, Ohio, which occasionally led to some interesting experiences, as the time when five polar bears escaped. A maddened elephant also once broke free, and before being subdued, it tore off the entire front porch of a house while the family inside cowered in fright.

46. The story of Annie Oakley is well known and won't be repeated here, except for a lesser-known incident that figured in the history of law. In 1903, a woman was arrested in Chicago and hauled before a court on the charge of "stealing the trousers of a negro in order to get money with which to buy cocaine." The woman pled guilty and threw herself on the mercy of the court, arguing that the stress of having toured as the most famous female rifle shot in the world had led to her current desperate situation. Although the woman identified herself as Lilian Cody, she admitted using a stage name of "Any Oak Lay," or "Any Oklay," perhaps inspired by her husband, one Frank Samuel Cowderly, who changed his last name to "Cody" in order to profit from the fame of Buffalo Bill Cody. The Hearst newspapers, and others, saw too good a story here to let mere facts stand in their way, and they blanketed the country with headlines and stories such as "Dope Caused Her Downfall. Annie Oakley is now in jail. Her Appetite for Drugs Drove Her to Steal the Trousers of a Negro." Although many of these newspapers printed retractions upon being appraised of the facts, the real Annie Oakley was neither amused nor satisfied, and she brought libel suits—which she eventually won—against the publishers of the original slur. This fascinating story is told in complete detail by Thomas R. Julin and D. Patricia Wallace, "Who's That Crack-Shot Trouser Thief?" (*Litigation* 28, no. 4 [summer 2002]).

CHAPTER 4

1. C. H. McKennon, *Iron Men* (New York: Doubleday, 1967), 95.

2. Another account states the cannon was procured from Fayetteville—see W. F. Jones, *The Experiences of a Deputy U.S. Marshal of the Indian Territory* (no date, place, or publisher). Still other sources say the cannon was from Ft. Scott, Kansas.

3. Glen Shirley, *Heck Thomas: Frontier Marshal* (Philadelphia: Chilton Company, 1962), 93–94.

4. A transcription of the telegram (if it is that) is included in the Alexander Lewis case files stored at the National Archives in Ft. Worth, Texas. I am indebted to Mr. Diron Ahlquist for providing this material and also for his supposition about who may have sent the telegram.

5. There's reason to believe that Thomas's posse joined forces with one commanded by Charles La Flore, as La Flore was also known to be in hot pursuit of the gang. Probably riding with La Flore was Mr. Bud T. Kell of the Indian Police, later among the train guards at Adair. Because both Kell and La Flore would later testify at Lewis's trial, and because there is no suggestion that they were present during the actual robbery, it must be their subsequent experiences in pursuit about which they could offer testimony. One of these posses also seems to have included noted man tracker Burrell Cox, later involved in the search for the Daltons just before Coffeyville. Thomas's posse had originally been after a ring of whiskey smugglers, two of whom (Tom Purdy and a gentleman known only as "Old Dad") managed to compound their crimes by somehow stealing Heck Thomas's own horse. Documentation for this information is in the handwritten letter by Thomas in the Lewis case files at the National Archives.

6. Samuel Harman, *Hell on the Border: He Hanged Eighty-Eight Men*, ed. Jack Gregory and Rennard Strickland (Muskogee, Okla.: Indian Heritage Publications, 1971), 32. The observation about the Black Hole of Calcutta is offered by the authorial voice, but the book's true author is not, as originally listed, Samuel Harman. Harman's role in publishing this work, which originally appeared in 1898, was that of a ghostwriter. Most historians agree that much of the book is based on the accounts, written or oral, of J. Warren Reed (sometimes spelled "Reid"), a famous Ft. Smith lawyer of the time. Why Reed declined to admit his authorship is not known, but one may suspect his anonymous role enabled him to comment on his own courtroom performances with seeming objectivity. The book's subtitle—"He Hanged Eighty-Eight Men"—also deserves comment. The Ft. Smith National Historic Site Web site reports that total executions between 1873 and 1896 were 86 men, but Judge Parker was not the only judge to preside over the court. Parker sentenced 160 people (including four women) to death, but only 79 were actually executed.

7. Harman, *Hell on the Border*, 37. Both the original jail under the courtroom and the newer facility have been preserved by the National Park Service at the Ft. Smith National Historic Site. A replica of the 1886 gallows, surrounded by a white fence, is similarly displayed, although visitors are admonished to stay off it and to respect it as an "instrument of justice."

8. Despite generations of TV Westerns and movies depicting characters wearing guns in hip holsters with the butt facing to the rear, Maledon's practice was not all that unusual. By one account, both bandit queen Belle Starr and legendary black lawman Bass Reeves wore their pistols similarly: "they both agreed this cross-body draw gave them quicker access to their deadly weapons, especially when riding horseback and a split second edge

meant life or death" (Charles Mooney, *Doctor Jesse* [Oklahoma City: Pro-Graphics, 1978], 116). Another authority on the matter noted that "pistols were generally carried butts forward." One reason was safety: "Because the thumb was locked over the hammer spur, releasing the spur was impossible until the barrel was clear of the body, making the cross-body or 'reverse' draw much safer than the hip draw. The later so-called 'conventional' hip-draw holsters did and do sometimes lead to accidents: when the barrel snags, jerking the trigger finger, the result can be a bad leg wound or, perhaps, a dead horse! (Eugene Cunningham, *Triggernometry: A Gallery of Gunfighters*, foreword by Eugene Manlove Rhodes, introduction by Joseph G. Rosa [Norman: University of Oklahoma Press, 1941, 1996], vxii).

9. Harman, *Hell on the Border*, 381.

10. Maledon's modest frame house, now partially restored, still stands in the 300 block of North 5th Street in Ft. Smith.

11. This quote, and the one immediately preceding, is from the Bristol, Pennsylvania, *Bucks County Gazette*, October 11, 1888, 4.

12. Decatur, Illinois, *Daily Republican*, April 22, 1896, 5.

13. Roger Tuller, *"Let No Guilty Man Escape": A Judicial Biography of "Hanging Judge" Isaac C. Parker* (Norman: University of Oklahoma Press, 2001), 60–61. For information on the hanging of Fulsom, see 67.

14. See Thomas Furlong, *Fifty Years a Detective* (St. Louis: C. E. Barnett, 1912), 330–32.

15. Full details of this episode can be found in Mark Essig, *Edison and the Electric Chair: A Story of Light and Death* (New York: Walker, 2003).

16. McKennon, *Iron Men*, 49–50.

17. *Indian Pioneer Papers*, interview with Ninnian Tannehill, April 22, 1938.

18. From Harman's *Hell on the Border*:

A draft of the official records for a period of ten years ending December 31, 1894, shows 7,419 criminal cases convicted; 305 of that number were for murder and manslaughter; 466 for assault with intent to kill; 1,910 for selling liquor to Indians; 2,860 for introducing liquor into the Indian Territory; 97 for illicit distilling; 124 for violating the internal revenue laws; 65 for violating the postal laws; 50 for counterfeiting; 24 for arson; 48 for perjury; 32 for bigamy; 27 for conspiracy to commit a crime; 59 for stealing government timber; 24 for resisting arrest; and 149 for other crimes not here enumerated; and added to this, be it known, that the years 1895 and 1896 placed more than 2,000 additional cases on the docket, and the reader commences to gather somewhat of an idea of the immense amount of work performed by this famous court. (185–86)

19. Colin Beavan, *Fingerprints: The Origins of Crime Detection and the Murder Case That Launched Forensic Science* (New York: Hyperion, 2001), 30.

20. Late in the evening of June 29, 1892, in Necochea, Argentina, Francisca Rojas ran to her neighbor's house, screaming that someone had killed her children. The local constable, summoned to her hut, discovered her two young children dead, their heads crushed. Ms. Rojas accused a local rancher, Mr. Velasquez, of committing the crime, and gave as his motive the fact that he had that same afternoon proposed marriage to her, which she rejected. Mr. Velasquez was arrested and interrogated using the time-honored and usually productive method of beating the hell out of him. But Velasquez would not confess. The constable, who was something of an amateur psychologist, switched from physical to mental torture and ordered Velasquez detained in the room containing the children's bodies, hoping the ghastly sight would shock his conscience. But this strategy didn't work either. Impressed with Velasquez's denials, and convinced that only an innocent man could withstand the methods he had employed, the constable let Velasquez go, which left Ms. Rojas herself as a suspect.

But she denied it. Too much of a gentleman to beat a confession out of her, the constable again employed his psychological methods and would at night sneak under her window while howling, moaning, and emitting ghostly, eerie noises, hoping she would interpret such scary sounds as the forlorn souls of her children, come back to torment her and force her confession. Perhaps hard of hearing, Ms. Rojas simply ignored this otherworldly din. The constable, completely frustrated, appealed for help from the larger and more sophisticated police force at La Plata, who sent Inspector Eduardo M. Alvarez to the scene. By chance, the La Plata constabulary had just become interested in this new science of fingerprinting and had trained some of the officers, including Mr. Alvarez, how best to gather such evidence. Examining the hut thoroughly, Alvarez discovered a bloody thumbprint on the door:

> He ordered Rojas's arrest. With an ink pad borrowed from the Necochea police chief, he took impressions from her thumbs and compared them under a magnifying glass with the bloody mark on the door. Rojas's right thumb matched perfectly. As Alvarez explained to Rojas how fingerprints identify the fingers they come from, she started shaking. When she saw for herself that the patterns under the magnifying glass were the same, she became hysterical, and, eventually, confessed everything. Because they stood between her and the man she loved, she had crushed her children's heads with a stone. She threw her murder weapon down a well and carefully washed the blood from her hands. She had forgotten that she had touched the door. (Beavan, *Fingerprints,* 114–15)

21. Two years after the Lewis trial had concluded, Kinney clipped an article (dated November 5, 1893) from the *Saint Louis Globe-Democrat* on this same subject. Subtitled "The Strongest Case of Circumstantial Evidence Is Weak at Best," the reporter asks the opinion of a "prominent criminal lawyer," who "swung his chair around to a revolving book-case, and selected a well-thumbed volume entitled 'Famous Cases of Circumstantial Evidence,' by S. M. Phillips, author of 'Phillips on Evidence.' This volume contains twenty-seven celebrated English and French cases of conviction on seemingly impregnable chains of circumstantial evidence, the falsity of which was only discovered after innocent men paid the penalty of their misfortunes with their lives. These cases are familiar to every student of law, and are always quoted by attorneys for the defense." The article concludes by mentioning the 1893 Missouri case of Mr. Andy Hedgepeth, a wealthy planter who fell in love with his neighbor's wife. After the neighbor disappeared, and upon the authorities finding a bloody hatchet (among other incriminating items) in Hedgepeth's possession, he was convicted by the circumstantial evidence further supported by the wife's confession that they had planned to kill her husband, although no body was ever found. After exhausting all appeals, Hedgepeth was hanged. But then the neighbor, the supposed victim (a man named Watkins), turned up alive, saying he had disappeared out of shame for his wife's behavior.

22. Beavan, *Fingerprints*, 18–19.

23. As spectacular as Reed's record was, it was probably eclipsed by that of Moman Pruiett, who specialized in defending murderers in the nearby Chickasaw Nation. "In his flamboyant career," writes Glen Shirley, "he defended 342 accused murderers. Of this number, 304 escaped punishment. The remaining 38 were found guilty and were given sentences ranging from four years to life imprisonment. The only client of his ever sentenced to death was granted presidential clemency" (*Shotgun for Hire: The Story of "Deacon" Jim Miller, Killer of Pat Garrett* [Norman: University of Oklahoma Press, 1970], 96–97). Yet Pruiett's successful record could actually work to his client's disadvantage. Learning that the infamous killer "Deacon" Jim Miller (suspected of killing Pat Garrett and perhaps as many as fifty other men) had retained Pruiett, a mob, fearing Pruiett's legal prowess, broke into the Ada, Oklahoma jail on April 19, 1909, and lynched Miller and three of his associates, all of whom were being held for the murder of Gus Bobbitt.

24. Glen Shirley, *Law West of Fort Smith* (Lincoln: University of Nebraska Press, 1968), 147.

25. Harman, *Hell on the Border*, 137.

26. Ibid., 152.

27. Jay Robert Nash, *Encyclopedia of Western Lawmen and Outlaws* (New York: Da Capo Press, 1994), 210.

28. Kinney certainly didn't think so. From the undated *Sedalia Gazette* article based on his interview: "The witnesses for the defense, with possibly one exception, were a very disreputable lot and stood ready to swear to anything that would clear the defendant. Three of their witnesses got into trouble at Ft. Smith and were ordered out of hotels; one of them, named Mounts, did not take the stand because the police had him under arrest; another one, named Dr. Johnson, did not take the stand because he was drunk. The two mentioned are a fair sample of the character of the witnesses for the defense."

29. Daniel F. Littlefield, from whose excellent book *Seminole Burning: A Story of Racial Vengeance* (Jackson: University Press of Mississippi, 1996) I first learned of the Lewis clan, was kind enough (in an e-mail dated August 17, 2004) to share his research on the extended family. And Alexander S. Lewis is not mentioned in a genealogy later compiled by one of the clan members.

30. Littlefield, *Seminole Burning*, 28.

31. Prosecutor William H. H. Clayton, who was originally a soldier, fought as a lieutenant in the Pennsylvania Infantry at Antietam, Fredericksburg, and the Battle of the Wilderness. "He was admitted to the Arkansas bar in 1871," writes Glen Shirley in *Law West of Fort Smith*, "and in March of the same year was appointed judge of the First Judicial Circuit, which office he resigned in July, 1874, to accept an appointment from Grant as United States Attorney for the Western District at Fort Smith. . . . During his fourteen years of service Clayton was to prosecute over ten thousand cases, convict eighty men of murder, and see forty of them hanged" (33–34). Clayton's beautifully restored house in Ft. Smith's Belle Grove historic district is now a popular tourist destination, located only a few blocks away from Miss Laura's whorehouse (the "hello bordello"), which now serves as the town's official visitors center.

32. On February 6, 1889, the United States Congress passed legislation permitting review of Parker's jurisdiction by the Supreme Court. Before that, the only recourse for a guilty defendant was presidential pardon. The case of Alexander Lewis was the fourth case to reach on appeal the Supreme Court, which seemed eager to overturn many of Parker's decisions on (as he phrased it) "legal technicalities."

33. Nash, *Encyclopedia*, 210. Reed was also a pioneer in the use of courtroom stage props: "by an ingeniously devised miniature train of cars, made of paste board, and arranged before the jury, Mr. Reed proceeded to demonstrate that his client was not one of the five robbers. He won his point and proved the possession of legal ability, competent to secure acquittals for men charged with high crimes, for which he afterwards became noted" (Harman, *Hell on the Border*, 327).

34. Harman, *Hell on the Border*, 28.

35. Furlong, *Fifty Years a Detective*, 269.

36. Harman, *Hell on the Border*, 48.

37. See Furlong, *Fifty Years a Detective*, 198–206.

CHAPTER 5

1. Dunn's indiscretions in Sedalia—which generated wide publicity—attracted the attention of Captain Amos Cartwright, late of the Confederate army, who showed up in town making inquiries. From an interview he provided to the *Sedalia Gazette* (September 29, 1891): "I knew the boy's father," said Captain Cartwright,

> and I want to say that the confederacy had no better or braver soldier than he. He was the soul of honor, and if the boy is anything like his father I don't see how he could have engaged in any questionable transactions.
>
> I remember as well as if it had happened only yesterday the "Battle of the Wilderness," in which Col. Dunn was wounded while leading his men in a charge. He never faltered after being shot, but continued at the head of the column, and although he was defeated there was not a wearer of the blue or gray who witnessed the fight that could not help admiring the gallant Mississippi colonel. I know nothing of the colonel's family, but for the sake of his memory and the "lost cause" for which he fought I hope the son will be acquitted.

It's significant that Captain Cartwright admits he knows "nothing of the colonel's family." He, like many others, is assuming that Dunn is who he claims to be.

2. Dueling, or ritualized individual combat, seems a practice (until fairly recently) common to most cultures and has probably existed since the invention of weapons. Certainly men seem quite adept at finding ever more creative ways to slaughter each other. For example, hardly had the aerial balloon been invented when, on May 3, 1808, two gentlemen used such in a spectacular duel over Paris, having selected blunderbusses as their weapons, the shot from one collapsing his opponent's conveyance, dumping his adversary and his second to their deaths from two thousand feet.

But history's most unusual duel, also fought near Paris but way back in 1400, involved a deadly dispute of honor between the Chevalier Maquer and a dog, the contest further remarkable in that the dog was deemed the challenger. The dog, a greyhound whose name has been forgotten, was owned by Aubry de Montdidier and accompanied him on walks through the forest. But after one such walk, the dog returned alone. It appeared at a neighbor's house and exhibited such frantic behavior that a party was formed to follow the dog back to the forest, where Montdidier was discovered murdered and buried in a shallow grave. There the matter might have ended except that the dog, by all accounts an otherwise placid and friendly animal, upon a number of subsequent occasions unaccountably attacked on sight Chevalier Maquer, a supposed friend of his late master. The local authorities, appraised of this unusual behavior, concluded that the dog was, in his canine way, accusing the chevalier of murdering his master and ruled that a duel must be fought to decide the matter. "The fight," writes Robert Baldick in *The Duel: A History of Dueling* (New York: Clarkson N. Potter, 1965),

> duly took place on the Isle of Notre-Dame, the dog being led into the lists . . . and then unleashed against Maquer. According to some chroniclers, the latter was armed with a lance, while others relate that he was buried waist-deep in the ground and had only a shield and stick with which to defend himself. Whatever the truth of the matter, he found it impossible to ward off the dog, which sprang at him and seized him by the throat, so that he screamed that he would confess if only the animal were pulled away. . . . For the aforementioned Maquer was hanged and strangled on the gibbet at Montfaucon, and Aubrey's body was taken by his friends and given an honourable burial. (20–21)

Baldick is also the source for the aerial duel, an incident he discusses at greater length on 161–62.

3. One might well wonder why Sickles was able to get away with such escapades, and the answer must involve influence and innate charm (the latter quality also amply possessed by James L. Dunn). For example, Sickles was able to befriend that notoriously difficult woman Mary Todd Lincoln and was an avid participant in the séances she held in her attempts to communicate with her dead children. He even managed to survive Mrs. Lincoln's jealous wrath after an incident in which he encouraged one of his high-spirited associates, a "Princess Salm-Salm," to kiss the blushing Abraham on his bristly cheek. The best account of Sickles's interesting life is Thomas Keneally, *American Scoundrel: The Life of the Notorious Civil War General Dan Sickles* (New York: Doubleday, 2002).

4. From the Web site http://www.pbs.org/duel.html.

5. See for example Baldick, *Duel*, 134.

6. "Skirt dancing" seems to have been invented by noted dancer Kate Vaughn sometime around 1876. The dance, presented in vaudeville and burlesque venues, featured a series of acrobatic kicks "performed in a flouncy skirt that would show just enough leg to keep the male spectators interested" (http://www .streetswing.com/histmain/z3shirt.htm). Less reputable performers of the dance would occasionally forget to wear tights under their skirts, an offense for which they could be arrested. Such

suggestive dancing, which signaled a decline in the age's strict Victorian morality and observance of propriety, reached new heights during the 1893 Chicago World's Fair, attended by over seven million visitors. The fair's most notorious (and therefore most popular) entertainment was entitled "The Streets of Cairo" and featured a dancer known as "Little Egypt, the hootchie-coochie girl of the Nile." Ms. Egypt's dance was unusual in that it involved not just movement of the legs, but the quivering of her exposed abdomen. Those wishing for less salacious entertainments and spectacles had plenty from which to choose. The fine folks up in Canada had sent down, for the world's admiration, a "mammoth" cheese, weighing in at 22,000 pounds. Other displays offered a detailed map of the United States made entirely out of pickles, a gigantic Liberty Bell composed of ripe California oranges (but was it cracked?), and a 1,500-pound *Venus de Milo* sculpted from dark chocolate. Appetites stimulated by such culinary masterpieces, visitors might be tempted to try a new sandwich popularized by the fair, called a "hamburger." (One must here note that the true provenance of the hamburger remains one of history's deepest mysteries.) This might be accompanied by sodas made effervescent by a novel process known as "carbonation." Those having a metallurgical interest would be sure to inspect what was billed as the largest single-piece metal casting in the world, an enormous axle, three feet thick and forty-five feet long, around which orbited a huge circular contraption, designed by a Mr. Ferris, capable of lifting over two thousand adventurous riders to a breathtaking height of two hundred fifty feet before depositing them back on the ground—all that for only 50 cents. Edison's "kinetoscope" was there first revealed, as were the first electric ovens. A new form of mail communication, called a "postcard," was passed out by various manufacturers as a marketing tool. One of these notably depicted a fierce group of Zulu warriors, their menacing spears temporarily stacked in the corner of a hut, marveling at one of their members operating an improved treadle-powered device for sewing stitches devised by Mr. Singer. Still, none of these displays, as awesome and ingenuous as they were, could rival Ms. Egypt's bare, vibrating tummy.

7. The *Saint Louis Globe-Democrat* (April 30, 1891) reported that after hanging around in Atlanta for a few days, "Miss Maurice, the New York skirt dancer, has left for New York. She said she did not care what became of Dunn, and was glad enough to get away from him when his money was about gone and he was behind the bars."

8. Thomas Furlong, in *Fifty Years a Detective* (St. Louis: C. E. Barnett, 1912), devotes an entire chapter (39–66) to a similar scam involving a large cotton shipment in Sherman, Texas, in 1883, when Captain Jack would have been working for him.

9. Dee Brown, *The American West* (New York: Charles Scribner's Sons, 1994), 48.

10. In the summer of 1885, the Southern Hotel was the scene of a murder which (so Thomas Furlong writes) "attracted the attention of the civilized world." The decaying body of Clarence Preller was discovered stuffed in a trunk. Suspicion almost immediately focused upon his traveling companion, Hugh M. Brookes, who had fled to New Zealand. After being extradited back to the United States (at great expense to the city of St. Louis), Brookes was jailed, but the legal authorities were not sure they had enough evidence to convict. They thus enlisted the services of Detective Furlong. Furlong staged an elaborate hoax involving a fake crime and the arrest of a "criminal" (actually one of his secret operatives) who, incarcerated in the same jail as Brookes, was able to collect incriminating statements. Brookes was found guilty and executed (see Furlong, *Fifty Years a Detective*, 9–39). One of the unwitting participants in Furlong's hoax was Judge Henry D. Laughlin, who was something of a mentor to Captain Jack, and who Kinney visited frequently (as recorded in his diary).

11. James McParland (1843–1919) was one of the most celebrated detectives of his time. McParland, an Irish immigrant, eventually ended up in Chicago and opened a saloon, which was destroyed during the great Chicago fire. He then found work with the Pinkerton Agency and spent years as an undercover operative infiltrating the ranks of the Molly Maguires, a band of labor terrorists active in the Pennsylvania coalfields in the early 1870s. His testimony was largely responsible for breaking up the gang, some ten (by other accounts as many as twenty) of whom were convicted of murder and hanged. McParland also seems to have been responsible, acting on the advice of his friend Sheriff "Doc" Shores, for recommending (a recommendation he surely later regretted) that the Pinkerton Agency hire an operative by the name of Tom Horn, later executed for murder with a rope he himself braided while awaiting hanging. See C. W. "Doc" Shores, *Memoirs of a Lawman,* ed. Wilson Rockwell (Denver: Sage Books, 1962), 273. Later, McParland was involved in the murder investigation after Idaho governor Frank Steuneberg was killed by a bomb, and brought charges against a number of prominent labor officials, including William "Big Bill" Hayward. The labor leaders were acquitted after a sensational trial in which they were defended by Clarence Darrow. McParland's exploits were even memorialized by Sir Arthur Conan Doyle, who has a fictional version of him meeting Sherlock Holmes in the novel *The Valley of Fear.*

12. This is probably William H. Reno, who would subsequently become a detective for the Colorado and Southern railroad and was a member of a posse who tracked "Black Jack" Ketchum, later hanged—beheaded,

actually—in 1901 for train robbery. Jay Nash, in his *Encyclopedia of Western Lawmen and Outlaws* (New York: Da Capo Press, 1994), writes that "train robbery was by then a capital offense in certain western states, although Ketchum seems to be the only outlaw who was ever executed for this crime" (199).

13. An early form of photography, the daguerreotype, had been introduced back in 1839. It involved a direct image cast on a silver-coated copper plate, with no negative, thereby prohibiting mass production. Still, the police potential of this new technology was soon recognized. On November 30, 1841, the *Philadelphia Public Ledger* observed that

> When a discovery has been made in science there is no telling at the time to what useful purpose it may be afterwards applied. The beautiful process invented by Daguerre, of painting with sunbeams, has been recently applied to aid the police in suppressing crime. When any suspicious person or criminal is arrested in France, the officers have him immediately daguerreotyped and he is likewise placed in the criminal cabinet for future reference. The rogues, to defeat this objective, resort to contortions of the visage and horrible grimaces. (from the Web site http://www.vernacularphotography.com.htm)

By 1851, Frederick Scott Archer had perfected the wet plate glass negative, allowing the easy reproduction of photos. But portrait or mug shot photography, despite the optimistic account quoted above, was chancy even with cooperative subjects as a result of the long exposure times required, which necessitated the use of instruments similar to those employed by Mr. George Maledon, including head clamps and other body restraints. By the early 1880s, various dry plate improvements were introduced that dramatically reduced the necessary exposure intervals and vastly simplified the development process. In 1888 George Eastman introduced the box camera, completely separating the taking of pictures (the slang term for which was "shadows") from their development (the camera was marketed under the slogan "You Press the Button, We Do the Rest"). The real impediment to effective police use of photography was the absence of a system of classification. A point to note is that as late as 1891, at least in Adrian, Michigan, some police forces did not even seem to have their own photographic equipment, forcing Captain Jack to march the prisoner from jail to an independent studio.

14. Another anthropometric system was offered by Francis Galton (1822–1911), a cousin of Charles Darwin. However, the purpose of Galton's measurements was eugenic. He believed that "superior" people could be identified on the basis of their physical characteristics and dimensions, and that they should be encouraged to breed with each other and thereby

improve humanity. This idea (by no means his alone) would bear evil consequence after his death. Galton's system was arguably superior to that of Bertillon in that it included fingerprints, for which Galton had to develop a system of classification and description, a system that formed the basis of that still in use today. Eventually, forensic scientists came to recognize that fingerprints alone could conclusively prove identity and had no need for any of the other measurements Galton and Bertillon recommended. An early effort to establish fingerprinting as the national standard for identifying criminals was made by Tom Furlong's protégé William Burns, in his capacity as the director of the United States Bureau of Investigation (a precursor to the FBI). See Gene Caesar, *Incredible Detective: The Biography of William J. Burns* (Englewood Cliffs, N.J.: Prentice-Hall, 1968), 216.

CHAPTER 6

1. Most accounts of Billington's fate describe his hanging as a legal execution. The issue turns on the question of whether or not the Plymouth Colony had a duly authorized government (in which case the hanging and the juridical proceedings that led up to it were legal) or only an informal "compact"—a document they in fact called the "Mayflower Compact"—to which forty-one adult male members of the colony had subscribed before even leaving the ship. In case of the latter, the Billington hanging can only be described, no matter how orderly it was carried out or however well deserved it might have been, as a vigilante lynching. In 1629 the Pilgrims would reorganize as the Massachusetts Bay Colony and would apply for a royal charter, but until that time the only royal charter extant belonged to Virginia, whose jurisdiction fell far short of New England. Not until 1634 would a true representative government elected by the "freemen" begin to function in the Plymouth colony.

2. Marshall Houts, *From Gun to Gavel: The Courtroom Recollections of James Mathers of Oklahoma* (New York: William Morrow, 1954), 235–36.

3. This gruesome practice of collecting body parts from the lynched victim was not uncommon. In 1878, train robber George Parrot, also known as "Big Nose George," attempted to derail and rob a Union Pacific train in Wyoming. He and his companion Dutch Charley then killed two members of the pursuing posse. Both were caught and lynched. Dr. John Osborne, a railroad doctor and future governor of Wyoming, obtained possession of Parrot's body. He stripped the skin from the chest, tanned it, and made it into a pair of shoes. See Wayne Gard, *Frontier Justice* [Norman: University of Oklahoma Press, 1949], 209–10.

4. From a report in the *Chicago Tribune*, January 1, 1894, in *A Red Record* (http://www.bedfordsmartins.com.history.html):

RECORD FOR THE YEAR 1892: While it is intended that the record here presented shall include specially the lynchings of 1893, it will not be amiss to give the record for the year preceding. The facts contended for will always appear manifest—that not one-third of the victims lynched were charged with rape, and further that the charges made embraced a range of offenses from murders to misdemeanors. In 1892 there were 241 persons lynched. The entire number is divided among the following states: Alabama, 22; Arkansas, 25; California, 3; Florida, 11; Georgia, 17; Idaho, 8; Illinois, 1; Kansas, 3; Kentucky, 9; Louisiana, 29; Maryland, 1; Mississippi, 16; Missouri, 6; Montana, 4; New York, 1; North Carolina, 5; North Dakota, 1; Ohio, 3; South Carolina, 5; Tennessee, 28; Texas, 15; Virginia, 7; West Virginia, 5; Wyoming, 9; Arizona Territory, 3; Oklahoma, 2. Of this number 160 were of Negro descent. Four of them were lynched in New York, Ohio and Kansas; the remainder were murdered in the South. Five of this number were females. The charges for which they were lynched cover a wide range. They are as follows: Rape, 46; murder, 58; rioting, 3; race prejudice, 6; no cause given, 4; incendiarism, 6; robbery, 6; assault and battery, 1; attempted rape, 11; suspected robbery, 4; larceny, 1; self defense, 1; insulting women, 2; desperadoes, 6; fraud, 1; attempted murder, 2; no offense stated, boy and girl, 2. In the case of the boy and girl above referred to, their father, named Hastings, was accused of the murder of a white man; his fourteen-year-old daughter and sixteen-year-old son were hanged and their bodies, filled with bullets, then the father was also lynched. This was in November 1892, at Jonesville, Louisiana.

5. The jewelry store had been founded by Charles's father, Charles G. Taylor, who also served a term as a judge (1878–1879) and was a prominent enough citizen to earn a biographical sketch in the *History of Pettis County, Missouri* ("Compiled with Great Care by Special Historians") published in 1882.

6. Omaha, Nebraska, *Morning World Herald*, February 29, 1892, 3.

7. On March 12, 1892, the *Chillicothe Constitution* reported that "it is now generally admitted that John Davis, the negro who assaulted Mrs. Chas. L. Taylor at Sedalia, is among negro miners at Vinita, I.T., and that they would successfully conceal him."

8. Another account of this incident ("He Has the Fiend," *Morning World Herald*, March 16, 1892, 2) differs significantly in some of the details. It reports Captain Jack as saying, "the negro now in custody at Houston answers the description of the rapist more minutely than any capture yet made, and I am strongly inclined to believe that we now have the right man. . . . When the officers went to have the fellow's picture taken he resisted desperately and said he would die first, and we got no picture."

9. For an excellent account of this incident, see Daniel F. Littlefield, *Seminole Burning: A Story of Racial Vengeance* (Jackson: University Press of Mississippi, 1996).

10. Denison, the "Gate City," is a perfect example of a town—one then of many—that owes its very existence to the railroads, as it was there that the Katy decided to cross over the Red River, which defines the border between Texas and Oklahoma. The town is named after George Denison, who was a vice president of the MKT Railroad. The red-light district, located on what was Skiddy Street, derives its name from (as Harry Sinclair Drago explains) "Francis Skiddy, the effete Easterner who was president of the Land Grant Railroad and a Katy director. He is said to have shuddered whenever Skiddy Street was mentioned in his presence" (*The Legend Makers* [New York: Dodd, Mead, 1975], 226). Some idea as to the character of early Denison is given by Edward King in the July 1873 *Scribner's Magazine* (quoted in Drago): "It is exceedingly remarkable, that in a community one-half of which is undoubtedly made up of professional ruffians, 'verminous' types and gamblers, and the off-scourings of society . . . that there is not more terrorism. Every third building in the place is a drinking saloon with gambling appurtenances, filled after nightfall with a depraved, adventurous crowd, whose profanity is appalling, whose aspect is hideous."

Certainly one of the more interesting features of Denison society, a practice said to be borrowed from Chicago, was that (until local officials outlawed it) each Sunday, the local madams would dress their employees in their finest and most regal apparel, then parade them in horse-drawn carriages through the streets, hoping to shame their rivals by the elegance and demeanor of their charges. But the high-spirited young ladies, bored with stately parades, would instead use the occasion to stage impromptu carriage races before large, admiring audiences. "Minor accidents occurred when the inexperienced drivers failed to resist the temptation to race," Drago notes; "the climax came when Frankie Green, Rowdy Joe's inamorata, drove her horses into Millie Hipps's speeding team. The wheels locked and two of Millie's girls were pitched into the road, both suffering multiple bruises and one a fractured arm" (215).

11. A contemporary account reads as if the town had just endured the crime of the millennium: "Denison is horror-stricken. History does not show a parallel. Four assassinations, and all of the defenseless women, is the record of last night. It was a night of horror, and Denison is to-day bowed down with grief and shame. All day long squads and groups of men have been standing about on street corners, and with expressions of deepest concern, discuss the deeds of some demon or demons whose existence is a menace to society." And later in the (undated, unidentified clipping): "If more than one man was engaged in the damnable work then humanity

has the more to fear. If only one did it then the demon is without a parallel in this or any other country, in this or any other age."

12. One reliable gauge of local prominence is when a newspaper can entitle an article, as this one, "Jack's Good Job," confident that readers will recognize the person to whom they are referring on only the basis of his first name.

CHAPTER 7

1. I haven't been able to find out anything about Mr. Ward. Mr. Diron Ahlquist, a noted researcher in the field and the editor of the *Oklahombres Journal,* has been kind enough (in an e-mail dated November 28, 2004) to share information on Bud Kell, who also testified at the Lewis trial: "Bud T. Kell was a deputy U.S. Marshal for the Western District of Arkansas in 1885–1887 and operated primarily in the Creek and Cherokee Nations. In 1888, he was the City Marshal of Muskogee and also a member of the U.S. Indian Police in which capacity he served in until at least 1892. In 1896, Kell was a 'night watchman' in Muskogee. In November 1896, Kell and Deputy U.S. Marshal Dave Moore shot and killed Joe Lacy at Muskogee while Lacy resisted arrest." As for Alfred McKay, Mr. Ahlquist informs me that he also served as a Deputy U.S. Marshal for the Western District of Arkansas between 1872 and 1896 as well as with the Indian Police from the early 1890s on.

2. "Free silver" advocates persisted even into the presidency of Franklin Roosevelt, and the issue did not end until the 1960s, when a decreasing supply of silver forced the U.S. Treasury to abandon silver entirely as a metal of coinage.

3. From the *Atlanta Constitution,* July 14, 1892, 1:

'TWAS BLOOD THEY WANTED
    The Negro Rioters at Paducah Tried to Lynch a White Man
    Louisville, Ky., July 13.—It became known last night that the negro mob at Paducah, on the previous night, was not intending to protect Burgess, colored, charged with thefts and assaults upon women, but to avenge the lynching of Hill by putting to death J. E. Randle, a white man, who, in February last, killed James Bennett, a negro liveryman. Randle's trial has been several times continued and by his family's influence it was believed he would get off with a light punishment. The governor yesterday sent Adjutant General Gross to Paducah to investigate the matter. The mayor during the day issued a proclamation for all citizens to remain within doors and a local company of state guards was called into service as deputies under the command of the sheriff. No further violence has been offered.

4. Quoted from the *Atlanta Constitution,* July 14, 1892, 4.

5. Carry Nation, *The Use and Need of the Life of Carry A. Nation,* rev. ed., chap. 8, n.p.

6. As noted in Chapter 1, La Flore was not a Cherokee but a Choctaw Indian.

7. Harry Sinclair Drago, *Outlaws on Horseback* (New York: Dodd, Mead, 1964), 219.

8. Ibid.

9. Harold Preece, *The Dalton Gang: End of an Outlaw Era* (New York: Hasting House, 1963), 193–94.

10. The *Sedalia Gazette* (July 17, 1892) notes that "Capt. Kinney was seen last evening by a Gazette reporter, at his home on South Prospect street. The captain's right arm was in a sling and his shoulder, where the leaden ball plowed its way into the flesh, was quite sore and painful, otherwise that official bore no evidence of having served as a target for a band of cut throats, who shot to kill. Mr. Kinney talked freely in regard to the Adair affair and threw much light on the action of the armed guard on the train. His statement in regard to the conduct of the Indian police shows that the accusations of cowardice on the part of the guard are unjust and unwarranted by the facts."

11. The historical record is confused as to whether the original depot was on the east or west side of the track, and a visit to modern Adair does not conclusively settle the question. Today, the existing business district is primarily on the west side. East of the main track (the freight spur and platform have long vanished) is a vacant field and some tin sheds with a residential district further behind. The clipping Captain Jack preserved (*Sedalia Gazette,* July 17, 1892)—which is probably incorrect—states that the east was the "depot side" of the track. Another contemporary account (Vinita, Indian Territory, *Indian Chieftain,* July 21, 1892) contradicts this by noting that as the robbery began, "the officers stepped out on the east side—the opposite side from the depot." An 1896 Sanborn-Perris plat map (the earliest available) clearly shows the depot—assuming it was not moved—on the west side of the main track. The Oklahoma Historical Society has a photograph entitled "Highballing Through Adair," showing what appears to be a diesel locomotive (not in use until well after these events) passing the Adair depot, but because it cannot be determined whether this train is heading north or south, the depot's location even at this latter date remains undetermined.

12. Some of the frightened passengers took extreme measures to protect their valuables. The *Saint Louis Globe-Democrat* reported, in a story dated July 16, 1892, that one passenger

SWALLOWED HIS DIAMONDS

DENISON, TEX., July 16—Capt. Harvey Thompson, of this city, and one of the leading sporting men of the State, was a passenger on the Missouri, Kansas and Texas train recently "held up" by robbers in the Indian Territory. Capt. Thompson wore on his person over $2000 in diamonds when the train robbers were making things pretty lively. Thompson deliberately swallowed the gems, which he had picked with a knife from the settings.

13. This account of the geometry of the battle is generally supported by the fireman's statement. Here is Brandenburg's statement in full:

Mr. O' Herrin [illegible], Sir this train arrived at Adair Station at 9:30 PM was Flagged[?] the train was stopped. When three armed men came in the Eng[ine] ordered us off taking the Engineer off on the right side of the train and me on the left I was ordered to take a pick and brake [sic] the express car door open I hammered on the door with the pick after some delay the door was opened from the inside too [sic] of the men went in the car every thing they got they put in a sack During this time there was a quite a number of shots fired on the East Side of the train. When they got through in the car they came out and all started West from the train there was 7 or 8 in number this work that I did was done under Heavy threats of Being Shot if I did not obey there [sic] orders.

Train delayed about one hour.

Signed, L. Brandenburg

From V. V. Masterson, *The Katy Railroad and the last Frontier* (Norman: University of Oklahoma Press, 1952), 256.

14. Actually, even by the standards of the day, the Winchester .44-40 was not an especially high-powered rifle. As early as 1881, Marlin offered a repeating rifle chambered in .45-70, making it almost twice as powerful as the Winchester. Or compare the Winchester with the Krag .30-40, which used a smokeless powder cartridge tested by the army in 1892. Both fired 200-grain bullets with 40 grains of powder load. But the Krag had close to double the muzzle velocity of the Winchester (2,000 vs. 1,300 ft/sec) and, at 100 yards' distance, nearly three times the delivered force (1,444 vs. 555 ft-lb). Even the venerable Sharps .40-90 delivered nearly four times the ballistic force of the Winchester at 100 yards (555 vs. 1,985 ft-lb). See John Walter, *The Guns that Won the West: Firearms on the American Frontier, 1848–1898* (London: Greenhill Books, 1999), 270.

15. Preece, *Dalton Gang*, 201.

16. One matter on which Drago disagrees with "Eye Witness" is about the presence of the spring wagon which, by many accounts, the Daltons

used to carry off their loot, an amount often stated (for example by Block) as $17,000 in coin. Drago writes, "we are told that the bandits 'backed a spring wagon up to the express car and in an almost leisurely manner loaded the loot into it.' That they required a wagon in which to make off with $17,000 passes belief. [This is so only if one assumes the $17,000 is in paper currency.] That they would have burdened themselves with a vehicle of any description is equally incredible" (*Outlaws on Horseback*, 217). Another point to be made concerning the wagon is from a contemporary report in the Vinita, Indian Territory, *Indian Chieftain* (July 21, 1892): "A surprise party was in progress at D. S. Cumming's residence the night of the robbery and it was a vehicle from there bringing the agent's sister in, which was mistaken for the plunder wagon of the robbers" (from Nancy B. Samuelson, *The Dalton Gang Story* [Eastford, Conn.: Shooting Star Press, 1992], 110).

Putting aside for the moment the question of how much, if anything, the Daltons actually got, whether or not the Daltons would have needed a wagon seems to depend on what types of coin the express car contained—and how, in advance, would they know this? One of the most popular gold coins then in wide circulation was the five-dollar gold Liberty ("Lib"), which weighs a quarter of an ounce. $17,000 would equal 3,400 Libs, or approximately 53 pounds of coin, surely not requiring a wagon. But if the coins were Morgan silver dollars, each weighing 26.73 grams, then 17,000 coins would weigh almost exactly 1,000 pounds.

17. Drago, *Outlaws on Horseback*, 218.

18. Bob Dalton was supposedly an especially fine marksman. Robert Barr Smith writes that "like the other brothers, he was an expert horseman, and he was the best shot of them all. Veteran U.S. Deputy Marshal Heck Thomas, who could shoot a little himself, called Bob 'one of the most accurate shots I ever saw . . . [he] fired his rifle mostly from his side or hip, very seldom bringing the gun to his shoulder. . . . ' Bob practiced his marksmanship every chance he got. A young frontier boy, son of the Osage agency doctor (and also a witness to Bob's whisky selling) said later that Bob paid him a quarter to throw tin cans into the air while Bob shot at them. The story goes that Bob could put three rounds into a thrown tomato can—from the hip—before his target hit the ground" (Robert Barr Smith, *Daltons! The Raid on Coffeyville* [Norman: University of Oklahoma Press, 1996], 46–47). The shooting ability of the gang's other members (particularly those who were not Daltons), if judged by their performance at Coffeyville, remains suspect. See Smith, *Daltons!*, 118–19.

19. See Samuelson, *Dalton Gang Story*, 128–30.

20. See the *Chillicothe Constitution*, May 11, 1891, 1.

21. Drago, *Outlaws on Horseback*, 219.

22. Ibid.

23. Oklahoma *Indian Pioneer Papers*, interview with Louise Rider dated April 16, 1938.

24. Both the Daltons and the railroad posse were probably firing Winchester Model 1873 rifles (see Chapter 1, n. 1). Cartridges chambered in 44-40 would have a muzzle velocity of nearly 1,300 ft/sec and an effective range of well over 500 yards. Even at 500 yards, the 203-grain bullets were moving at 805 ft/sec. Stray bullets, of course, could travel much farther, although at reduced velocity. At the distance specified by Drago, such slugs could have easily hit the doctors whether they were inside or outside.

Still, as one expert notes, "comparatively little is known about the Daltons' guns, though a .38-calibre Webley Bulldog was taken from the waistcoat pocket of the slain Bob Dalton after the Coffeyville raid. His holster gun was apparently a Colt Single Action Army revolver. An 1886-pattern Winchester rifle was pictured with the corpses, but it is not known whether it was one of the Daltons' own guns" (Walter, *Guns that Won the West*, 177). The contemporary accounts of the Adair robbery contain many references to "Winchesters," but I suspect that the term was used generically to refer to any type of repeating rifle.

25. One contemporary account (Vinita, Indian Territory, *Indian Chieftain*, July 21, 1892) does mention a "coal house" in which the officers were wounded. A very brief account of these events recently posted on a Web site by the Adair Chamber of Commerce also mentions a "coal bin" constructed from railroad ties and located south of the depot. Supposedly, "school boys dug bullets out of the ties years afterwards for souvenirs." One problem with this is that the Sanborn-Perris plat maps, drawn specifically for the purpose of writing fire insurance, might be expected to show the location of a building or a shed in which large stores of combustibles were housed. And while the June 1896 map shows, south of the depot, such ephemeral structures as two granaries and a corncrib, no coal house or bin is depicted.

26. Glen Shirley, *Law West of Fort Smith*, 102. Shirley's qualifying footnote about this robbery is as follows: "Although the identity of the raiders was never established, it has always been the general, though perhaps erroneous, opinion that the Daltons tried their hands bank-robbing at the expense of this little Oklahoma community. In his book Emmett Dalton states: 'Until toward the very end, when we held up some banks, our activities were directed at the express company and its allies.'"

27. Drago, *Outlaws on Horseback*, 217.

28. Another point of confusion is exactly how many participants there were on both sides of the engagement. Shirley contends the train carried "thirteen Indian police and special guards." Block counts nine, as does the *Stillwater Gazette*. Drago says ten. Preece has "a baker's dozen." Mr. Hearn

thought "there seemed to be about fifteen of the detectives." Emmett Dalton estimated fourteen. Paul Wellman counts eleven. James D. Horan, in a wildly inaccurate account of the robbery (*The Outlaws: Accounts by Eyewitnesses and the Outlaws Themselves* [New York: Gramercy Books, 1977], 151), says the battle involved "three deputies." Smith says eight, as does Captain Jack.

As for the Dalton gang, Block (and Emmett Dalton) says there were eight members. Drago lists six. "Eye Witness" has La Flore say at least seven and maybe more than twelve. Hearn counts seven or eight. Wellman says six. The *Globe-Democrat* writes that "when asked as to the number of robbers, Kinney said reports differed, but that the station agent at Adair, who was held up before the train arrived, said there were fifteen in the party" (July 16, 1892).

29. Glen Shirley, *Heck Thomas: Frontier Marshal* (New York: Chilton Company, 1962), 141. Shirley probably means not the Pacific railroad but the Pacific express company, because it was their car that was robbed at Adair. "Eye Witness" reproduces a reward poster (also included in this book) that supposedly appeared the day after the robbery. Also in the immediate aftermath, some suspected (probably unjustly) that the express car messenger might have been involved. So reported the *Atlanta Constitution*, July 19, 1892:

The Messenger Suspected.

St. Louis, July 18.—George P. Williams, the messenger who was in charge of the express company's car, which was robbed at Adair, I.T., Thursday night last by the Dalton gang, has been suspended pending an examination by the company.

30. Smith, *Daltons!*, 65.

31. Ibid., 71.

32. Such a common attitude, which it helped to create, encouraged the political movement of Populism to flourish. From one of their manifestos: "There are but two sides in the conflict that is being waged in this country today. On the one side are the allied hosts of monopolies, the money power, great trusts and railroad corporations who seek the enactment of laws to benefit them and impoverish the people. On the other are the farmers, laborers, merchants, and all other people who produce wealth and bear the burdens of taxation. . . . Between these two there is no middle group" (Harold C. Faulkner, *Politics, Reform and Expansion* [New York: Harper and Row, 1959], 58).

33. Some train robbers actually seemed to believe they were modern Robin Hoods and acted accordingly, as is made clear in the following unidentified, undated clipping saved by Captain Jack (from which I quote excerpts):

Train Robbers Murder Conductor J. P. McNally

Seven Masked Men Go Through a Train in Daring Style—Said They Did Not Want Workingmen's Money, But They Robbed Some Laborers Just the Same

LITTLE ROCK, Ark., Nov. 4—At 10 o'clock last night seven masked men held up and robbed express train No. 51 of the St. Louis, Iron Mountain & Southern railroad at Olyphant, a station about seven miles from Newport. Passenger Conductor J. P. McNally was shot dead while trying to protect his train. After robbing the express car the passengers were relieved of their valuables.

Those who were passengers on the train . . . say that it was the announced policy of the train robbers that they did not want any workman's money; that they only wanted contributions from those who were able to give. They also said they wanted nothing from the ladies and told the ladies to rest easy. They did not adhere strictly to the policy announced, for several workingmen lost all they had while others were not molested.

Callous growth on the hands of a passenger was the evidence on which the robbers relied to prove that the passenger was a workingman. G. W. Crawford of Colorado City, Tex., was one of the men who escaped on this policy. The robbers who were going through the car he was in ordered him to hand out his money. He says he was getting it out as fast as he could when one of the robbers ran his fingers across the palm of Crawford's hand and said "You are all right; keep your money."

There was a party of six cowboys from Texas on board of the train. The robbers took their money from them, but when they found out they were workingmen they gave them their money back.

The robbers told the passengers they wanted only good watches, and when a passenger handed over a cheap watch it was handed back to him.

34. Smith, *Daltons!*, 67.

35. "Eye Witness," *The Dalton Brothers and Their Astounding Career of Crime*, introduction by Burton Rascoe (1892; reprint, New York: Frederick Fell, 1954), 15.

36. See the Decatur, Illinois, *Daily Review*, June 16, 1892, 7. Compare this with Emmett Dalton's breezy assertion that "Kinney, La Flore and Johnson, the only men who really showed fight, soon recovered from the effects of their wounds" (*Beyond the Law* [Coffeyville, Kans.: Coffeyville Historical Society, (1918)], 121).

37. Glen Shirley, *The Fourth Guardsman* (Austin, Tex.: Eakin Press, 1997), 40–41.

38. The ATSF, which was a larger railroad than the Katy, would have been a step up for Captain Jack. He was soon prosperous enough to build his own

three-story house in Topeka (since razed), located at 1435 Topeka Avenue. I have included in this book a picture, taken probably around 1902, showing Captain Jack and his family posed on the front porch of the house. With him is his wife Elizabeth (who would live until July 29, 1938) and their seven children (four sons and three daughters). Also shown is Reuben Taylor, his son-in-law, who had married his daughter Mamie. The occasion for the picture is probably the christening of his first grandchild.

39. Preece, *Dalton Gang,* 201.

40. Ibid., 200.

41. Detective Pat Lawler, as best I can tell, has been almost completely forgotten by history, as have the criminals he successfully fought. Lawler, a thirty-year veteran of the St. Louis police force, as noted in his obituary, which is probably from the *Saint Louis Globe-Democrat,*

> was the man who captured Wat Jones, Johnny Morgan, George Walsh and Johnny Murphy, the quartette of bank sneaks who "tore Chicago wide open" a couple of years ago. The four came down to St. Louis to repeat their operations, but were at once "spotted" by Lawler, who nipped their schemes in the bud by locking them up. He also captured Eddie Guerin, the celebrated Chicago bank thief, and Vincent, the great London and Union Pacific forger. It would take volumes to narrate the work done by Lawler and the adventures he underwent. His loss is a misfortune to the department that can never be repaired.

Quiet, though genial, good-natured, but perfectly firm, Patrick Lawler, in his prime, stood in the front rank of American thief-takers.

Tom Furlong, who did not always enjoy cordial relations with the St. Louis police, described him as "the best detective on the city force" (*Fifty Years a Detective* [St. Louis: C. E. Barnett, 1912], 168). Lawler died of consumption and was survived by a wife and daughter, with whom Captain Jack kept in contact, as on November 12 and 13, 1891, when they were guests at his home.

42. Was Captain Jack right- or left-handed? I have no idea. But if he was right-handed, as he assumed his firing position behind the depot's northwest corner when the battle began, this might mean that in order to reduce his own exposure, he was forced to fire his Winchester from his left shoulder. Such may have contributed to his missing what were apparently well-lit targets only some twenty yards away. Another factor may have been that, remembering La Flore's stories about Dick Glass, and Detective Brady's similar assertion that many train robbers wore body armor, he was attempting head shots, notoriously difficult under even the best of circumstances.

43. Emmett Dalton's account of the guards' conduct is as follows: "The only ones who had any courage were La Flore, Marshal Sid Johnson and L.

L. [*sic*] Kinney, who stood their ground until they were badly wounded and had to retire. The others piled off the train with a whoop and then when Bob and the boys opened upon them, they rushed pell-mell back into the cars or made a break for town. One of the passengers on the train told that several of the brave deputies took off their guns and hid them in the seats" (*Beyond the Law*, 120–21). Emmett also embellishes his report with a story—repeated nowhere else in the record—that the express car contained a special guard, a huge and muscular "Texas bad man" hired to protect the safe but who promptly hid once the action started.

CHAPTER 8

1. Benjamin Franklin, *Autobiography* (New York: Holt, Rinehart and Winston, 1964), 7.

2. Ibid., 126.

3. Ibid., 131.

4. This account is "surely an error," as Robert Barr Smith asserts (*Daltons! The Raid on Coffeyville* [Norman: University of Oklahoma Press, 1996], 91).

5. Most contemporary reports of the Coffeyville raid, supported by some eyewitness accounts, claim that six robbers were in the gang, and that one escaped or turned back before the gang arrived. Most modern writers insist that only five robbers raided Coffeyville. Smith, in *Daltons!* (the best examination by far of the incident), concludes that only five participated. Smith devotes an entire chapter of his book to this much-debated subject of the "sixth man." If there was a sixth man, it was probably Bill Doolin, although Emmett Dalton later wrote that Doolin's arrogant and reckless conduct at Adair displeased them, causing his separation from the gang. Doolin was also a natural leader, competing with Bob Dalton for the top spot, and would afterward form his own gang, lasting until August 1896, when he was shot and killed by Heck Thomas. Thomas always claimed that he himself had killed Doolin (with a shotgun firing No. 8 buckshot), but his account is disputed by Frank Canton, who ascribed the honor to Thomas's posseman Bill Dunn, brother of Rosa and Bee, whom Frank himself killed. See Robert K. DeArment, *Alias Frank Canton* (Norman: University of Oklahoma Press, 1996), 190–91.

6. Smith, *Daltons!*, 91.

7. Ibid., 125.

8. A photograph included in this book shows a lawman I believe to be Ransom Payne posing with the upright corpses, but to my knowledge, this officer has not been conclusively identified. Payne seemed to be obsessed with the Daltons and would be naturally attracted to the scene of their de-

mise. Marshal Grimes, in the letter firing Payne, places him at Coffeyville immediately after the raid and for the express purpose of obtaining photographs: "you [Payne] never did a thing except to go up to Coffeyville and get their pictures after they were dead, and trying to get their bodies and take them to California for the reward" (quoted in Nancy B. Samuelson, *The Dalton Gang Story* [Eastford, Conn.: Shooting Star Press, 1992], 130).

9. Payne's unsuccessful effort to profit from the dead Daltons was not the first time he attempted to use his credentials for private gain. Payne, who was something of a litigious sort, was on duty just before the 1889 Oklahoma land rush, patrolling the territory to evict trespassers ("sooners"). This gave him a considerable advantage in the race to follow over all the other prospective settlers forced to await the starting gun at the borders. Payne immediately filed on some choice plots near Guthrie. Other claimants disputed his ownership on the grounds that his status as a deputy marshal gave him an unfair advantage in staking out land. The following legal battle would reach the Supreme Court nine years later (169 U.S. 323 *Payne v. Robertson et al.*, No. 20, February 28, 1898). The Court upheld the lower courts' denial of Payne's title.

10. Quoted from Smith, *Daltons!*, 162. Another (surely false) rumor in the aftermath of the battle was that Bill Dalton had secured an appointment as a United States deputy marshal and was returning to Coffeyville to seek revenge generally upon the citizenry (including unnamed "newspaper correspondents") and specifically upon a Mr. Chapman, who had somehow ended up with Emmett's horse, a horse Bill claimed was thereby stolen. See the Olean, New York, *Olean Democrat*, December 27, 1892, 1.

11. *Atlanta Constitution*, October 14, 1892, 1.

12. A writer for the *Atlanta Constitution* (October 29, 1892, 4), echoing the sentiments of an editorial that appeared in the *Chattanooga Times*, observed "that Bill's attempt to collect from the people of Coffeyville money he claims was found on the body of one of the slain murderers in excess of the sums rifled from the banks, points out Bill as a fit subject for the vigorous attention of Judge Lynch, if ever lynching is justifiable. If the Daltons had any money it was stolen money, according to the story of the one yet alive, and Bill has no right to it, [no] more than has any other thievish scoundrel."

Another oddity after the raid was that a gentleman calling himself "Byron Dalton" came to the attention of the press, falsely claiming to be the father of the Dalton clan. (James Lewis Dalton, their real father, died on July 16, 1890.) This Mr. Dalton, when asked as to the cause of their criminal behavior, offered the novel explanation that his younger boys had read too many novels. See the *Atlanta Constitution*, October 12, 1892, 2.

13. See Samuelson, *Dalton Gang Story*, 142–43.

14. Samuelson has recently uncovered evidence suggesting that George "Bitter Creek" Newcomb died in either late 1894 or October 1895 of wounds received in the Battle of Ingalls, and that the Newcomb killed with Charley Pierce was in fact George's brother Alfred Newcomb. See her letter to the editor, *Wild West Magazine*, August 2002. Most of the historians I have questioned on this matter accept Samuelson's conclusion.

15. The title Captain Jack preferred to use was "Special Agent," and he is so listed on the ATSF stationery letterhead ("Special Service Department") in 1893.

16. Arguably one of the most underappreciated inventions in history, at least in terms of its cultural impact, is the bicycle, which dates back to a device patented in 1817 by the Baron von Drais. Although recognizably a bicycle, this contraption (popularly known as a "hobbyhorse") was constructed entirely from wood and lacked pedals. By 1870, high-wheel designs were introduced and featured all-metal construction. In the Gay Nineties, bicycles became immensely popular, the demand for such leading to numerous innovations in techniques for mass manufacturing and assembly, techniques later put to good effect by Mr. Henry Ford. Many cycling clubs were established, such as the League of American Wheelmen, who successfully lobbied for improved roads, literally paving the way for the automobile. In perfecting bicycle design, inventors developed pneumatic tires, self-sealing and internally lubricated bearings, and metallurgical refinements producing lighter-weight and stronger steels. Two bicycle mechanics in Dayton, Ohio, would use such advances in a conveyance that flew for all of twelve seconds in the sky above Kitty Hawk, North Carolina, on December 17, 1903.

The cultural impact of the bicycle was perhaps even greater than any commensurate advances in mechanical engineering. In order to ride them, women had to adopt less restrictive styles of clothing, notably bloomers (or "knickerbockers"), which many thought a shocking sight, leading to laws—widely ignored—prohibiting such apparel. The newspapers of the time are filled with articles describing the arrests of woman cyclists for "public indecency." Not infrequently, women were subjected to punishments considerably beyond the embarrassment of arrest. Such was the case (reported by the *Atlanta Constitution*, September 29, 1894, 1) of

"JACK, THE WHIPPER."
A Fellow Who Is the Terror of Female Bicyclists
Chicago, September 28.—"Jack the Whipper" has broken loose and is making life full of terrors to the female bicyclists who ride in Washington park during the evening. Jack has a frantic aversion to bloomers

and his method of expressing his disapproval is to plant a few lusty welts with a raw-hide whip on every pair of bloomers that he can find with a girl inside of them. His plan for the last two nights has been to wait behind a tree until a bicycle with bloomers on it comes along, then he springs out and plies his rawhide vigorously. He has severely whipped two young women and pursued several others. The park policemen have so far been unable to catch him.

It would be misleading to report that women achieved any overwhelming solidarity of opinion on this issue. So reports the *Atlanta Constitution* on April 9, 1895, in a front-page article:

Orlando, Fla., April 4—(Special)—The question of bloomers has put the women of this town by the ears. For a year bicycling has been growing more and more popular, until at present every young woman in the town and many of the middle-aged matrons are experts on the wheel.

About two months ago the women formed a bicycle club and last Saturday evening, the question of adopting a costume came up. One young lady, noted for expertness on the wheel, introduced a resolution requiring members to adopt the bloomer costume. This resolution led to a heated debate, which grew so warm at times that hair pulling seemed to be imminent.

A similar question would even reach the Pope, who felt compelled to appoint a distinguished ecclesiastical committee to "examine the question of priests riding bicycles and the hygienic and moral aspects of the practice. A section of the bishops oppose bicycling because the riders are unable to wear their clerical gowns" (Hamilton, Ohio, *Hamilton Daily Republic,* December 28, 1894, 1). But no less an authority than Susan B. Anthony herself remarked that "I think it [bicycling] has done more to emancipate women than anything else in the world" (*New York World,* February 2, 1896).

17. Harold Faulkner, *Politics, Reform and Expansion* (New York: Harper and Row, 1959) 142.

18. Another account has it that upon first being approached by the bandits, McDaniels immediately sought the advice of his lawyer, A. J. Daggs, whereupon the two of them traveled to Chicago to notify the authorities: "Then General Manager Frey was informed, and the case was placed in Kinney's hands" (Frederick, Maryland, *News,* September 22, 1894, 1).

19. The article referred to immediately above provides further details:

After the plans of the conspirators had been formed they elected McDaniels leader. McDaniels notified Kinney of this and Kinney instructed McDaniels that he must not be the leader; that it was not the desire of the railroad or express company to lead men into the commission of crime, and he must put one of the others forward. Accordingly, McDaniels declined to act as leader, and Abrams was chosen.

Kinney says McDaniels was not promised $5,000 or any other sum for exposing the conspiracy. He will receive only expenses actually incurred. McDaniels has been a saloon keeper, deputy sheriff and school teacher.

20. *Reno Weekly Gazette and Stockman,* September 20, 1894, 1. Exactly who gave the "orders" is not made clear. As at Adair, there didn't seem to be, in the force assembled to defend the train, a clear chain of command. Captain Jack would have been in command of the railroad guards, and he would also have had authority over the railroad personnel. Wells Fargo provided a force under the command of District Superintendent Stockton. Sheriff Saling and his deputies were present representing the local jurisdiction.

21. *Fort Wayne Weekly Sentinel,* September 18, 1894, 1.

22. As, for example, by the *Arizona Republican,* September 19, 1894, 1.

23. *Fort Wayne Weekly Sentinel,* September 18, 1894, 1.

24. Philip Fradkin, *Stagecoach: Wells Fargo and the American West* (New York: Simon and Schuster, 2002), 107–8.

25. *Fort Wayne Weeekly Sentinel,* September 18, 1894, 1. Because Bill Dalton was killed only three months before the Gorin robbery, Stockton may have meant Bob Dalton. After the Coffeyville raid, as reported by the *New York Times* (January 16, 1893, 1), the personal effects of the gang members were auctioned off to repay creditors to their estate. Bob Dalton's saddle was bought (for $23.50) by John Kloehr, one of the Coffeyville heroes, and is today displayed in the Dalton Defenders Museum: "Professional relic hunters bought the other effects. Bill Powers's watch brought $25. Bob Dalton's Winchester brought $60 and his revolver $31. The total realized by the sale was $294.25."

26. *Fort Wayne Weekly Sentinel,* September 18, 1894, 1.

27. As had happened at Adair, some of Captain Jack's superiors were quick to second-guess his actions. A director of the ATSF, returning from a board meeting, happened to be a passenger aboard the train. He remarked (as reported by the Frederick, Maryland, *News,* September 19, 1894, 1), "I see no reason why, with seven or eight men ready and watching for robbers, they were allowed to escape. It is very strange."

28. "Dad" certainly had more than his fair share of misfortune during his tenure driving trains. On December 28, 1891, and on the same route as the Gorin robbery, he survived a spectacular train wreck, with his engine and a number of cars skidding off the rails and plunging down an eighteen-

foot embankment near Newcomb, Missouri. Fifteen people were injured, some seriously. See the *Chillicothe Constitution*, December 28, 1891, 1.

29. This is speculation on my part; I've been unable to locate any records of the actual trials. It may be that some of them died before any court appearance. The Delphos, Ohio, *Daily Herald* reported (September 19, 1894, 1) that "two of them were captured at Memphis, Mo., one being shot six times with a Winchester—he cannot live."

30. Frederick, Maryland, *News*, September 22, 1894, 1.

CONCLUSION

1. Another source refers to him in 1910 as the "assistant night chief of detectives."

2. Walter Lord writes, "on April 1, 1898, an adventurous soul bought the first American machine ever made specifically for sale. By 1900 some eight thousand cars sputtered about the country. Over one hundred taxis graced the streets of New York; Chicago even had a motor ambulance" (*The Good Years: From 1900 to the First World War* [New York: Harper, 1960], 4).

3. The Knights of Columbus took out a series of newspaper advertisements promoting this effort. My source is the Clearfield, Pennsylvania, *Clearfield Progress*, January 10, 1918, 4. One suspects the recreation centers might be needed because in 1917 Congress passed the Eighteenth Amendment, which, when ratified, would deprive the three million doughboys, over there and still here, of their traditional arenas of relaxation: saloons and bars. Carry's Crandall hammer had smashingly triumphed.

BIBLIOGRAPHY

BOOKS

Baldick, Robert. *The Duel: A History of Dueling.* New York: Clarkson N. Potter, 1965.

Beavan, Colin. *Fingerprints: The Origins of Crime Detection and the Murder Case That Launched Forensic Science.* New York: Hyperion, 2001.

Beaver, Frank. *On Film: A History of the Motion Picture.* New York: McGraw-Hill, 1983.

Block, Eugene. *Great Train Robberies of the West.* New York: Coward-McCann, 1959.

Boorman, Dean K. *The History of Winchester Firearms.* New York: Lyons Press, 2001.

Bristow, Joseph. *Tales of Old Fort Gibson.* New York: Exposition Press, 1961.

Brown, Dee. *The American West.* New York: Charles Scribner's Sons, 1994.

Browne, Sir Thomas. *Hydriotaphia (Urn Burial) and The Garden of Cyrus.* Edited by F. L. Huntley. Northbrook, Ill.: AHM Publishing, 1966.

Burton, Art. *Black, Red, and Deadly.* Austin, Tex.: Eakin Press, 1991.

———. *Black, Buckskin, and Blue: African-American Scouts and Soldiers on the Western Frontier.* Austin, Tex.: Eakin Press, 1999.

Caesar, Gene. *Incredible Detective: The Biography of William J. Burns.* Englewood Cliffs, N.J.: Prentice-Hall, 1968.

Coogan, Tim Pat. *The Man Who Made Ireland: The Life and Death of Michael Collins.* Niwot, Colo.: Roberts Rinehart, 1992.

Cook, David. *A History of Narrative Film.* New York: W. W. Norton, 1981.

Cunningham, Eugene. *Triggernometry: A Gallery of Gunfighters.* Introduction by Joseph G. Rosa. Foreword by Eugene Manlove Rhodes. Norman: University of Oklahoma Press, 1941, 1996.

Dalton, Emmett. *Beyond the Law.* Coffeyville, Kans.: Coffeyville Historical Society, [1918]. This book is a photocopy of the original, copyrighted in 1918.

DeArment, Robert K. *Alias Frank Canton.* Norman: University of Oklahoma Press, 1996.

Dillon, Richard. *Wells, Fargo Detective: The Biography of James B. Hume.* New York: Coward-McCann, 1969.

Dodge, Fred. *Under Cover for Wells Fargo.* Edited by Carolyn Lake. Norman: University of Oklahoma Press, 1969.

Drago, Harry Sinclair. *Outlaws on Horseback.* New York: Dodd, Mead, 1964.

———. *Road Agents and Train Robbers.* New York: Dodd, Mead, 1973.

———. *The Legend Makers.* New York: Dodd, Mead, 1975.

Essig, Mark. *Edison and the Electric Chair: A Story of Light and Death.* New York: Walker, 2003.

"Eye Witness." *The Dalton Brothers and Their Astounding Career of Crime.* Introduction by Burton Rascoe. 1892. Reprint, New York: Frederick Fell, 1954.

Faulkner, Harold. *Politics, Reform and Expansion.* New York: Harper and Row, 1959.

Fradkin, Philip L. *Stagecoach: Wells Fargo and the American West.* New York: Simon and Schuster, 2002.

Franklin, Benjamin. *Autobiography.* New York: Holt, Rinehart and Winston, 1964.

Fry, Peter, and Fiona Somerset Fry. *A History of Ireland.* New York: Barnes and Noble, 1988.

Furlong, Thomas. *Fifty Years a Detective.* St. Louis: C. E. Barnett, 1912.

Gard, Wayne. *Frontier Justice.* Norman: University of Oklahoma Press, 1949.

Hagan, William T. *Indian Police and Judges.* Lincoln: University of Nebraska Press, 1966.

Harman, Samuel. *Hell on the Border: He Hanged Eighty-Eight Men.* Edited by Jack Gregory and Rennard Strickland. Muskogee, Okla.: Indian Heritage Publications, 1971.

Harrington, Fred Harvey. *Hanging Judge.* Foreword by Larry D. Ball. Norman: University of Oklahoma Press, 1951, 1995.

Hartman, Mary, and Elmo Ingenthron. *Bald Knobbers: Vigilantes on the Ozarks Frontier.* Gretna, La.: Pelican, 1988.

Henry, O. *The Complete Works of O. Henry.* New York: Doubleday, 1953.

Horan, James D. *The Outlaws: Accounts by Eyewitnesses and the Outlaws Themselves.* New York: Gramercy Books, 1977.

Houts, Marshall. *From Gun to Gavel: The Courtroom Recollections of James Mathers of Oklahoma.* New York: William Morrow, 1954.

Jones, W. F. *The Experiences of a Deputy U.S. Marshal of the Indian Territory.* No date, place, or publisher. This pamphlet appears to be a reproduction of interviews conducted by the WPA Federal Writers' Project during the 1930s.

Julin, Thomas R., and D. Patricia Wallace, "Who's That Crack-Shot Trouser Thief?" *Litigation* 28, no. 4 (summer 2002).

Keneally, Thomas. *American Scoundrel: The Life of the Notorious Civil War General Dan Sickles.* New York: Doubleday, 2002.

Klein, Maury. *The Life and Legend of Jay Gould.* Baltimore: Johns Hopkins University Press, 1986.

Littlefield, Daniel F. *Seminole Burning: A Story of Racial Vengeance.* Jackson: University Press of Mississippi, 1996.

Long, Jeff. *Duel of Eagles: The Mexican and U.S. Fight for the Alamo.* New York: William Morrow, 1990.

Lord, Walter. *The Good Years: From 1900 to the First World War.* New York: Harper, 1960.

Masterson, V. V. *The Katy Railroad and the last Frontier.* Norman: University of Oklahoma Press, 1952.

McKennon, C. H. *Iron Men.* New York: Doubleday, 1967.

McMath Jr., Robert C. *American Populism: A Social History 1877–1898.* New York: Hill and Wang, 1993.

Miller, Floyd. *Bill Tilghman: Marshal of the Last Frontier.* New York: Doubleday, 1968.

Mooney, Colonel Charles W. *Doctor in Belle Starr Country.* Oklahoma City: Century Press, 1975.

———. *Doctor Jesse.* Oklahoma City: Pro-Graphics, 1978.

Nash, Jay Robert. *Encyclopedia of Western Lawmen and Outlaws.* New York: Da Capo Press, 1994.

Nation, Carry. *The Use and Need of the Life of Carry A. Nation.* Rev. ed. 1905. N.p.

Neeley, Bill. *The Last Comanche Chief.* New York: Wiley, 1995.

Nix, E. D. *Oklahombres: Particularly the Wilder Ones.* 1929. Reprint, Lincoln: University of Nebraska Press, 1993.

Nolan, Frederick. *The West of Billy the Kid.* Norman: University of Oklahoma Press, 1998.

O'Beirne, H. F. *Leaders and Leading Men of the Indian Territory: Choctaws and Chickasaws.* Vol. 1. Chicago: American Publishers' Association, 1891.

Painter, Nell Irvin. *Standing at Armageddon: The United States, 1877–1919.* New York: W. W. Norton, 1987.

Patterson, Richard. *Train Robbery.* Boulder, Colo.: Johnson Books, 1981.

Preece, Harold. *The Dalton Gang: End of an Outlaw Era.* New York: Hasting House, 1963.

Rosa, Joseph. *The Gunfighter: Man or Myth?* Norman: University of Oklahoma Press, 1969.

Samuelson, Nancy B. *The Dalton Gang Story.* Eastford, Conn.: Shooting Star Press, 1992.

———. *Shoot from the Lip: The Lives, Legends, and Lies of the Three Guardsmen of Oklahoma and U.S. Marshal Nix.* Eastford, Conn.: Shooting Star Press, 1998.

Schlereth, Thomas J. *Victorian America: Transformations in Everyday Life.* New York: Harper Collins, 1991.

Shirley, Glen. *Heck Thomas: Frontier Marshal.* New York: Chilton Company, 1962.

———. *Law West of Fort Smith.* Lincoln: University of Nebraska Press, 1968.

———. *The Fourth Guardsman.* Austin, Tex.: Eakin Press, 1997.

———. *Shotgun for Hire: The Story of "Deacon" Jim Miller, Killer of Pat Garrett.* Norman: University of Oklahoma Press, 1970.

———. *Temple Houston: Lawyer with a Gun.* Norman: University of Oklahoma Press, 1980.

Shores, C. W. "Doc." *Memoirs of a Lawman.* Edited by Wilson Rockwell. Denver: Sage Books, 1962.

Smith, Robert Barr. *Daltons! The Raid on Coffeyville.* Norman: University of Oklahoma Press, 1996.

Svenvold, Mark. *Elmer McCurdy: The Misadventures in Life and Afterlife of an American Outlaw.* New York: Basic Books, 2002.

Tilghman, Zoe. *Marshal of the Last Frontier.* Glendale, Calif.: Arthur H. Clark, 1949.

Tillotson, Geoffrey, with Paul Fussell Jr. and Marshal Waingrow, eds. *Eighteenth Century Literature.* New York: Harcourt Brace and World, 1969.

Tower, Michael. *Dialing "911" Was Not an Option! Tales of Lawlessness Along the Middle Washita River.* Privately published, 2004.

Tuller, Roger H. *"Let No Guilty Man Escape": A Judicial Biography of "Hanging Judge" Isaac C. Parker.* Norman: University of Oklahoma Press, 2001.

Walker, Dale. *Legends and Lies: Great Mysteries of the American West.* New York: Tom Doherty, 1997.

Waller, Brown. *Last of the Great Western Train Robbers.* New York: A. S. Barnes, 1968.

Walter, John. *The Guns that Won the West: Firearms on the American Frontier, 1848–1898.* London: Greenhill Books, 1999.

Wellman, Paul. *A Dynasty of Western Outlaws.* New York: Bonanza Books, 1961.

ORAL HISTORIES

Oklahoma *Indian Pioneer Papers,* interview with Mrs. Katie (Whiteturkey) Day, April 21, 1937

Oklahoma *Indian Pioneer Papers,* interview with Louise Rider, April 16, 1938

Oklahoma *Indian Pioneer Papers,* interview with Ninnian Tannehill, April 22, 1938

Oklahoma *Indian Pioneer Papers,* interview with Claude Timmons, n.d.

JOURNALS AND PERIODICALS

Harper's Weekly
Lost Treasure Magazine
Master Detective
New Yorker
Wild West Magazine

NEWSPAPERS

Ada, Oklahoma, *Evening News*
Albert Lea, Minnesota, *Freeborn County Standard*
Arizona Republican
Atchison Daily Globe
Atchison Globe
Atlanta Constitution
Atlanta Journal
Bristol, Pennsylvania, *Bucks County Gazette*
Chillicothe, Missouri, *Chillicothe Constitution*
Clearfield, Pennsylvania, *Clearfield Progress*
Colorado Springs Gazette
Decatur, Illinois, *Daily Republican*
Decatur, Illinois, *Daily Review*
Delphos, Ohio, *Daily Herald*
Edwardsville, Illinois, *Edwardsville Intelligencier*
Fort Wayne Weekly Sentinel
Frederick, Maryland, *News*
Fresno Weekly Republican
Ft. Smith, Arkansas, *Fort Smith Elevator*
Ft. Wayne, Indiana, *Fort Wayne Sentinel*
Galveston Times
Hagerstown, Maryland, *Herald and Torch Light*
Hamilton, Ohio, *Hamilton Daily Republic*
Indian Journal
Kansas City Journal
Kansas City Times
New York Times
New York World
Olean, New York, *Olean Democrat*
Omaha, Nebraska, *Morning World Herald*
Reno Weekly Gazette and Stockman
Saint Louis Globe-Democrat
Sandusky, Ohio, *Register*
Sedalia, Missouri, *Sedalia Bazoo*

Sedalia, Missouri, *Sedalia Daily Democrat*
Sedalia, Missouri, *Sedalia Gazette*
Stevens Point, Wisconsin, *Gazette*
Stillwater, Indian Territory, *Stillwater Gazette*
Trenton, New Jersey, *Times*
Vinita, Indian Territory, *Indian Chieftain*

INDEX